Hist
2.99

Number Two: Texas A&M Southwestern Studies

ROBERT A. CALVERT AND LARRY D. HILL
General Editors

D1567737

WOMEN OF THE DEPRESSION

Women of the Depression

CASTE AND CULTURE IN SAN ANTONIO, 1929–1939

BY

Julia Kirk Blackwelder

TEXAS A&M UNIVERSITY PRESS

College Station

Library of Congress Cataloging in Publication Data

Blackwelder, Julia Kirk, 1943–
    Women of the Depression.

    (Texas A&M southwestern studies; no. 2)
    Bibliography: p.
    Includes index.
        1. Women—Texas—San Antonio—Economic conditions.
2. Working class women—Texas—San Antonio—Economic
conditions. 3. Afro-American women—Texas—San Antonio—
Economic conditions. 4. Mexican American women—Texas—
San Antonio—Economic conditions. 5. San Antonio (Tex.)—
Race relations. 6. Depressions—1929—United States.
I. Title. II. Series.
HQ1439.S2B42   1984   305.4'09764'351   83-40496
ISBN 0-89096-177-8 (cloth); 0-89096-864-0 (pbk.)

Manufactured in the United States of America
SECOND EDITION, 1998

For Jere

Contents

List of Illustrations

MAP

List of Tables

Preface

THIS book is about women in Depression San Antonio, not women as a single group but women as members of particular economic groups and women as members of distinct ethnic groups whose circumstances determined how the Depression affected their lives. "Anglo," "black," and "Hispanic," terms currently in use, are employed in this book to designate Depression San Antonio's three major ethnic groupings. Although the terms obscure significant intra-group differences, broad public recognition of the three groupings has defined and continues to define the discriminatory social structure of the Southwest. The differences among Anglo, black, and Hispanic women's lives in Depression San Antonio are both measurable and describable, and the following pages analyze these quantitative and qualitative differences.

Group definitions in the Southwest rest on distinctions that are partly national and partly racial. The designation "Hispanic" applies to all persons of Spanish or Latin-American heritage, but virtually all Hispanics in Depression San Antonio were Mexican American and the two terms are used interchangeably in this text. Some Hispanics in present-day San Antonio regard themselves as Caucasians of Spanish descent. Still others identify themselves as Indians. Race, therefore, does not define Mexican American, but race is an important component of identity for individual Mexican Americans.

Blacks were and are distinguished from others solely on the basis of race. There were virtually no Negro or black Hispanics in Depression San Antonio and the distinction between the two groups was clear. The blacks of Depression San Antonio were the descendants of Afro-American slaves and freedmen.

The term "Anglo" distinguishes all whites of non-Spanish European extraction from all Hispanics; Mexican Americans have adopted "Anglo" as a label for a group regarded as their oppressors. For such purposes a term that blurs ethnic distinctions among the dominant group is functional. Non-Hispanic whites have accepted "Anglo" as a descriptor that sets them apart from the minority groups of the Southwest.

In attempting to understand and explain ethnic discrimination and the social structure of early-twentieth century San Antonio, I have found the concept of caste most helpful and have presented a highly qualified definition of caste in the chapter that follows. One scholar who might quarrel with my interpretation is Mario Barrera, who has utilized the idea of internal colonization to describe ethnic and racial relationships in the Southwest. Barrera objects to the application of the term "caste" because the United States has never been a classic caste society.[1] Internal colonization is helpful in understanding the sources and the process of social stratification in the United States, and Barrera's work significantly deepens that understanding. I concur with his thesis that capitalists actively encouraged immigration from Mexico and the economic segregation of Hispanics in order to lower labor costs. I prefer a model of discrimination built on the notion of caste because the status of blacks and Mexican Americans has differed and because Anglos clung to habits of discrimination when their economic interests dictated otherwise. The experience of Mexican Americans in the twentieth century has been different from that of blacks, in San Antonio at least, in that Mexican Americans have had more occupational mobility and have not been legally segregated. In favor of the comparative aspects of the black and Hispanic experience, Mexican Americans have faced much greater barriers to citizenship and to permanent alien status than have earlier immigrants. Mexican Americans have experienced exploitation and discrimination that Anglo immigrants in the Southwest have not known. Caste describes racial and ethnic relations in the Southwest somewhat better than internal colony because the process itself has been different—marginal labor versus slavery and black codes—and because Anglos clung to occupational distinctions of caste when it was in the interest of neither employer nor employee to do so. In addition, Anglos in the Southwest have clearly defined Hispanics as both different from and preferable to blacks by establishing less social distance between Mexican Americans and Anglos than between blacks and Anglos.

[1]Yet Barrera himself writes that "designating a certain relationship as neocolonial does not mean that it is exactly the same as classic colonialism, but only that the same general relationship exists." Mario Barrera, *Race and Class in the Southwest: A Theory of Racial Inequality*, p. 195.

Acknowledgments

NEARLY a decade has passed since I began the research for this book. Through these years I have accumulated debts of all sorts that I cannot begin to repay. I thank all who assisted me.

The book could not have taken its present form without the generous contributions of several San Antonians who shared with me their memories of everyday life in the Depression. Dora Guerra, of the University of Texas at San Antonio Library, and Lou Nelle Sutton, member of the Texas House of Representatives, were particularly helpful in introducing me to the women whose recollections appear here. Thelma Gavin, Bexar County Archivist, helped me locate and gain access to county court records. Tom Shelton of the Institute of Texan Cultures at San Antonio spent several days researching and locating photos in the Institute's Collection for inclusion in the book. The photodocumentation that accompanies the text witnesses the thoroughness of Tom's work.

Sections of this book were drafted during a Summer Seminar for College Teachers, sponsored by the National Endowment for the Humanities and directed by Stanley L. Engerman. Through numerous conversations, Stan aided in the development of my ideas, and he subsequently improved the manuscript through his careful reading and criticism. Paul Escott, Carole Haber, and J. Harvey Young offered helpful suggestions and made several important corrections. Sandy Bergo and Mary Bottomly typed the manuscript from the first to the final draft.

The research presented here was funded in part by the Wellesley College Center for Research on Women in Higher Education and the Professions, the Foundation of the University of North Carolina at Charlotte, and the Southern Regional Education Board.

The deepest of my debts is to my family: to my mother and father, Zilpha and Karl Kirk, who parented my children through the several summers that I was away from home; to my children, Kirk and Dallas, for the gifts of their affection and spontaneous humor. I especially thank my husband, Jere, who cheerfully allowed this project to rearrange his life and who, by never reading a word of this book, remains its only totally enthusiastic admirer.

WOMEN OF THE DEPRESSION

Introduction

San Antonio, Texas
March 12, 1939

To Mr and Mrs Roosevelt

Dear president I am coming to yo in the lowest manner I ever been taught asking is there any way yo can help me to get some work on the p w a. I have been trying to get some work on the p w a for over 2 years but they will turn me away. I am a poor widow and has a little grandson to take care of has no way to pay my rent was put out of doors a few days a goe. I beleave you are a servant of god and I beleave yo will help those who will ask yo in the name of the lord.

Yours truly

Katie Lee Ackles
112 Armstrong St[1]

THIS work recounts the experiences and describes the behavior of women who lived through the Depression in San Antonio, one of America's poorest cities. The Depression exacerbated problems of low wages, substandard housing, and poor health conditions that afflicted San Antonio before the crash. Separately and together San Antonio women experienced economic disasters and dislocations that were worse than those of most other American communities. Not all groups bore San Antonio's distress equally.

In a geographic sense the women of San Antonio's racial and ethnic groups frequently were separated from each other, residing in distinct enclaves. Anglos dominated the North Side, blacks clustered on the East Side, and Mexican Americans concentrated in West Side slums. Differences in wealth and surroundings reinforced the geographic separation.

The casual visitor who strayed from the North Side or the Central Business District into the neighborhoods of the poor immediately confronted the realities of residential segregation. In the 1930s a three-to-four-block stretch of shops and other businesses on East Commerce Street com-

[1] Records of the Work Projects Administration, Record Group 69, State Series, Texas, National Archives. Hereafter cited as Records of the Work Projects Administration.

prised the center of the black trade district. Although not as massive or as depressed as the West Side, the black community was ringed by substandard housing on its northern, western, and southern extremes. In the early 1940s the completion of Victoria Courts, a public housing project, eliminated the worst of the East Side slums, but throughout the 1930s the economic and health problems of the East Side received little attention from public officials. Civic leaders claimed that a black politician, Charlie Bellinger, delivered to his constituents more than their share of public services and improvements.

A substantial commercial district stood on the near West Side and served Mexican Americans of all income levels. West Side businesses acted as a buffer between the Central Business District and the West Side slums. Businesses that printed or sold Spanish-language publications, Spanish-language film theaters, sidewalk cafes serving Mexican dishes, Mexican-American groceries, pharmacies carrying Mexican folk remedies, and the Mexican Clinic served the needs of the city's large Hispanic community and provided the incomes of the Mexican-American middle class. Spreading out west of the business district were the most miserable slums in urban America.

The economic and social life of San Antonio inevitably brought Anglo, black, and Mexican-American women in contact with one another, though they resided in separate neighborhoods. During the Depression such interaction often revealed the distances that separated life-styles, for San Antonio's ethnic and cultural complexity and the unequal distribution of wealth in the city made it a place of remarkable and frequently painful contrasts.

The staging of the Battle of the Flowers, a ball and parade in celebration of San Jacinto Day, revealed the complexities of the city's socioeconomic structure in a single shared experience. On San Antonio's North Side grand houses with luxurious courtyards and tropical gardens testified to the persistence of ease, despite the Depression, for a small group of Anglos. The preference of the wealthy for architecture of the Spanish colonial style suggested the fondness of the Anglo elite for selected remnants of Mexican influence in Texas. In homes such as these, even at the height of the Depression, young girls eagerly looked forward to the spring social season, which centered on the Battle of the Flowers. From among the daughters of San Antonio's business and professional elite, the Order of the Alamo selected a queen and a court of princesses to reign over the year's

Marie Louise Guenther, queen of the Battle of the Flowers Parade, 1933. The annual celebration of San Jacinto Day symbolized the superior position of Anglo women in Depression San Antonio.
(*San Antonio Light* Collection, University of Texas Institute of Texan Cultures, San Antonio.)

most important social event. The queen and her court, costumed in elaborate and bejeweled gowns and robes, rode flower-decked floats through the heart of the city to the Alamo.

During the 1930s the Battle of the Flowers was an annual distraction from the daily concerns of a city under the siege of the Depression, but it demonstrated in full irony the social and economic inequities of a racist society. Anglo girls were the only candidates for queen and princesses of the Battle of the Flowers. Anglo wives planned teas, lunches, and parties and awaited invitations to events planned by other Anglo wives. Behind the scenes black and Mexican-American women cooked, cleaned, and served. From December to April the most skilled seamstresses of the West Side Hispanic community labored over the robes and gowns that would be

Onlookers at the Battle of the Flowers Parade, 1937. Black and Mexican-American women participated in the Battle of the Flowers only as maids and seamstresses to the queen and her court.
(*San Antonio Light* Collection, University of Texas Institute of Texan Cultures, San Antonio.)

worn for a single occasion, afterward to be cleaned and preserved by a black dry cleaner on the East Side. Mexican-American men pruned shrubs and manicured lawns and gardens of Anglo homes. On the East Side and on the West Side the Battle of the Flowers reminded residents of their lot in the city's socioeconomic system rather than creating a festive mood of distraction from daily chores. The place of blacks and Mexican Americans at the parade was on the sidelines, observing from the sidewalks as the more fortunate passed by. In the homes of the East Side and the West Side women wrestled each day with the effects of discrimination, effects that were documented in statistics of death and disease.

The physical and economic deterioration suffered by San Antonio women during the Depression was greater than most histories suggest. General discussions of working women in twentieth-century America describe the 1930s as basically continuous with the rest of the century. While no historian has denied the catastrophic effects of female unemployment, the effects of the Depression have been regarded as temporary, the situation of women workers gradually improving as the economy moved away from the 1932 nadir to the boom of wartime. Sympathetic treatments of New Deal liberalism stress that state-level concern for women workers and measures of the Roosevelt administration resulted in permanent improvements in the wages and conditions of women's work. William H. Chafe has written:

Prompted by reports of women receiving starvation wages and sleeping on subways, public officials started a new campaign to safeguard female workers from exploitation. Seven state legislatures enacted minimum-wage laws in the early 1930's; governors throughout the Northeast banded together to regulate women's working conditions; and the Roosevelt administration established the National Recovery Administration (NRA) with authority to institute industry-wide codes regulating wages and hours. Perhaps the most important step forward was the enactment of the federal Fair Labor Standards Act (FSLA) of 1938. The statute established the unprecedented principle that the federal government had the right to control wages and hours of both men and women engaged in occupations related to interstate commerce.[2]

Chafe goes on to argue that "the minimum wage laws passed during the 1930's substantially improved the situation of women workers on the lowest rung of the economic ladder." Chafe cites wage improvements in a number of cities and industries, but the figures, like the analysis, refer to the Northeast and consider neither wage-code violations nor the displacement of workers under the new codes.

In San Antonio a few more women were employed at the end of the 1930s than at the beginning, but women rarely if ever benefited from federal wage codes, and Texas adopted no codes of its own. In several instances San Antonio businessmen succeeded in obtaining exemptions from enforcement agencies. Many large local employers of women closed their doors permanently with the eventual enforcement of the Fair Labor Standards Act. Other employers closed because of the general business decline, and still others moved their plants to other locations because of union activity in San Antonio. Although employment levels recovered in the 1940s, the jobs that had disappeared during the Depression were not replaced by equivalent positions during the war. Many women experienced long-term unemployment because their skills did not match those demanded in new jobs or because of discrimination by employers.

Twin themes run through the stories of women in Depression San Antonio, ethnicity and family. Ethnic prejudices divided women into what

[2]William H. Chafe, *The American Woman: Her Changing Social, Economic, and Political Roles, 1920–1970*, p. 81.

were virtually three separate worlds. Women understood the Depression largely in the context of the collective experiences of Anglos, blacks, and Mexican Americans. Ethnicity was the most important single indicator of socioeconomic status in San Antonio, and the Depression reinforced the pattern of segregation. Anglos, who were predominantly middle class, saw the Depression as a difficult time, but as a group they were callous to the city's high death rate from disease and malnutrition that almost never touched them personally. Black San Antonians comprised a small, overwhelmingly working-class community who experienced high unemployment. The black community knew hunger but rarely starvation. A cooperative spirit helped many black families through the most difficult periods. In contrast, Mexican Americans lived daily with the specter of disease and death. It was an unusual Hispanic family that was not touched by the death of a child or young adult. Unlike middle-class Anglos, middle-class Mexican Americans could not turn their backs on the misery in their midst. Unlike blacks, Hispanics found that community resources were too few for cooperation to provide substantial relief for their numbers. Depression recollections of middle-class women from each ethnic group appear in the following pages. The centrality of ethnicity emerges in the women's sensitivity to the problems of others in their ethnic group rather than others of their social class.

Among all ethnic groups family was the emotional anchor of female identity and the focus of female concern during the Depression. The attention to family and the interdependence of its members across generations gave most women emotional ballast and financial assistance. Some women, however, found themselves totally alone or alone with dependents. When unemployment struck and persisted, the latter group suffered intense feelings of isolation and helplessness. In a city with few social services, the Depression was a particularly terrifying experience for women alone and those with children to support. As one unemployed worker expressed it, women without supportive families lived in a community where "no one helps but God in heaven."

This book traces the personal dimension of life in the Depression for many San Antonio women who left letters, reports, and diaries or consented to oral interviews. One of the goals of this book is to portray the impact of the Depression on women's lives and the suffering it caused. The broader purpose, however, is to analyze the behavior of San Antonio's women and the system in which they lived. The subjects selected for analysis include the problems of women in the work force, the roles of women in family and community, and the effects of the Depression on the female life cycle. Relief, emergency jobs, and criminal activities are discussed as alternatives to regular employment and as subjects that illuminate the contrasts among the city's Anglo, black, and Mexican-American women.

I selected the women of San Antonio for study because of the city's demographic complexity, the poverty of the area, and the importance of women in the local economy. San Antonio differed from all other medium-sized and large cities in the nation in having proportionally the largest Mexican-American community. San Antonio contrasted with northern cities in maintaining legalized segregation of blacks in its schools and public accommodations. It differed from most other southern cities in that Mexican Americans rather than blacks occupied the bottom of the economic ladder. Unlike most southern cities, San Antonio counted a significant number of European immigrants among its inhabitants. In the ambience created by the interaction of its many racial and national groups, San Antonio was and is unique. Tourism, light industries, and commerce all drew Alamo City women into the work force in the decades preceding the Depression and locked them in the sectors of the economy most vulnerable to economic fluctuations.

San Antonio in the early twentieth century manifested a tripartite social system that is more nearly described by caste than by class. Social segregation did not reflect a classic caste system in several respects. Caste carried no religious sanctions, heredity was not an inviolable badge of occupation, and each "caste" displayed a class structure among its members. The vast majority of blacks and Mexican Americans, however, could not reasonably expect to acquire middle-class status. They attended inferior schools, and they did not interact socially with Anglos. Blacks and Mexican Americans were marked by Anglos as inferior on the basis of real or imagined distinctions of race or color. The three caste groups, Anglos, blacks, and Mexican Americans, were segregated from each other geographically, in occupational status, and by marriage patterns.

This caste system based on race, color, or ethnicity was a dominant force shaping women's lives. Both employers and relief agencies discriminated among women on the basis of caste, and the kind and the degree of discrimination deeply affected women's abilities to cope with the Depression. Most San Antonio women understood that prejudices of one kind or another circumscribed their options, and they adjusted their behavior accordingly.

Each caste had its own culture, however, and cultural differences by race or ethnicity also shaped women's behavior. Culture influenced both women's perceptions of the Depression and their reactions to personal economic problems. Differences among Anglos, blacks, and Mexican Americans were evident in family composition, in the cultural institutions supported by each group, and in values and attitudes. Familial values and traditions frequently weighed as heavily as need in women's decisions about meeting economic emergencies.

Throughout the Depression, Anglo women in San Antonio were materially better off than minority women and had access to better jobs. Proportionally, then, Anglo women had the most to lose in the uncertain 1930s. While they had the most at stake, Anglo women were least likely to face the direst consequences of their losses. Anglo women had broader opportunities, stronger financial resources, and greater access to relief. Black women suffered deprivation during the Depression and subsisted at a standard below that of most Anglo women. Most black women had always been poor, but cooperation and sharing were techniques of surviving poverty that they had mastered. For many black women the Depression was basically consistent with the experience of the difficult 1920s. For the most part, Hispanic women also had always been poor, but the Depression had two radical effects on Mexican Americans that were felt not at all or to a lesser degree by other populations. Fear of deportation inhibited many Mexican-American families from seeking public or private relief during the repatriation drive of the 1930s. The curtailment of migrant agricultural labor throughout the nation drove thousands of Mexican Americans with little or no urban work experience to seek year-round survival in San Antonio. Unlike urban blacks, displaced Hispanic migrant workers usually had no mutual-support networks to fall back on.

In the following analysis both the separateness of the female as opposed to the male experience in Depression San Antonio and the distinctiveness of the ethnic experience are evident. Men appear in these pages as family members whose decisions and employment difficulties shaped women's lives. As women tell their own stories of the Depression and as statistics tell the stories of other women, the increasing dependence of individual families on women's abilities to cope and on women's earnings emerges. The Depression and the city are dual protagonists in the drama, but the central focus is women's behavior in a difficult environment.

The first two chapters of the book outline the socioeconomic and family settings in which San Antonio women found themselves. Chapter 3 recounts the reactions of middle-class and upper-class women to the Depression. Chapters 4 and 5 explore the factors that propelled women into the labor force and the effects of occupational segregation. Chapters 6 and 7 detail the fruits of caste with respect to working conditions, wages, and emergency jobs. Chapter 8 outlines both the caste orientation of the labor movement and the economic factors that worked against successful unionization. Chapter 9 presents women's criminal activities as a further expression of occupational segregation, as a reaction to the Depression, and as an area in which women were treated differently from men. Chapter 10, the final chapter, summarizes the consequences of caste for women in Depression San Antonio and the long-run persistence of occupational segregation. Each chapter demonstrates the primacy of race or ethnicity in shaping women's Depression experiences. Collectively the chapters illustrate the interaction of discrimination and culture and the strength of both in the face of crisis. Appendix A explores occupational segregation and caste in a theoretical perspective.

[1]

The Neglected City

So it was a case of begging from the government to give you food to bring home to your children. They used to be sitting in a line out in the back yard of our office, a hundred at a time on a Saturday morning to get a grocery list so they could take home the food that was necessary for their family: three, four, five, one—an old man by himself, a woman. And I was moved by every age, whether it was a family with children, whether it was an old man or old woman. It just got me, that I could not stand it.

—Adela Navarro, caseworker in Depression San Antonio[1]

As a caseworker, Adela Navarro knew well the plight of the city's unemployed. She also understood that when a hungry person begged for food in San Antonio few heard the cry. Men and women gave generously of their time and money in efforts to feed and clothe the needy, but volunteer campaigns could make little progress in battling the suffering that afflicted the city. Throughout the 1930s city and county officials were adamant in their resistance to dispersing local tax revenues for relief or on public projects. As Navarro recalled, it was President Franklin Delano Roosevelt who "threw open the doors of the warehouses and fed the people of San Antonio."

San Antonio in 1930 was an urban center of about 230,000 persons with an additional population of 60,000 in the rest of Bexar County (appendix B, table 1). Approximately 8,000 residents of Depression San Antonio were European immigrants, among whom Germans were the most numerous. There were few persons of Oriental or American Indian extraction, and the city's 18,000 blacks formed an unusually small community for a southern city of such size. More than 83,000 residents of the city were Mexican immigrants or persons of Mexican extraction, making San Antonio the second-largest Mexican-American community in the United States and placing blacks far behind Hispanics numerically as a minority population (table 2). Los Angeles, with a population of more than 1,000,000—90,000 of whom were Mexican-American—was the only city

[1]Interview with Adela Navarro, May 29, 1979.

in the United States with a larger Mexican-American population than that of San Antonio.

Many Anglo San Antonians brooded about the presence of so many Mexican Americans in the population, though blacks were rarely perceived as a threat to Anglo well-being. Throughout the Depression voices were raised urging the repatriation of Mexican immigrants, and public officials rigorously enforced regulations against the employment of aliens on public works projects. From 1929 through 1939, twenty-five Mexican women and many more men were prosecuted in the federal court in San Antonio on charges of illegal entry into the United States and were ordered deported. Countless other Mexican Americans left the country voluntarily or under the fear of deportation. Although repatriation had public support in San Antonio, removal of Mexican Americans from relief rolls was not formally organized there as it was in Los Angeles, Saint Paul, and other cities with proportionally fewer Hispanics seeking assistance.[2] The explanation for San Antonio's relatively lenient behavior on repatriation lies most probably in the city's heavy dependence on the marginal labor of Hispanics, especially women.

Although both blacks and Mexican Americans had a per capita income well below that of Anglos, black San Antonians were more likely to own their own homes than were Mexican Americans and less likely to live in overcrowded conditions. Mexican Americans suffered higher infant and adult death rates than did blacks and were more likely to contract tuberculosis or venereal disease. Despite the social, economic, and medical problems it faced during the Depression, the Hispanic community in San Antonio grew substantially during the 1930s, while Mexican-American sectors of other urban places lost population (table 3).[3]

Spatially, San Antonio's black population was concentrated in an area of about sixty square blocks on the city's East Side and a smaller neighborhood on the North Side composed primarily of household servants of affluent Anglo San Antonians. Pockets of black residences were sprinkled through the West Side of the city. Mexican Americans were confined largely to the West Side, where population density was heaviest, in some of the worst slums in the United States. Although residential segregation has eroded considerably since World War II, a stable black community re-

[2]Abraham Hoffman, *Unwanted Mexican Americans in the Great Depression: Repatriation Pressures, 1929–1939.*

[3]Ibid.

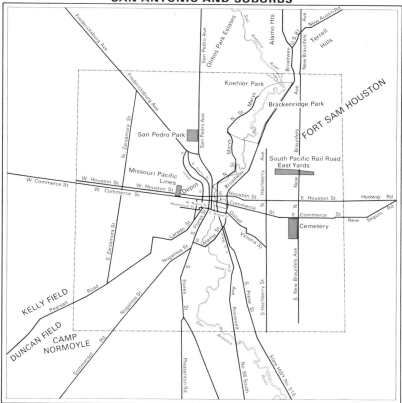

San Antonio and suburbs, 1936

mains intact on the East Side, and the West Side remains both predominantly Hispanic and the area of the city most plagued by unhealthful living conditions. During the Depression the West Side was distinguished from the rest of the city not only by poverty and disease but also by the concentration there of prostitution and exploitative working conditions in scores of small factories employing women, two of the particular problems that burdened the women of the city during the 1930s.

Although San Antonio is not unique in the racial and ethnic prejudices its citizens have practiced, the citizens' behavior has been especially incongruous with the myths and facts of local history that they have cherished. The culture of Mexico pervades all aspects of life in San Antonio that are visible to the eye or audible to the ear. Food, place-names, architecture, and public entertainments all reveal the more than 250 years of Mexican heritage in San Antonio. Migrants from Mexico were the first residents of the settlement that became San Antonio, yet thousands of Hispanics born in San Antonio were treated like second-class citizens in the twentieth century. San Antonio, like many other cities of the Southwest, owes much of its physical charm to the efforts of the Spanish priests who came north in the eighteenth century to build a network of missions throughout Mexico. Although the Alamo is the most famous Mexican mission in the United States, it is but one of many structures in San Antonio that were built before Texas independence.

The missionaries who came to Texas arrived with the encouragement and support of the military, which began quartering troops in the area in the 1720s. In the 1730s a small band of refugees from the Canary Islands arrived to augment the community of approximately two hundred Spanish-speaking residents. Despite Indian raids and squabbles among the missionaries and settlers, by the end of the American Revolution San Antonio had grown to a population of two thousand.

Anglos, primarily from the southern states, began settling in San Antonio under the charter granted to Moses Austin in 1821, and the success of the campaign for Texas independence settled the question of Anglo dominance. Even though Anglo migration continued, the decline of the missions and the removal of the Mexican military reduced San Antonio to a ghost of its former self. After Texas achieved statehood in 1845, European visitors and immigrants began arriving in a steady stream. A few blacks had been taken to San Antonio as slaves, but a larger group migrated there after Emancipation.

After the Civil War cattle and sheep ranchers exploited the free ranges of West Texas, bringing commercial prosperity to San Antonio. The one employer that most affected the local economy over the next century, the United States government, had established a permanent army post, Fort Sam Houston, on the city's outskirts at the time of the Civil War. By the turn of the century San Antonio had grown to a population of 53,000, and a number of small manufacturers had opened for business.

The prosperity of the 1880s and 1890s changed the atmosphere of San Antonio in a number of ways. Both as a military town and as a trading center the city developed various entertainments from vaudeville to prostitution that gave the town a reputation as a place of bawdy good times.

The city's opulent bordellos, concentrated in a small district on the West Side, appeared and flourished during these years. Not far from the houses of prostitution the King William area of handsome homes belonging to the city's commercial elite developed simultaneously.

As the city grew, its cultural institutions expanded as well, and the ethnic diversity of San Antonio marked their growth. German Americans established a school before the Civil War, and in 1851 they built Beethoven Hall, an auditorium used principally for musical performances. German Americans founded both Catholic and Lutheran churches in the city. Irish Americans were an important component of the city's laboring and commercial classes, though their cultural institutions were not as strong as the Germans'. Scandinavians and eastern Europeans also joined the city's population before the turn of the century. By the early twentieth century a small Polish community had formed around its own church in central San Antonio. Although a number of immigrant cultures flowered in San Antonio, Mexican influence always had the strongest impact on the look and tone of the city.

As the twentieth century opened, all the basic demographic, cultural, and economic characteristics that were to describe San Antonio in the Depression were manifest, though there were important developments and changes in the three decades before the great crash. There was no substantial immigration from Mexico during the period from Texas independence through the remainder of the nineteenth century. The approximately three hundred Mexicans who crossed the border into Texas each year during the 1880s and 1890s tended to settle in rural areas or towns south of San Antonio. Immigration increased dramatically after 1900, but most of the newcomers also found homes in rural areas. The Mexican Revolution and the demand for agricultural labor during World War I accelerated immigration in the next decade, and economic and political conditions in Mexico during the 1920s brought the exodus to a crest on the eve of the Depression. Between 1900 and 1930 an estimated 500,000 persons migrated to the United States from Mexico, and after 1920 an increasing proportion of the migrants headed for urban areas.[4] Mexican agricultural laborers, who had worked the fields during the war years and were set adrift after demobilization, began clustering in towns and cities. The cities of the Southwest, par-

[4]Mark Reisler, *By The Sweat of Their Brow: Mexican Immigrant Labor in the United States, 1900–1940*. Reisler discusses the pattern of Mexican immigration and the problems of enumerating Mexican immigrants to the United States.

ticularly San Antonio, emerged as centers for seasonal labor. Farm agents came from as far away as Michigan to recruit Mexican-American workers who wintered in San Antonio. Although black migrant workers in the United States tended to travel singly or in small groups of men, Mexican-American workers usually moved their entire families from place to place as they followed the crops. Many Mexican-American children who spent much of their lives in San Antonio never established permanent roots in the city. Thousands never completed elementary school because of their root-lessness or because they participated in migrant field labor.

The twentieth-century immigrants included a large number of edu-cated and formerly wealthy landowners who fled Mexico during the revo-lution, but most were peasant farm workers driven out by poverty. In the sudden crush of San Antonio's population growth in the 1920s residential building did not keep pace. Impoverished immigrants crowded together in small homes and hastily constructed shacks on the West Side; often two or three families were packed into two or three rooms. Mexican-American residences filled in the remaining open spaces between rail lines and ware-houses and surrounded the red-light district. The West Side from the 1920s onward was marked by poor housing and high death and disease rates.

No major city in the United States fought the Depression with fewer weapons than did San Antonio. The political and economic development of the city after Texas statehood created circumstances that foreshadowed the city's inability to attack the hunger and disease that stalked its people. The major sources of income and tax revenue had always been visitors or temporary residents who had little concern for the city's welfare. Since the nineteenth century cattle barons and oil tycoons have found San Antonio a pleasant distraction from their cares and an important center for commer-cial transactions, but few have called it home. World War I brought the expansion of Fort Sam Houston and the building of new military installa-tions, including a flight school, at the southwestern edge of the city. During the Depression, Fort Sam Houston, Camp Normoyle, Kelly Field, and Duncan Field all employed workers from San Antonio. Since then, the military has overshadowed all other contributors to the local economy. The military has been the major consumer of labor and resources in San An-tonio, but it has not directly generated city tax revenues. During the 1920s the United States Army spent about $38 million annually in Bexar County. Army personnel, however, turned their backs on the city, knowing that they would soon be reassigned or discharged. The vast majority of government employees lived outside the city limits and consequently did not participate in city politics.

With so many residents and investors uninvolved in the life of the city, machine politics emerged early and forcibly in San Antonio and persisted into the Depression decade. An article in *Survey Graphic* signaled the death of the Democratic machine with the election of Maury Maverick as mayor in 1939.[5] The machine and boss rule, the *Graphic* article argued, dated from 1846, when Bryan Callaghan wrested political control from the local Mexican elite. Absentee investment and a heavy economic reliance on tourism and commercial entertainment not only left a leadership void where machine politics could flourish but also created opportunities for graft and vice that left their marks on all aspects of life in the city.

In the early twentieth century Anglo San Antonians saw black ward boss Charlie Bellinger as the most important link between machine politics and prostitution, gambling, and the liquor traffic. While little concrete evidence of Bellinger's career remains, his critics attributed his influence to extensive real estate holdings and a loan business in the black community. Bellinger had purportedly raised capital for investment in legitimate businesses through a career in vice during the first decade of the twentieth century. After World War I, Bellinger emerged as the strongest political voice in the black community by promising and delivering neighborhood improvements and better schools for blacks in exchange for black votes for Democratic machine candidates. Bellinger never sought public office himself; his power depended on delivering a bloc vote that was never more than a small minority of the city's total electorate. His disproportionate influence derived partly from the fact that the black San Antonians were much more likely to be registered voters than were Mexican-American citizens. In 1934 approximately 5,000 blacks as opposed to 7,000 Mexican Americans had paid poll taxes. Bellinger went to prison in 1927 on a tax-evasion conviction, but his opponents maintained that he continued to dominate black voting until his death in 1936. The victory of New Deal advocate Maury Maverick in the 1934 congressional race was credited to the disqualification of black voters in the Democratic primary that year. It has also been claimed that Mexican-American citizens voted down the line for the machine until Maverick's election.[6]

[5]Audrey Granneberg, "Maury Maverick's San Antonio," *Survey Graphic* 28, no. 7 (July, 1939):421–26.

[6]Ibid.; Owen P. White, "Machine Made," *Collier's*, September 18, 1937, pp. 32–33.

Thus when San Antonio entered the 1930s, its major employers were not participating in community leadership, it had an entrenched political machine that exacerbated ethnic and racial hostilities, and the more substantial elements of the permanent middle class lived outside the city limits. As thousands of immigrants poured into the West Side in the 1920s, the need for public services greatly outweighed both the desire and the ability of the modest middle class to provide public services of any kind. The course of San Antonio's development and Anglo understanding of social and economic conditions in the city produced a sterile environment for the development of social and relief services. Anglo politicians and influential businessmen ignored calls for street and sanitation improvements that were sorely needed on the Hispanic West Side before the great crash.

In a city with few public services and woefully inadequate private social services even in the "prosperous" twenties, the quality of life and even life itself depended almost entirely on personal income. Black San Antonians, who were concentrated in low-paying domestic and laboring jobs, lived more modestly than most Anglos and had a shorter life span. The black population, however, did not suffer so widely as Mexican Americans the ravages of malnutrition and enteritis that killed many children before they reached adulthood. The *San Antonio Light* reported that 90 percent of the children who were registered in West Side clinics suffered from malnutrition.[7] Poverty and disease were so pervasive in the 1920s that San Antonians were slow to recognize the Depression as a qualitative change.

In San Antonio as elsewhere in the nation investment declined immediately after the Wall Street panic, but the consequences of Black Friday were not immediately evident to the average worker. The reality that hard times were at hand was suggested by the behavior of the Hoover administration in the closing months of 1929. President Hoover verbally assured the nation that the economy was sound and that it was folly to doubt prosperity. A gathering of corporate leaders at the White House in November and subsequent efforts to enlist the support of business and state officials for White House policy were clear signs of the severity of the economic setback. In December, Hoover carried a message to Congress that economic confidence among investors had been restored since the crash, but declining bank deposits, the near standstill in auto production, and the appearance of breadlines in the nation's cities were but a few signs of the coming Depression. For most San Antonians the Depression existed pri-

---

[7]*San Antonio Light*, May 20, 1939.

Communist-led demonstration at city hall, 1930. The demonstration was peaceful and provoked no backlash from public officials. The press did not publish photos of the event.
(*San Antonio Light* Collection, University of Texas Institute of Texan Cultures, San Antonio.)

marily in the newspaper headlines until the spring of 1930. A decline in construction starts had occurred in Bexar County almost immediately after the crash, but it was several months before most local citizens appreciated the consequences.[8]

[8]Hoover's later recollections cast the mood of late 1929 and early 1930 as uncertain but not depressed. In his memoirs the former president dated the coming of the Depression as March, 1930, a year after his inauguration. Herbert Hoover, *The Memoirs of Herbert Hoover: The Cabinet and the Presidency, 1920–1933*, pp. 312–13; Harris Gaylord Warren, *Herbert Hoover and the Great Depression*, p. 118; Albert U. Romasco, *The Poverty of Abundance: Hoover, the Nation, the Depression*, pp. 10–28; Mary Maverick McMillan Fisher, "San Antonio I: The Hoover Era," in Robert C. Cotner, ed., *Texas Cities and the Great Depression*, pp. 53–55.

In the last three months of 1929 the demand for food, clothing, and shelter at the Bexar County Red Cross and other charitable organizations rose rapidly. Unemployment increased, though few citizens recognized its proportions until April 7, 1930. On that day a parade of about one thousand persons, mostly Mexican Americans, passed through town to City Hall. The demonstrators presented Mayor C. M. Chambers with demands for public works projects to relieve unemployment. Before the march took place, Governor Dan Moody intervened in an attempt to reroute the parade so that it would not pass the Mexican consulate as its organizers had planned. The consul had kept the Mexican government informed of the problems facing San Antonio's Hispanics and had used his good offices to protect the civil rights of Mexican citizens in the city. Throughout the Depression the consul represented the plight of Mexican citizens in San Antonio to local administrators as best he could, but he rarely found a sympathetic ear. The governor's office, fearful of diplomatic complications that might follow if the demonstrators included the consul among officials they wished to alert to their demands, asked Mayor Chambers to reroute the parade and warned that the U.S. Department of State had reported that the march would be linked to a Communist demonstration. The mayor did not interfere, and the parade subsequently passed the Mexican consulate without incident. At city hall the demonstrators presented the mayor with a resolution requesting immediate employment assistance. Later that spring voters approved a five-million-dollar bond package for public improvements.[9]

Symptoms of the Depression in San Antonio and surrounding Bexar County multiplied in 1931. Default and delinquency in tax payments forced the dismissal of more than three hundred city employees. The board of the San Antonio Independent School District cut its budget and eliminated many teaching, administrative, and maintenance positions. Five banks closed in 1931, and before the end of the year "Hoovervilles," shanty towns built from scrap materials and named after the seemingly unsympathetic president, had begun appearing on the city's outskirts. In the summer of 1932 the school board resorted to payment in scrip and cut teachers' salaries drastically. Continuing declines in revenues forced cutbacks and payment in scrip by Bexar County as well, though the county's fiscal problems were less severe than the city's. Late in 1932 remnants of the Bonus Army, World War I veterans who had demonstrated in Washington to seek early payment of their military pensions, swelled the population of Bexar

[9]*San Antonio Express*, April 8, 1930; Fisher, "San Antonio I," p. 63.

In 1933, at the height of the Depression, unemployed workers gather at Bexar County Courthouse to register for jobs and relief.
(*San Antonio Light* Collection, University of Texas Institute of Texan Cultures, San Antonio.)

County's shanty villages, and in October the Veterans of Foreign Wars organized a relief camp for veterans, finding them temporary work on nearby farms to generate food donations for the camp.[10]

Despite deepening indications of local and national distress, the *San Antonio Express* tried to persuade readers late in 1932 that "in San Antonio and its trade area—as throughout the country—signs are multiplying that business recovery is well under way and that the improvement is more than seasonal."[11] In 1933 city employment was cut further, but San Antonio could not meet its June payroll. Relief figures and estimates of unemploy-

[10]Fisher, "San Antonio I," pp. 57–68, *San Antonio Express*, October 18, 1932.
[11]*San Antonio Express*, October 23, 1932.

ment indicate that San Antonio passed through the nadir of the Depression in 1933, but recovery was slow and incomplete as the nation entered World War II. Throughout the Depression local civic leaders and public officials resisted acknowledging the severity of the disaster and the need for publicly funded county and city relief programs. Both the denial of the depth of the problem and the refusal to foster public responsibility for massive unemployment exacerbated physical and psychological suffering in the city. Despite the commencement in the late thirties of the military buildup that brought jobs and consumer dollars to San Antonio, the city was still deeply depressed in 1940. Among cities with populations of 200,000 or more, San Antonio had the lowest median wage. A prominent San Antonian blamed the city's low income on the fact that the Mexican-American community, which had low earning power relative to that of both blacks and Anglos, had grown more than other groups in the population.[12]

As the Depression waxed in San Antonio, individual women perceived and reacted to the emergency in a multitude of ways. Ethnic prejudices as well as differing notions of women's proper role during a time of high unemployment divided women when solidarity would have benefited all. Women were also isolated from meaningful cooperation with each other by their overwhelming preoccupation with the problems of their own families. The women who did provide leadership in fighting the Depression came from all sectors of the economy. Many were middle-class women who knew the Depression as relief administrators. Other leaders were members of the leisure class who had previous experience in civic work or industrial workers who believed that organization was their only weapon against personal powerlessness.

[12]T. R. Picnot, "Socio-Economic Status in Low Income Groups of San Antonio" (address before San Antonio Social Workers Association, mimeographed copy, n.d.).

[2]

The Family and the Female Life Cycle

Maybe sometimes situations like that have their own advantages. The family is more together. Today every kid has a car to go their own way. They live in apartments. We wouldn't have thought of that. . . . But like I said, families stuck together and could depend on each other.

—Carmen Perry[1]

As San Antonio women articulated their concerns during the Depression and as they remembered the past, their thoughts ran first and last to family. Social worker Adela Navarro remembered her mother's watchful supervision of her children's education and her insistence on respectful behavior. Homemaker Ruby Cude recalled how hard her husband worked, sometimes holding down two jobs at one time, to make a comfortable life for his family. Store clerk Beatrice Clay reminisced about neighborhood sharing and backyard picnics that helped and cheered each of the families in her community. Family commanded deepest personal loyalties and constituted the primary economic unit in which a woman participated.

Marriage and the arrival of children were events that the average young girl expected in her life as well as the circumstances that most narrowly defined the roles she played in adulthood. Most girls coming of age in San Antonio in the 1920s married before or after a period of paid employment, stayed at home to rear the children, and did not enter the paid work force after marriage. The well-being of wives and of daughters living at home usually depended on the labors of male wage earners. For women who did not enter the work force, the vagaries of the labor market and the wage cuts of the 1930s were experienced second-hand in the form of sharply reduced household budgets, the sometimes awkward presence of husbands and fathers at home during their usual working hours, and male depression. The first responses of wives and daughters to financial setbacks were to adapt to a life-style of leftovers and hand-me-downs and to show support for male family members who felt shame for economic problems

[1]Interview with Carmen Perry, May 22, 1979.

not of their making. As Navarro remembered of her father and her brothers, "I could see what had happened in my own family, that they just couldn't bear it." [2]

Regardless of their family status, women's experiences during the Depression were not individual or solitary experiences. Their dependence on male wage earners profoundly influenced most women's perceptions and roles during the Depression. Women saw the Depression through the filter of emotional concerns and attachments that affect wives, mothers, and daughters in prosperous times as well. A woman did not achieve independence by remaining single and entering the work force; life was more comfortable if economic resources were pooled, and regard for parents or siblings was paramount if the woman had neither spouse nor child. The composition of the family and family changes over time defined the responsibilities of women as they moved through the Depression decade, but for most women family concerns of one kind or another were ever present. Women who wished or needed to work weighed their household responsibilties and the attitudes of family members in the balance with the benefits of market labor and the difficulty of finding work. The death of a husband or the serious illness of a child was a catastrophe that was outside a young girl's expectations of her adult life and might leave deep personal scars. The Depression intensified the economic hardship caused by a serious illness or a death in the family. Considerations of family were primary in a woman's decision to seek work or not to seek work at any stage of her life.

In 1930 and in 1940 the vast majority of adult women were married. Marriage patterns were not the same for all population groupings, however, and marriage did not bring the same responsibilities to all women. Among San Antonio women blacks married earliest, 22 percent of all black women between the ages of fifteen and nineteen being married, widowed, or divorced in 1930 (tables 4 to 6). Mexican-American and native-born Anglo women married slightly later than blacks, but foreign-born Anglo women almost never married in their teens. As women reached their early twenties, life-cycle patterns manifested their greatest differences by ethnicity, though only among foreign-born Anglos was the majority single. After age twenty-five, differences in the percentages of the population who were married began to even out, but Anglo immigrant women remained the least likely to have married.

[2]Interview with Adela Navarro, May 22, 1979.

The wedding of Mr. and Mrs. Theron Beckwith at the Civil Works Administration camp in Bexar County, ca. 1934. The Depression caused many men and women to postpone marriage, with a resulting rise in age of marriage between 1930 and 1940. (*San Antonio Light* Collection, University of Texas Institute of Texan Cultures, San Antonio.)

The age of marriage increased slightly between 1930 and 1940 with women in all age brackets somewhat more likely to be single at the end of the decade. Contrary to the notion that the Depression brought a drop in the divorce rate, only women under age thirty were less likely to be divorced in 1940 than were women in the same age group in 1930. Black women, a small percentage of the total female population, recorded a decline in both the number and the percentage of women reporting themselves as divorced, but the chances of other women experiencing divorce increased. The women who reported themselves as widows in 1940 were a somewhat older group than widows recorded in the census of 1930. Both the number and the percentage of women in the total population who were widows increased over the course of the Depression.

Census statistics on marital status provide the broad outlines of the family cycle through which women passed, but reporting of this information is a sensitive area that individuals may choose to protect through inaccurate responses. Some hints of problems in reporting emerge from a comparison of statistics on males and females. Substantially fewer married men than married women appear in the census count of 1930, and the difference increased over the decade. The discrepancy indicates that, whether the husbands were absent or nonexistent, many married women were not protected from the responsibilities of family headship by their spouses.[3]

Women's family responsibilities were different from men's regardless of family headship and regardless of the presence or absence of children. Virtually every family enumerated in the census of 1930 included a home-maker, a woman who fulfilled the role of caring for the home but was not a paid housekeeper (table 7).[4] Many homemakers were also household heads, though the majority of families were male-headed. Anglo families were most likely to be male-headed, and black families had the lowest inci-dence of male headship. The percentage of families of each ethnic group that were headed by males reflects sex ratios in the city. The male-female ratio was lowest among blacks and highest among Anglos (tables 4, 5, and 8).

The Depression exacerbated emotional as well as economic stress on the family, and either kind of stress might lead to the dissolution of the family unit or the temporary separation of its members. Admissions of men and women to the state mental hospital in San Antonio increased dramat-ically during the early 1930s.[5] Suicide increased, though it remained rare among women. The tensions created by poverty and overcrowded living conditions proved overwhelming to Janie Brown Katlan, who lived with her husband, two sisters, and four nieces in a two-room apartment. In 1938, after nine months of marriage, the twenty-year-old woman shot her-self through the heart.[6] Another San Antonio woman, Kate Clark, poi-soned herself. She left a note in which she explained that she knew it was wrong to take her life but that she could not find work and suicide was "the only way out."[7]

---

[3]Given the presence of the military, which drew married men away from homes else-where in the nation, the number of San Antonio wives with absent husbands may actually have been larger than the census suggests. An estimation of the military's impact on the com-position of the city's population can be derived from the number of people living outside pri-vate households. In San Antonio, 8,463 men and 2,469 women lived outside private house-holds in such places as hotels, large boardinghouses, and military barracks. In Houston, a city with considerably larger population, fewer men but more women lived outside private house-holds. Virtually all the San Antonio men were white, and most were between the ages of twenty and thirty-four.

[4]In 1930 the Census Bureau defined a homemaker as a female household member who was primarily responsible for the care of the home and who performed those duties without receiving wages.

[5] Fisher, "San Antonio I," p. 56.

[6]*San Antonio Light*, March 3, 1938.

[7]*San Antonio Light*, August 11, 1933.

Abandonment was more likely to break up families than was mental illness or suicide. Unemployed fathers deserted their wives and children, who often had nowhere to turn for support. There were also instances of mothers abandoning their children. In May, 1936, an unemployed single mother left her three-month-old infant on the steps of the Salvation Army headquarters. The baby wore a note in which the mother said that she had gone to Austin in hope of finding a job. She promised, "I will send money every week if I have it." [8]

In 1930 the state of Texas tried to minimize the effects of desertion by a spouse or parent in a law that facilitated support suits. As the law took effect in Bexar County, local officials reported encouraging signs that the legislation was slowing desertion. The county tried to counsel husbands, who were the primary targets, to keep families together. County-court records reveal, however, that mediation failed in many cases as wives took to the courts in hopes of forcing payments from their spouses or former spouses.

The reactions of Hispanic women to the new law reveal the limitations of cultural values in the depths of economic crisis. Despite cultural proscriptions that forbade wives from publicly shaming their husbands or even admitting that they had left home, Hispanic women were prominent among nonsupport plaintiffs. [9] While they were unlikely to violate their husbands' authority as long as they remained at home, wives exercised considerable autonomy if their spouses deserted them.

Female family heads in all ethnic groups faced frightening circumstances during the Depression. When unemployment threatened the survival of their families, many women beseeched members of the Roosevelt administration to help them in some way. One mother wrote to Eleanor Roosevelt:

Aug 23—1939
San Antonio, Tex

Dear Mrs. Roosevelt:

I am trying hard to get on W.P.A. I'm a typist and just can't seem to find work. I have four little children depending on me. And I have no home and no money to

---

[8] *San Antonio Light*, May 16, 1936.

[9] From 1929 through 1933, 204 Spanish-surnamed women and 262 other women sued their spouses on charges of desertion or nonsupport in Bexar County's Thirty-seventh District Court. See also Kathleen M. Gonzales, "The Mexican Family in San Antonio, Texas" (Master's thesis, Unviersity of Texas, 1928), p. 29.

buy food or pay rent. the relief has rejected me for W.P.A. work, because I have a three months old baby girl. The oldest boy is 6 and will go to school this year, but I dont know how I can send him if I dont get work.

My little baby needs milk and I can't buy it. am living in one room in a basement which is warm and damp. . . .

Mrs. Roosevelt I'm begging you with all my heart to *please* help me if you can. I love my babies dearly and won't submit to them being put in a home away from me. I would simply die apart from them.

Mrs. Renee Lohrback[10]

Another San Antonio woman wrote the president and Mrs. Roosevelt the Depression had separated her from her children:

I am desperately in need of a job, I wish to beg that you will please help me to get one on W.P.A. Will be satisfied what ever it is.

I am a widow, one son to care for. I've never been on W.P.A. but I have been on relief. I can't find employment in any private home. I've tried for the last two months—I find a week of work or so then it play out so I can't find any thing steady enough to make a living.

I tried to get on W.P.A. and they refuse to take me on because they say I am a good maid and I ought to stay in the private homes, but I have tried to find employment there for last two mos. and failed.

I had to send my son away to the country until I can find work to care for him on. . . .

Please sir, & Madam, I feel unworthy to worry your highness but please be merciful unto me.

Very truly yours,

Myrtle Ford.[11]

Despite the pressures of the Depression, most San Antonio families remained intact. In all ethnic groups most parents of young children stayed together during the Depression, but there were significant differences in family composition among Anglo, black, and Hispanic families. Overall, Anglo girls had greater chances than other San Antonio females of growing to adulthood in a family composed of two parents and their children and of imitating this pattern in their adult lives. Throughout the Depression the Anglo family was more stable than the minority family. The black family was the most likely of all San Antonio families to be broken by separation or abandonment, and the Mexican-American family was the most likely to be broken by death of a parent or child.

[10]Records of the Works Projects Administration, file 661.
[11]Ibid.

Mexican-American families were both larger and younger than other families, black families being the smallest (table 9). In 1930, Mexican Americans accounted for less than one-third of San Antonio families, but they constituted three-fourths of families with three or more children under ten years of age and nearly two-thirds of families with four or more children under age twenty-one. Foreign-born Anglo families were nearly identical to native-born Anglo families with respect to size and age structure. Across all ethnic groupings the majority of families with young children had only one or two under age ten.

The San Antonio Health Department reported a decline in the birthrate during the Depression, especially during the early 1930s (table 10).[12] A comparison of the age structure of the total population in 1940 with the figures in 1930 confirms the change. Both the ratio of children under ten years of age to women fifteen years of age and older and the absolute number of children under age ten decreased between 1930 and 1940.

The postponement of marriage and the practice of birth control were obvious factors in the declining birthrate, but abortion also persisted throughout the Depression as a means of family limitation. When undertaken without proper medical assistance, abortion was dangerous. Each year a few San Antonio women died at the hands of untrained abortionists. The story of Mrs. Antonia Mena illustrates both the desperation of poor wives and the crude conditions under which abortionists operated. When she discovered that she was pregnant, Mrs. Mena, aged twenty-eight, sought the aid of an abortionist.[13] With her sister she went to the home of Mrs. Leota Mowers, who told them that she had performed many abortions and that her clients had suffered no ill effects. Mrs. Mena paid Mrs. Mowers her last ten dollars and gave her a radio as security for the additional twenty-five dollars that Mrs. Mowers required. After the abortion had been performed, police were called to Mrs. Mowers's home, where Mrs. Mena was found dead on the living-room floor.

The declining birthrate that characterized the Depression, especially its early years, did not necessarily mean that household size decreased as well. The Depression discouraged persons in their late teens and early twenties from leaving home to begin their own households either as newlyweds or as single persons. Carmen Perry's brothers postponed marriage and remained in the parental home longer than they wished. A young

[12]See also San Antonio Department of Health, *Annual Report* (1936), table 1.
[13]*San Antonio Light*, February 1, 1938.

Mrs. Antonia Mena, who died at age twenty-eight following an illegal abortion performed by Mrs. Leota Mowers (*right*). Mrs. Mowers collected ten dollars and a radio for performing the fatal abortion.
(*San Antonio Light* Collection, University of Texas Institute of Texan Cultures, San Antonio.)

single woman named Schild lost her clerical job early in the Depression and returned to her parents' home after a period of independence.[14] In 1940 a substantial number of young adults were living in the homes of their parents. Married children might also share quarters with their parents. Ruby Cude and her husband and children moved in with her parents after a period of being on their own. As the Depression neared its end, large numbers of young adults found themselves in the same situation as Miss Schild and the Perrys.

The chances of a female living outside the nuclear or extended family were slim (table 11). In 1940 nearly two-fifths of San Antonio females of all ages lived with parents or grandparents. Of females in this category more than one-fourth were twenty years of age or older. A small percentage of females lived in the homes of their grown children, more than one-tenth

[14]Homework interview no. 30, Records of the Women's Bureau, Correspondence and Survey Materials Relating to Bulletin no. 126, Record Group 86, National Archives. Hereafter cited as Records of the Women's Bureau, Materials Relating to Bulletin no. 126.

headed households, and more than one-third were wives living with their spouses. Less than 1 percent of the city's female population lived in the homes of their employers, a slightly larger percentage lodged in private households, and less than 6 percent lived in the households of relatives other than spouses, parents, or grandparents.

Black women were slightly more likely to be live-in employees than were white women, but the vast majority of women who lived with their employers were not black. Nonwhite women were somewhat more likely than whites to live as lodgers or servants in the households of others or to live with relatives outside the immediate family (table 11).[15] Black children were more likely than other children to live in the home of a relative other than a parent. Anna Graves left Seguin to live with her aunt in San Antonio because there was no high school for blacks in Seguin in the 1930s. Graves was one of many black children whose lives were enriched when they reached out from the nuclear to the extended family. Anglo and Mexican-American families held their children more strictly to nuclear bonds.

Ethnicity was also a significant indicator of other life-cycle differences. The school-leaving age of boys and of girls varied among Anglos, blacks, and Hispanics. Whether or not there was a causal relationship between school-leaving age and work-force participation, Mexican-American girls, who entered the work force at a younger age than that of other San Antonio females, were also the first to leave school. Chapters 4 and 5 reveal that familial values and occupational segregation operated jointly to push young Hispanic girls who had left school into the labor force while their mothers remained at home.

Black females stayed in school longer than Anglo girls and entered the work force later. The census data reveal that black women differed from Anglos and Hispanics in that young girls who left school tended to marry before entering the labor market rather than finding work and marrying after entering the work force. For all groups the average school-leaving age increased over the decade, and youthful employment declined (tables 15 and 21).[16]

One of the most common concerns of women who wrote letters to Eleanor Roosevelt and New Deal administrators asking for help was the

---

[15]Anonymous interview, May 16, 1978.

[16]While individuals cannot be traced through the census data, the school-leaving age and the age at marriage of black females were closer together than the school-leaving age and the age at entering the work force. For a discussion of the pattern see chapter 4.

reality that poverty could interfere with the education of their children. Few families considered allowing children to drop out of school to seek employment because almost no jobs were available for teenagers as the Depression deepened. Many mothers, however, confronted the prospect or the reality of children leaving school because they could not pay for books and supplies or because they did not have enough clothes to leave the house. One mother laid off from WPA employment wrote Eleanor Roosevelt that "in September when school starts it will be impossible for mine to attend, they will have no shoes & there clothing is no better than rags." [17]

In 1930 one in every ten San Antonio families included lodgers, who might be live-in servants, guests, boarders, or rent-paying family members (tables 12 and 13). [18] Beatrice Clay described the economic circumstances under which homeowners took in family members as boarders:

I think there were some people who had a very very tough time because I had an uncle who lived almost on the same block that I lived. [He] was buying his home and he had not had a job for almost six months. And we were renting and he was buying so he came to me and asked me if I would move in with him. And he had his mother which is my grandmother and another nephew whose parents were both dead. And he said that they could make room and we could move in and what money we were paying for rent could pay the interest on his note to keep him from losing his house, which we did. [19]

Black households like Clay's were the most likely to include boarders, and Mexican-American families were the least likely. [20] The absence of lodgers from Mexican homes is consistent with the extreme poverty and small housing units in the Mexican-American community, but it conflicts with contemporary accounts of multiple-family households. Mexican values stressing the integrity of the family unit and the vulnerability of young girls to outside influences may have generally discouraged lodging arrangements and, in the exceptional cases, may have contributed to an undercount of lodgers by census takers. While black San Antonians suffered

[17]Records of the Works Project Administration, file 662.

[18]While it is reasonable to suspect that lodgers in Anglo households were more likely to be household employees than were the nonfamily residents in black and Hispanic homes, the census of 1930 does not discriminate between employees and boarders.

[19]Interview with Beatrice Clay, May 24, 1979.

[20]*San Antonio Light*, May 22, 1930. See also San Antonio Housing Authority, *San Antonio Housing Survey, 1930*. For a thorough discussion of boarding arrangements in urban America see John Modell and Tamara K. Hareven, "Urbanization and the Malleable Household: An Examination of Boarding and Lodging in American Families, *Journal of Marriage and the Family* 35 (August, 1973):467–79.

Pablo and Antonia Martinez, who lived in this one-room house with Pablo's parents and his older brother, photographed in June, 1937. Poverty forced many Mexican Americans into cramped, unsanitary housing.
(*San Antonio Light* Collection, University of Texas Institute of Texan Cultures, San Antonio.)

residential segregation, they never experienced the intense overcrowding and slum conditions of the Mexican West Side. As Mexican immigrants flooded into the city in the 1920s, houses in the Mexican community were subdivided, and new one-room shacks were thrown up to accommodate the newcomers. Such close quarters discouraged adding outsiders to the household but probably contributed as well to an undercount of West Side residents by the 1930 census takers, a situation suspected by city leaders once the fifteenth census was published.

Regardless of the reasons, black households included more lodgers than did Mexican-American households. Since both the income from boarders and the responsibilities of caring for them may have discouraged married women from seeking work outside the home, it is surprising that black married women were both most likely to be in the labor force and most likely to keep lodgers. Conversely, married Hispanic women were least likely to seek work and least likely to have lodgers in their homes. Lodging arrangements are but one facet of the interaction between culture and economic conditions in San Antonio. The economic situation of the black family encouraged married women to bring money into the home in either wages or rent. Cultural values supported these economic motivations in black families. Female protectiveness in Hispanic families discouraged similar responses to need.

Although census statistics indicate that significant differences in the composition of families and households did exist, the statistics suggest little about the structure of families. Secondary literature on family life in America has consistently emphasized that familial values and the structure of authority within the family have varied widely among the many racial and national groups that comprise the nation's population.[21] San Antonio women, like their sisters elsewhere in the United States, grew up under cultural prescriptions that affected women's roles and family life, attitudes that were peculiar to their ethnic or racial groups. Mexican Americans preserved a culture that emphasized male authority and family loyalty above other values. Mexican wives were expected to be unquestioningly obedient to their husbands, and daughters were expected to defer to the wishes of brothers as well as fathers. Sons might dictate the actions of their mothers in the fathers' absence. Wives had a duty to protect the manliness of their husbands by refraining from active lives outside the home and by not criticizing the behavior of their husbands before friends or relatives. Likewise, daughters had an obligation to preserve the moral reputation of the family through obedience and the avoidance of persons outside the family.

In a thesis of 1928 on the Mexican-American family in San Antonio, Kathleen Gonzales argued that Hispanics in the city preserved Mexican values and that for women and girls these values dictated a life very different from Anglo expectations. After marriage a woman was to confine her attentions to home and family. Even church-related activities, accept-

---

[21]On the black family see Herbert G. Gutman, *The Black Family in Slavery and Freedom, 1750–1925*; Elmer P. Martin and Joanne Mitchell Martin, *The Black Extended Family*; Carol B. Stack, *All Our Kin: Strategies for Survival in a Black Community*. On the Mexican-American family see Gonzales, "The Mexican Family in San Antonio, Texas."

Mrs. C. C. de la Garza preparing the altar at a West Side church, ca. 1935. Service on the altar guild was one of the few culturally acceptable activities of Mexican-American married women.
(*San Antonio Light* Collection, University of Texas Institute of Texan Cultures, San Antonio.)

able social engagements for most American women, were strictly limited: "The Church expects a woman to give all her time to her husband and home after marriage and for that reason does not provide organized clubs for married women." [22] Gonzales argued that overall the maintenance of Mexican values undermined the well-being of women. Daughters were

[22]Gonzales, "The Mexican Family in San Antonio, Texas," p. 5.

born into families that preferred and favored male children. Pointing out that many Mexican-American wives preferred out of modesty to have babies delivered by midwives rather than by doctors, Gonzales concluded that "some would rather die than go through a medical exam." [23] The family cycle itself was destructive of a wife's health, but it was a process that she was powerless to change:

> The woman does not care for a large family because her husband's salary is too small to support one. The woman is quick to see the opportunities her children would miss which are enjoyed in homes where there are few children. In her desire for fewer children, she is hampered by two very strong forces. The church denounces it as a crime not to bear all the children God sends, and the husband dislikes it because he wants the wife to be tied hand and foot, so to speak. [24]

The consequences of unlimited fertility and low income, as Gonzales understood them, were exhaustion and malnutrition among women.

Mexican Americans carried their regard for family beyond the nuclear unit. Parents might continue to demand the obedience of their adult children, and siblings comprised the strongest social relationship of adults. Compadres, the godparents of one's children, were friends to whom mutual obligations of kinship extended, though persons selected to be compadres might or might not be blood relatives.

Cultural ideals do not reflect the behavior of an entire population. Familial values differed somewhat according to social class in Mexico, and acculturation eroded the observance of Mexican values among Mexican Americans. Mexican-American wives frequently exercised subtle influence on family decisions. A 1965 study of Mexican Americans in the Southwest argues that women assumed considerable autonomy when husbands abandoned the home. [25] In San Antonio there was also some evidence that women exercised authority or acted independently, as in the suits for alimony or support brought by Hispanic women in the 1930s. Considerable numbers of Mexican-American women also acted independently of men in the labor movement. Even with deviation from the ideal, however, in comparison with black and Anglo women the Mexican-American wives lived tightly circumscribed lives without expectations of companionate relationships with their husbands. For Mexican-American families generally a

[23]Ibid., p. 34.
[24]Ibid., p. 16.
[25]Ruth Landes, *Latin Americans of the Southwest* (New York, 1965), pp. 81–87.

predictable pattern of internal conflict emerged around intergenerational differences over Mexican as opposed to Anglo-American values. The emphasis on individual achievement or personal advancement in American society conflicted with Mexican expectations of self-sacrifice for the sake of family. For women, a taste for individual accomplishment involved the risk of worldliness, an indication of impurity. Such conflict was more likely in relatively affluent families that could afford both to keep their women at home and to educate them.

Despite the recent flood of historical and sociological literature on the Afro-American family, little has been written about the internal dynamics of the black family.[26] From the high rate of labor-force participation among married black women it has been argued either that the black family was matriarchal or that husbands and wives were equals, but almost no attention has been given to the relationships between husbands and wives or the relationship of resident fathers to their children. Beatrice Clay, whose husband was a dry cleaner in Depression San Antonio, took pride in her husband's work and his abilities, but she was equally proud of her own accomplishments.[27] A basic disagreement over the career course that her husband ought to pursue encouraged Clay to divorce her husband and begin a business of her own. The statistics of 1940 on household composition reveal that black children were more likely than other children to live outside the nuclear family. As Anna's migration to her aunt's home in San Antonio illustrates, however, the extended family might not necessarily be a home of last resort for children who could not be cared for by parents. The extended family might well serve to broaden children's opportunities. In matters that were not wholly economic, the extended black family enriched the lives of members in active relationships that were not so deeply cultivated in other families.

Just as statistics on household composition and the literature on Mexican-American and Afro-American culture do not describe or adequately define family life and women's roles in those groups, the relationships of Anglo family members to each other are largely a mystery. "Anglos" are an ethnic group including Germans, Poles, and other first- and second-generation immigrants. Immigrant groups such as the Poles were

[26]Robert B. Hill, *The Strengths of the Black Family: A National Urban League Research Study* (New York, 1971), pp. 18–20.

[27]Interview with Beatrice Clay, May 24, 1979.

small but unified. The Polish community in San Antonio centered cultur-ally and geographically around a Catholic church that encouraged the re-tention of Polish language, culture, and family structure.[28] On the other hand, young German and Polish girls often left home daily for domestic jobs in the homes of native-born families whose family structures were dif-ferent from their own. In comparison with European and Mexican fam-ilies, the typical American family was more child-centered and more egali-tarian. While husbands might exercise ultimate authority, companionate marriage was the American ideal, an ideal shocking to many immigrant groups but familiar to black Americans.[29]

In contrast to young Mexican-American women, young Anglo women had considerable freedom, and they did not surrender all expectations of independent activity when they married. In her married life Ruby Cude found satisfaction in church-related social projects. Ruby's husband, Elton, was sometimes skeptical of her social involvements, but he never at-tempted to interfere in her decisions. During the many years of their mar-ried lives the Cudes have assisted and welcomed into their home a number of young people, some related and some not, and they have always entered into such commitments as partners.[30] As mothers, both Anglo and black women worked with different goals from those of Mexican-American wives. Whereas a Hispanic mother taught her child obedience and devotion to family, an Anglo or black mother educated her child to "be somebody." In their adult lives Anglo women had a broader range of social contacts than either black or Hispanic women had and less emotional reliance on the extended family. Unlike Mexican-American wives, black wives frequently had close relationships with a few nonrelated women that involved some mutual dependence. Beatrice Clay, a black employee of Washer Brothers Department Store, maintained a mutually supportive friendship with a coworker that allowed both women to maintain steady incomes during the early years of the Depression. Anglo women, who were less likely to be employed, formed their extrafamilial friendships through churches, neigh-

---

[28]Sister Jan Maria Wozniak, "St. Michael's Church: The Polish National Church in San Antonio, Texas, 1855–1950" (Master's thesis, University of Texas, 1964).

[29]For a historical analysis of white middle-class family ideals see Paula S. Fass, "The Family Redivivus: 1880–1930," *The Damned and the Beautiful, American Youth in the 1920s* (New York, 1977), pp. 119–67.

[30]Interview with Mr. and Mrs. Elton R. Cude, May 21, 1979.

bors, social clubs, and their husbands. Even in the Depression years entertainment among Anglo women focused more around peer groups than around family. An evening's entertainment with other couples was an expected social activity of most wives, though the Depression may have reduced outings to a covered-dish supper at a friend's home. As an unmarried office clerk, May Eckles participated in similar activities with other unmarried friends or with a group of friends and relatives. Such get-togethers and group outings were not unknown to black and Mexican-American women, but they were less likely to center in relationships outside the family.

Women's understanding of their roles and responsibilities as daughters, wives, and mothers and as Anglos, blacks, or Hispanics predisposed them to cope with the realities of the Depression in different ways. A Hispanic mother ideally stayed at home to protect her family and her reputation, but there was no social disgrace for either her or her daughters if they sought pay for sewing or other tasks that they could undertake in their own homes. Black wives, accustomed to some autonomy in decision making, found employment outside the home easier to accept. Native-born Anglo wives generally felt the least economic pressure to enter the work force, and most had not expected to work after marriage. Nevertheless, work outside the home did not carry the same stigma for the Anglo wife as for a Mexican-American wife. Regardless of marital status or cultural role definitions, women weighed a number of familial considerations in reaching their decisions about seeking employment. In such deliberations the pull of the labor market increasingly won out over the pull of the home, but the transition involved changes in the work lives of all family members, not just wives or daughters and not just the members of one racial or ethnic group.

In Depression San Antonio the ideal of a family economy in which the father worked to support his wife and sustain their children until they completed secondary school and began independent lives was not a reality for most families, whether Anglo, black, or Hispanic. Anglos had a much stronger probability of passing through the life cycle as members of single-worker families than did minority persons. The pressures of the Depression, however, lessened the striking ethnic differences in the work patterns of families. The Depression reduced the employment options of the youngest and the oldest workers, making the reliance of black and Hispanic families on these workers more difficult. The expansion of employment opportunities for Anglo women encouraged the movement of wives and adult or nearly adult daughters into the labor force during a period when their incomes were most needed to maintain the family.

[3]

Coping: Middle- and Upper-Class Women

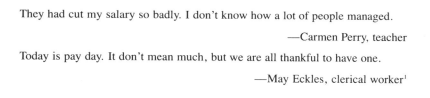

They had cut my salary so badly. I don't know how a lot of people managed.

—Carmen Perry, teacher

Today is pay day. It don't mean much, but we are all thankful to have one.

—May Eckles, clerical worker[1]

MAY ECKLES was fifty-four years old at the time of the great crash. Her life revolved around family and work. She lived with a sister in a comfortable but not luxurious home on the North Side. With family members she had invested in property in San Antonio and in the Rio Grande Valley. She was secure in her job as a clerk in a realty title office in the Bexar County Courthouse. She filled her evenings talking with friends and relatives. They talked of local politics, family and children, job dissatisfaction, unsatisfactory household help, and others' marital problems. Holidays brought family visits and feasting. Two days before Christmas, 1929, May and her sister bought a live turkey and trembled at the prospect of killing and dressing it. As the Depression set in, holidays passed without special treats and with little or no excitement or comment. From time to time May entertained Mr. Pugh, a gentleman friend from the Valley. When Pugh received a ticket for running a stop sign, May took the citation to the courthouse and asked a friend to look into the case.

Although May and her sister, "Buzzie," lived on modest incomes, they could afford to hire help with household chores. "Maria, the Mexican girl," came in to cook and clean from time to time. The laundry was taken to the home of a laundress, but May shopped around and drove a hard bargain as an employer:

We took wash over to a Mexican woman in the alley behind Mrs. Hughes this morning, as we are so disgusted with the way Irene, Deliah's daughter is doing the

[1]Interview with Carmen Perry, May 22, 1979; "A Diary Setting Out the Life of May Eckles," February 15, 1932 (typed copy, Daughters of the Republic of Texas Library, San Antonio); subsequent details and quotations are taken from this diary, hereafter cited as Eckles diary.

work and we told the Mexican woman we would pay her $2.00 a week summer and winter, but at noon her son came over to tell us she wanted $3.00 for that wash, so we went and got it this evening and we are going to send it to the laundry.

Some days later Deliah died. May and Buzzie bought Irene a pair of gloves for the funeral and took flowers to the cemetery. After Deliah's death Irene was reinstated as laundress. There were obligations that did not end with an impulsive dismissal. Such were the events that preoccupied May Eckles in 1929, though on the last day of the year she concluded, "Well, the old year of 1929 is fast coming to a close, I sure hope the New Year will be a little more business like than the old has been."

The coming year, however, proved more difficult than the last. By February the Depression dominated May's thoughts. She and Buzzie budgeted carefully, but May was relieved early in 1930 when they were able to rent one of their empty bedrooms. On all sides the signs of distress multiplied. News of local suicides and the disturbing presence of the unemployed filled her diary. One evening after she returned from work,

a young boy came in and asked for something to eat and we gave him some supper and he ate like he was starved to death, poor fellow. There was a man at the Court House to-day that Mrs. Shipley and I were talking to in the hall and he was crying, and we asked him if he was sick and he said no, but he was up against it and did not know which way to turn and could not get anything to do and his money had given out, and Theodore Semmang came along about that time and gave him a dollar and later Mrs. Shipley gave him 50¢. There are hundreds of people roaming the country and looking for jobs and hungry.

The Depression touched the Eckles household more personally when May's employer announced an officewide pay cut of 15 percent to begin in March. Although the suffering of the unemployed surrounded her, and she herself engaged in some private charity, May stood resolutely against increasing public relief efforts in San Antonio. In April she and her sister attended a mass meeting to protest passage of a public bond program that would have provided jobs for some of San Antonio's unemployed. The protest followed a march of bond supporters with "about 1,000 men, women and children in it, about 7 Americans, 2 negroes, and the rest Mexicans who are not even naturalized citizens."

Although 1930 was difficult, 1931 and 1932 brought additional distress. May and Buzzie could not meet all their financial obligations. May had difficulty obtaining payment from her renter, and her paycheck did not always arrive on time. Banks closed, and coworkers lost their jobs. After a second pay cut in August, 1931, Eckles concluded that "if they cut us much more we won't have enough to live on" and told her maid, Maria, that she would have to let her go for the rest of the year. In the coming months May watched as hunger grew in San Antonio and people begged for help:

Bessie [not further identified] fed one man this morning, and just as Buzzie came home another man was knocking at the door, and while we were giving him something to eat on the back porch another man knocked at the front door and I sent him across the street, and later about 5 o'clock a negro man came for something to eat.

As 1931 ended, May summarized her feelings that the year had been "the worst financially the world ever knew, let's hope 1932 will be the best." She hoped for improvement in 1932, but a request to her boss for a raise brought an emphatic no. After her sister also suffered a pay cut, May commented that "it sure goes hard, but guess we will have to do the best we can." The pay cut, however, forced May and Buzzie to seek a rescheduling of their mortgage payments. During 1932, May's preoccupation with personal financial matters was temporarily interrupted by news of the Lindbergh kidnapping and Amelia Earhart's flight across the Atlantic, but at the end of the year she again remembered that it had "been one awful year as far as finances are concerned."

The financial situation of the Eckles household continued to deteriorate in 1933. Maria, who had been brought back to work at the end of 1932, was again discharged, and more stringent measures were considered:

We were knocked cold today when they phoned us this morning from the office we had to take another 20% cut, effective the 15th, but later it developed that neither Jack nor Buzzie were affected, but I do, taking $19.90 a month off my salary. Well we got to figuring and decided to let Maria go and maybe try and trade our house for a duplex. Guess we will get through some way.

A few days later May attempted to work out a compromise to keep Maria on: "I had a talk with Maria, and asked her if she would work for $3.00 a week and she said no, so I told her that next week would be her last week here and she is all wrought up about it, but I don't know whether she will stay on or not." After a week had passed, "Maria came by to tell us that she would work for $3.00, so guess she will be back in the morning. Guess she found out work was scarce."

Although May believed that the family's finances had been brought under control by mid-February, subsequent pay cuts forced the Eckles household to resort to the most severe readjustments they were to face in the Depression. A few short diary entries record May's and Buzzie's passage into despair:

February 28, 1933

Well to-day is the last of February and we all got paid, so we all have one more month to go. George Huntress has cut his force down to one-half time, half of them work until the 15th and the other half come on and work until the first.

March 1, 1933

I am sure on a hop this morning getting money into the bank to meet the payment on our note on the house, but I made it. We are starting out on a cash basis with the groceries to-day, but Maria not knowing it went over to Crutcher's and got some things. I failed to tell Mr. Crutcher that we were going to shop here and there from now on to see if we could save a little.

March 7, 1933

Well, there are no girls in Geo. Huntress' office this morning but Julia Haas and a Mrs. Riley who came down but was not supposed to.

March 15, 1933

Well, to-day is pay-day and we were all a little worried, but thank goodness all got paid, Buzzie along with the rest of the Alamo Abstract people got a notice that they would be paid a percentage according to the amount that the Company made after all expenses were paid, so Buzzie is worried to death.

March 17, 1933

I spoke to Mr. McNamee about the chance of Ansley reducing our note and he said all we could do would be to ask him to waive the payment on the principal for a time or two.

September 30, 1933

. . . the lady who held the note on our Alamo Heights lot said she would extend the loan six months until April 9, 1934 and then what, I don't know.

November 15, 1933

Today is payday and Buzzie got her usual 50% cut from the Alamo.

Harassed by her financial obligations, May sought additional income early in 1933 by taking on a line of silk stockings and underwear that she could sell from home in her spare time. After a month, however, she returned her samples, saying that she did not have enough time to make the sales. Early in 1934 she secured a loan on an additional house she owned with several family members. The proceeds of the loan paid current expenses, and by March her worst fears had subsided. May was encouraged by a $5-a-month raise, though Buzzie did not receive additional income. April brought May a $10 raise in addition to the previous month's increase. Loans to cover mortgage and tax payments were obtained through the Home Loan Office and the Federal Land Bank, and Buzzie was able to borrow $125 for home improvements later in the year. In the title offices where May and her sister were employed, business picked up markedly during the fall of 1934.

For May Eckles the fall of 1934 was also the beginning of a new life. Through August and September she was busy planning her wedding to Pugh. The house again filled temporarily with the kinds of family activity and excitement of the days before the Depression. After her October wedding May moved to the Valley, where her husband maintained a farm. She kept in close contact with relatives in San Antonio and made frequent visits to the city. For May and for Buzzie the financial crisis had passed.

As other San Antonio women look back on the Depression from a contemporary perspective, they recall personal problems, poignant vignettes of public suffering or outrage, bitter experiences of discrimination, and the joys of sharing and family life that pulled them through difficult times. Adela Navarro, one of the few Mexican-American caseworkers in Depression San Antonio, particularly remembers the pain of men who could no longer provide for their families:

> I used to see men cry because they didn't have a job where they could bring home the food for the children. And I was very moved. Men moved me so much to see them in that plight. They were belittled before the eyes of their families and they couldn't take it. And you know that's lowering the pride of manhood.[2]

Mrs. G. J. Moore, a Mexican American who has lived in San Antonio all her adult life, remembered "finding people going through trash cans looking for food because nobody could get help that was not an American citizen. And these were people who had been living here for fifty, sixty, seventy years."[3] Adela Navarro remembers that the Depression intensified prejudice against Mexican Americans and that no degree of education or genteel comportment could protect them from charges that they were backward Mexicans. May Eckles's diary revealed particular ways in which racism might influence Anglo reactions to the problems of

[2] Interview with Adela Navarro, May 29, 1979. Perceptions of the Depression and the coping mechanisms of American women are discussed in Jeane Westin, *Making Do: How Women Survived the '30s*; and Caroline Bird, *The Invisible Scar*.

[3] Interview with Mrs. G. J. Moore, May 23, 1979.

the Depression. Minority women like Eckles's maid and laundress were expected to accept wage cuts as their employers' incomes dwindled even though they already existed at poverty levels. When thefts of food and clothing occurred during the Depression, minorities attracted suspicion. As Eckles noted after her laundry was stolen from the clothesline, "Just before I left for the office this morning I went out to bring in my dresses I washed yesterday evening and both of them were gone, they had been stolen off the line, my, I was mad, and you bet if I see a nigger or Mexican with those dresses on, they will take them off right now." [4]

Prejudice was a constant companion to minority persons during the Depression, but family was an important protection against the outside world. Adela Navarro understood that all the members of her family contributed to their well-being and their self-respect through chores at home or wages earned outside the home. Carmen Perry, a Mexican American of European heritage, recalled the support of both family and friends. She secured a teaching position in the public schools. The teachers had their difficulties, including salary reductions and payment in scrip. Perry remembers:

They had cut my salary so badly. I don't know how a lot of people managed. Our main problem as teachers was that, of course. We used the bus, we didn't have cars, and we made our own clothes because we had time in those days. We could buy material for 25 cents a yard. We could buy T-bones for 25 cents a pound, and hamburger for a dime and things like that. You can't believe now that it really happened. They'd give you soup bones. And you pay what now, $1.30 for soup bones?

But one thing, I think with conditions like that, people kind of unite. We had to help each other. Sometimes at the end of the week we'd say, can you spare me a quarter until Monday? We'd share. We'd entertain ourselves by getting together and chatting. . . .

Of course at school we put on plays and things like that. One play by the faculty was a riot. . . . I think those were some of the best days we ever had. [5]

The Depression kept families together as working members supported the unemployed, but it also forced many young people to postpone beginning their own families. Perry's two older brothers could not marry until Perry herself gained a teaching job:

My brother went with the girl he married seven years, waiting for things to get better and they could afford it. And then my other brother not quite that long and

---

[4] Eckles diary, June 1, 1931.
[5] Interview with Carmen Perry, May 22, 1979.

then they finally married, one in June, the other in September. It was the year I got
a job. . . . They just couldn't do anything else. We needed help at home and their
wives were working also, helping in their homes. It all works out if there's love and
affection, and a desire to do it. Maybe sometimes situations like that have their
advantages.

Young people who did marry during the Depression sometimes in-
curred the wrath of the older generation. When the son of a friend married,
May Eckles commented, "Beats the jews how these boys marry on nothing
and let their mothers struggle for themselves." [6]
Not all San Antonians remember the Depression as having been much
more difficult than other periods. Beatrice Clay is grateful that she kept her
job through the Depression. She believes that her work experiences during
the 1930s laid the groundwork for a successful business career in later
years. For only a few cents, Clay and her neighbors could entertain themselves, sharing their resources: "We went to dances and picture shows. We
could go to the Majestic and the Empire. Of course they were segregated. . . . Sometimes we had people gather in the yard. We have a big
yard right out there and that's what I did for the children." [7] Clay cooperated with her coworkers at Washer Brothers, where they divided up the
tasks among themselves to protect their jobs. She traded clothing that the
store discarded at the end of a season for food that a neighbor could obtain
more easily.
For middle-class San Antonians of all ethnic groups the Depression
was a time of making do, but not necessarily of suffering. Ramona Garcia
grew up in San Antonio during the Depression. [8] Although she wanted
things that the family could not afford, there was no real deprivation in her
home. Breadlines and beggars at the door were so common that she simply
perceived them as normal aspects of daily life. Judy Grice recalled that
middle-class San Antonians eased the difficulties of the lean years by ex-
changing goods and services. [9] When she graduated from high school, she
wore a dress that a San Antonio clothier had given her father in exchange
for his professional services as a physician. As a teenager Ruby Cude was
impressed by the sudden transformation of daily life in San Antonio at the
outset of the Depression:

[6] Eckles diary, April 16, 1933.
[7] Interview with Beatrice Clay, May 24, 1979.
[8] Anonymous interview, May 18, 1979.
[9] Anonymous interview, May 22, 1979.

I think the food lines were most terrible. They made a terrible impression on me. Of course we were quite young and our grandfather owned an ice plant. As a child I never had to do without anything, and even after our marriage Elton and I lived very well on his salary. But there was never a day that we didn't have two or three, in those days called hoboes, men that were out of work and traveling from one place to another. . . . My father and grandfather had to feed them and they were never turned away.[10]

Ruby and Elton Cude married in 1932, when she was seventeen and he was twenty. They set up housekeeping in a small apartment on Elton's $80-a-month salary at Gulf Oil. Soon after their marriage his salary was cut 10 percent, but unlike the years from 1929 through 1931, when he had moved from job to job as the Depression forced cutbacks, Cude held on to the Gulf job until he went to work in the sheriff's office in 1937. Ruby's mother had helped her put a trousseau together for the wedding. Her mother was a good seamstress, and Ruby's aunt passed along some of her clothes to the young bride. Coats were very expensive, however, and the Cudes had been married ten years before Ruby had her first new coat.

In 1933 the Cudes' first child arrived, and a second son was born in 1936. Mrs. Cude is thankful that she and her family made it through the Depression without any real deprivation, but she remembers having to scrimp and cut corners to get by. Occasionally she resented the relative ease of friends or relatives. She and her husband and children lived in an old house that needed repairs. One of the things that aggravated her in the house was that the sash windows would not stay open. Her small son was cut and bruised by a window that slammed shut on his hands. "Just out of clear blue they would bang down, you know, if you didn't keep them propped up. And I went to Maureen's one day and everything was new and I went home and told Elton I'm not going back again. I don't mean that I want her house, but I would like windows that didn't fall down all the time."

In 1936 the financial burdens of rearing children as well as the problems of other family members forced the Cudes to move in with Ruby's parents. Also living in the house were Ruby's two younger sisters, an unemployed uncle who had come to San Antonio from Mississippi, another uncle with his wife and two children, and a boarder. While the family never went hungry, it was difficult to meet expenses throughout the thirties. Mrs. Cude recalled:

[10] Interview with Mr. and Mrs. Elton R. Cude, May 21, 1979.

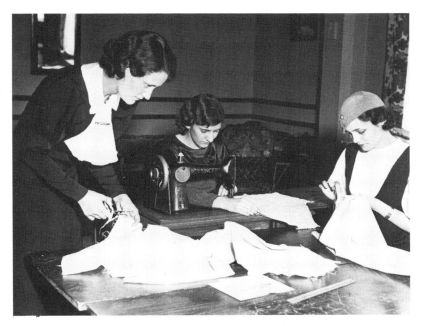

Middle-class Anglo women sewing, ca. 1935. Left to right: Etta Goldsmith, Jean Jameton, and Louella Matteson. Anglo women gained emotional support and mutual aid in peer-group activities. The Depression also drew well-off middle-class women into many relief activities.
(*San Antonio Light* Collection, University of Texas Institute of Texan Cultures, San Antonio.)

There were times when Elton had to take more than one job at one time and he was working three jobs and only sleeping 3 or 4 hours a night. . . . Elton used to get aggravated at me because I'd pay the bills first and I'd run short on grocery money. So then I'd change and I'd buy what we needed for groceries and I'd cut down on bills, maybe two dollars a month or something. If I couldn't pay every 1st and 15th, I'd have a crying spell."

Middle-class women also reacted to the Depression by practicing the community volunteerism they had learned in the 1920s. In San Antonio as in other American cities the twenties brought a proliferation of women's clubs, most of which affiliated with the General Federation of Women's Clubs. Nearly all of the associations in the San Antonio Federation of Women's Clubs had committees on charity, and some clubs were wholly charitable in their orientation. In addition to the club movement women had a long tradition of participation in church missionary societies that

practiced relief work as part of their religious commitment. With the
onslaught of the Depression middle-class women redirected the established
organizational structures of the clubs and church groups to make relief
their central concern.

Club women sponsored benefit performances and other fund-raising
programs for the needy throughout the Depression. The city federation was
proud of its members' work. After a federation-sponsored appearance by
comedian Will Rogers had generated $9,000 for relief assistance, the *San
Antonio Home and Club* editor commented:

The City Federation's sponsoring and management of the Will Rogers perfor-
mance in the city and the distribution of the funds derived therefrom is an outstand-
ing example of what women in the city have done in the relief of unemployment;
but there are doubtless dozens and dozens of other cases when women and their
organizations have been doing much good along this line and their deeds have gone
unheralded.[11]

Nationally, members of the Federation of Women's Clubs supported
the National Recovery Administration by organizing and executing local
campaigns to get merchants and employers to pledge to observe NRA
wage, production, and price codes. A *Home and Club* editorial asserted
that, while some Americans might not support the New Deal, "in women's
support of it there will be unanimity."[12] In the early years of the Depression
the federation in San Antonio and elsewhere encouraged housewives to
find odd jobs around the house for which the unemployed could be hired.
In the belief that consumer spending would cure the ailing economy, the
federation exhorted its members to buy. *Home and Club* readers were told
that saving was unpatriotic because it decreased the consumption of goods
and thus caused cutbacks in employment. The homemaker, as the individual responsible for most household purchases, could assist recovery
through careful spending. The city federation staunchly supported federal
recovery programs but criticized the more radical ideas proposed by some
citizens. In response to the bonus soldiers' attacks on the Reconstruction
Finance Corporation as a welfare program for bankers, the editor of *Home
and Club* argued that the RFC aided bank customers primarily.[13]

The San Antonio Junior League maintained a baby-and-child clinic in
a transitional neighborhood adjoining the West Side. As the Depression

[11] *San Antonio Home and Club* 1 (May, 1931): 12.
[12] *San Antonio Home and Club* 4 (August, 1933): 8.
[13] *San Antonio Home and Club* 3 (August, 1932): 3–4, 8.

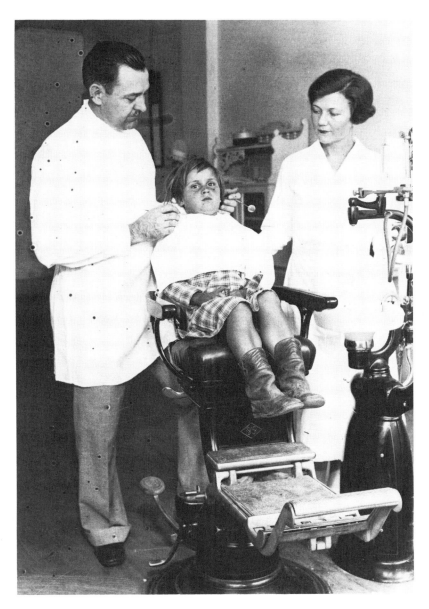

Patient at Junior League clinic, May, 1933. The clinic provided free medical and dental care to needy Anglo children.
(*San Antonio Light* Collection, University of Texas Institute of Texan Cultures, San Antonio.)

deepened, the league expanded its services and extended its reach into other neighborhoods, but it never attempted to serve the areas of the city that were predominantly black or Mexican. The clinic began in 1924 as a visiting-doctors program. Pediatricians quickly pinpointed malnutrition as the major health problem, and in 1930 the league opened a soup kitchen. From the kitchen the league also dispensed clothing, bedding, fuel, and rent money. The soup kitchen closed in 1934, when the programs of the Civil Works Administration and the Public Works Administration went into effect.

All but one of the families given assistance in the soup kitchen and the clinic were Anglo. Sarah Bailey Williamson, a graduate student at the University of Texas who interviewed several clinic families, viewed the impoverished workers as honest and willing to work but slovenly and unambitious. While sympathetic toward their plight, she concluded that most residents in the area did not measure up to her standards of cleanliness and hard work. Williamson described her impressions of the neighborhood:

> The men in almost perpetual state of unemployment congregated at the little store at the end of the street and swapped yarns, pitched horseshoes in the street, or dug in their small gardens, or tinkered with a tool or a lawn mower. Fat women in none too clean dresses and old felt slippers rocked placidly back and forth on the tiny porches while children and dogs romped noisily over yards and in the street. This shiftlessness, no doubt, resulted from inherent mental limitations and acquired easy-going habits of tenant farm life.[14]

League members who assisted in the clinic had various reactions to the poverty and suffering to which they were exposed, but all felt deeply the contrast between their daily lives and the experiences of their clients. The league workers were impatient with members of their own social set who complained of the austerity of their situations and were grateful for the ease of their own lives. Almost all of the league women whom Williamson interviewed argued that the middle and upper classes would be more concerned with economic and political measures to improve health and living conditions if they were exposed to the suffering and misery that the women had observed. Clinic workers, however, were also judgmental about their clients. They tended to divide the clinic population into two groups, those who worked for self-improvement and those who could not or would

---

[14]"Children's Free Clinic of the San Antonio Junior League" (Master's thesis, University of Texas, 1934), pp. 87–88.

not help themselves. Toward the latter category the women occasionally grew hardened or indifferent, but the first group inspired admiration. As one league worker said:

> I had led a life which I didn't realize had been sheltered, until I met up with my first carload of patients, whom I was to deliver to the Clinic for medical attention. Always a bit over-sensitive, my first selfish thought was a resolve to spend as little time as possible among such unhappy circumstances. However, I was sent out to a pitiful little shack, without doors or windows where a mother was fighting to keep life in four little ones, one of whom was two weeks old. I had a lovely little layette for the baby. The sweetness and cheer which I found in that little home, and surely it was more of a home than some very fine houses I have seen, shamed me greatly I assure you and never from that day on did I draw back from these people.[15]

The Mexican clinic on the West Side provided free medical care to the Hispanic community. Middle-class Mexican-American women worked through such volunteer groups as Beneficencia Mexicana to support the clinic, but never in highly visible roles as did Anglo women. Hispanics who needed food, clothing, or shelter rather than medical care looked first to the Catholic church.

Our Lady of Guadalupe Church, under the direction of Father Carmine Tranchese, provided the margin of survival for many Mexican families on the West Side in the 1930s. After his arrival in 1932, Father Tranchese initiated a food-distribution program, and Mexican-American women donated their time and skills to prepare food for themselves and unfortunate neighbors. The church was the one place in San Antonio where a needy Mexican could be sure of not being turned away and of not being forced to submit to seemingly endless examination by caseworkers. Father Tranchese was also instrumental in securing federal approval for a public housing project sponsored by the Works Progress Administration on the West side, the first such complex built in San Antonio.[16]

Protestant settlement houses on the West Side also served the Mexican-American community during the Depression, providing essential medical and dental services for indigent patients. The Mexican Christian Institute was founded in 1913 to aid political refugees of the Mexican Revolution, but by the 1920s the country's economic refugees had become the primary clients of the facilities. The Presbyterian church also maintained a settle-

[15]Ibid., pp. 103–104.
[16]From 1939 the Work Projects Administration.

ment house in the northwest section of the city. The Wesley Community
Center, sponsored by the Methodist church, likewise offered recreational
facilities, language classes, and medical assistance to residents of the West
Side. Working mothers of the three major ethnic groups were aided by nur-
series for their children sponsored by a number of churches and religious
organizations, but such facilities were always inadequate to meet the demand for inexpensive child care. Black women received assistance from
Protestant and Catholic churches and from the Salvation Army, but settlement houses did not operate on the East Side.

As the Junior League clinic demonstrated, middle- and upper-class
women sincerely wished to remedy the problems of inadequate housing,
hunger, and disease, but they moved first to aid their Anglo brothers and
sisters. In 1933 the San Antonio Federation of Women's Clubs proposed
building a shelter for single working girls. An editorial in the *Home and
Club* pointed out that temporary shelter was available for only 123 women
and that the many homeless girls seeking work in the city would inevitably
turn to prostitution if facilities were not provided.[17] The federation's concern always focused on the city's clerks and shopgirls rather than on the
domestic and factory workers, most of whom were minority women. In the
tone of *Home and Club* articles federation authors revealed that their sympathy for Anglo workers was based on their ability to identify with the
women, to see that clubwomen were potentially clerks themselves or the
mothers of clerks. They were concerned with preserving the virtue and respect of the Anglo working girl as well as relieving her despair. The plight
of the Anglo working girl received brief citywide attention after the shooting death of fifteen-year-old Mattie Mae Pierson in March of 1935. Mattie
Mae had recently moved to San Antonio from the small town of Cuero,
Texas. She reportedly came to the city alone in hopes of earning money for
her parents. She found a job at the Main Street Taxi Dance, where she
earned three cents for every dance and for every glass of beer that she induced a patron to buy. In a dance-floor scuffle between two patrons, a gun
went off, and Mattie Mae was killed. The public responded with demands
for the closing of the city's dance halls, but with no apparent results.[18]
Throughout the Depression women's groups reached out to women with
special problems such as unwed mothers and the recently widowed, but
despite rhetoric and the public outcry that followed the death of Mattie

[17]*San Antonio Home and Club* 4 (September, 1933):8.
[18]*San Antonio Express*, March 30, 1935; *San Antonio Light*, March 29, 31, 1935.

Mattie Mae Pierson, who was shot and killed at the Main Street Taxi Dance in March, 1935. Taxi-dance halls were believed to foster prostitution, but not until the shooting of fifteen-year-old Mattie Mae was there a public outcry against the dance halls.
(*San Antonio Light* Collection, University of Texas Institute of Texan Cultures, San Antonio.)

Mae Pierson, women's clubs did not assist female transients or exploited women workers.

Many relief activities of women's groups during the Depression, such as the Junior League clinic, were projects that had been ongoing from the 1920s or earlier. The YWCA had long provided short-term shelter to women. One of San Antonio's most successful charitable organizations in the early 1930s was the Milk and Ice Fund, which provided sanitary milk and food for children. The organization was credited with reducing San Antonio's infant death rate from its all-time high of 142 per 1,000 in 1922. By 1935, however, the Milk and Ice Fund could no longer draw enough contributions to continue operations, which had been sponsored by the San Antonio Council of Parents and Teachers.[19]

During the early 1930s women were exhorted to do their part to overcome the Depression. In efforts to encourage charity among women, sisterhood was stressed. The president of the San Antonio Altrusa Club reminded clubwomen:

> The woman in business who has a reasonable sense of security in her own position as owner, executive, or employee in any capacity, owes it to her less fortunate sister, a victim of the economic crisis resulting from the general depression of the past two years to do all in her power to aid in preserving the latter's morale both by word of encouragement and by contribution to the Relief Fund which is now being raised by six local clubs of business and professional women.[20]

As individuals, women understood only those aspects of Depression San Antonio to which they personally were exposed. Some women had little knowledge of the malnutrition and disease in their midst. Caseworker Adela Navarro daily confronted family after family living on the edge of survival. She found it difficult to remember the Depression as a time of generosity and familial strength in the community as a whole, though she has rich memories of her own family. For women like Ruby Cude and Beatrice Clay memories of familial sharing and mutual support overshadow their recollection of breadlines, want, and unemployment. Minority women well understood that occupational segregation and other manifestations of prejudice limited their options and those of their male relatives in fighting the Depression, but Anglo women did not fully comprehend their advantages. On the other hand, all the women whose recollections have been presented here, most of whom were personally fortunate in weathering the Depression without hunger or long periods of unemployment, believe that they were poor during these years. They understand little about the causes of their poverty; the Depression remains an enigma. Women acted on their primary loyalties to family during the Depression, and all women understood that the family was the essential institution and economic unit that protected individual well-being in hard times.

[19]*San Antonio Express*, January 22, 1932; January 9, 1935; Angela Marie Chappelle, "Local Welfare Work of Religious Organizations in San Antonio, Texas" (Master's thesis, University of Texas, 1939).

[20]*San Antonio Home and Club* 2 (February, 1932):8.

San Antonio women remember deprivation and despair during the Depression. They watched the painful decline of male self-respect as fathers and brothers could no longer feed and clothe their families. Minority women remember the stings of ethnic prejudice that have pursued them into the present. Women also recall, however, how they made the best of scarce commodities, how families banded together, and how the more fortunate shared with the less fortunate. In San Antonio, as elsewhere in the nation, middle- and upper-class women mobilized emergency funds and relief commodities, but charitable contributions could not begin to meet a disaster of such catastrophic proportions, and women who wished to help the poor often circumscribed their assistance according to class and ethnic prejudices. Hundreds of San Antonio women workers joined the ranks of the unemployed. Others clung to their jobs tenaciously despite pay cut after pay cut.

[4]

Working: Women's Participation in the Labor Force

I am writing you this letter asking you to help me in getting work. I am willing to work at most any thing I can do and I realy kneed work if any one in this world does. I have 4 children out of school because I haven't the money to buy their school supplies. My husband is a carpenter and he don't draw much salary and dont get much work at that and is not able to work on account of his back. And I have tried to get work ever-where and they turn me down. . . .

If you don't help me I dont know what I am going to do for part of the time we don't have any thing to eat ever thing has gone up so high. I have done ever-thing I can to keep things going. I have made over old clothes for the children and I have saved in ever way I could to keep things going and we have gotten behind in ever-thing.

—San Antonio, Texas, September 27, 1939

Mrs. Samuel Bush to Eleanor Roosevelt[1]

THE trend toward paid work outside the home has dramatically altered the style and the quality of the lives of twentieth-century women. From the establishment of the New England textile mills in the 1820s through the twentieth century, changes in the overall occupational structure have pulled women into the work force.[2] The Depression highlighted the importance of occupational segregation and the transformation of work in drawing women into employment. Neither public fears that women might take the jobs of male family heads nor the employment collapse of the decade stopped the flow of women into the labor market during the 1930s. In San Antonio and elsewhere, however, women increased their representation only in "female" occupations that expanded as a consequence of changing technology or consumer tastes despite the grim state of the economy.

[1]Records of the Work Projects Adminsitration, RG 69, Texas, file 690.

[2]Thomas Dublin, *Women at Work: The Transformation of Work and Community in Lowell, Massachusetts, 1826–69*; Valerie Kincade Oppenheimer, *The Female Labor Force in the United States*, pp. 156–67; Elyce J. Rotella, "Women's Labor Force Behavior and the Growth of Clerical Employment in the United States, 1870–1930" (Ph.D. diss., University of Pennsylvania, 1977).

During the Depression thousands of San Antonio women like Mrs. Bush repeatedly and vainly sought employment to counterbalance their husbands' loss of jobs. Other women with employed spouses or working children found that no amount of scrimping would enable the families to meet expenses from their incomes. These women might seek work as well, despite the dim prospects of success. Between 1930 and 1940 both the number of women seeking work and the number of women employed in the city increased. Countless other women, never enumerated as members of the labor force, felt the need to work but were discouraged by high levels of unemployment and sex and ethnic discrimination in the labor market.

Overall, more San Antonio women, married and single, entered the labor market during the thirties than had in the previous decade. The increase, however, was restricted to Anglo women. Labor-force participation declined slightly among black women, but the exact impact of the Depression on Hispanic women's work rates cannot be measured with certainty. Between 1930 and 1950 the percentage of Hispanic women significantly decreased in the labor market (table 18), and the decrease appears to have come primarily during the thirties. This chapter explores the pattern of ethnic differences in labor-force participation, and the next chapter examines occupational segregation as a source of those differences.

The labor-force participation rates of Anglo, black, and Hispanic women demonstrate that ethnicity was a primary indicator if not a determinant of the work experience of women in Depression San Antonio. In both 1930 and 1940 black women were about twice as likely as other women to be in the paid work force (table 17). In 1930 more than half of all black women (based on the population ten years of age or older) had entered the labor market. In contrast, only one-fourth of Anglo and Hispanic women had sought paid work. Among white women foreign-born Anglos demonstrated the highest rates of labor-force participation and Mexican Americans the lowest. The high level of black participation in the San Antonio labor market paralleled statistics for other cities in both the nineteenth and the twentieth centuries. Black labor-force patterns are consistent with the conclusion that women's work-force behavior is negatively related to income levels of fathers, brothers, and husbands, as is the fact that Anglo immigrant women had higher rates of labor-force participation rates than those of native-born Anglos.

The one statistic in the census of 1930 that stands out from the broader pattern is the low rate of labor-force participation among Mexican-American women. If women's entrance into the labor market was simply and directly related to economic need, clearly more Hispanic women should have been paid workers. Cultural factors, the state of the economy, and occupational segregation all discouraged employment among Hispanic women, while need propelled them into the labor market. Unlike black families, Hispanic families were reluctant to send daughters outside the home and even more reluctant to allow wives to work. Large families also kept Mexican-American mothers homebound longer than Anglo or black mothers. Largely unskilled, geographically segregated, and greeted with prejudice, prospective Hispanic workers had few job choices. Those who did work clustered in a few industrial occupations. In small industrial plants female family members could work together or under the watchful eyes of fathers and brothers. Domestic work presented opportunities for Mexican-American employment, but the dangers of working in strangers' homes and the language barrier kept many women from seeking such work.

Within the pattern of ethnic differences in work rates there were additional contrasts in the marital status and ages of female workers. Although less likely to work outside the home than other women, both Mexican-American and foreign-born Anglo women who did work entered the labor market at younger ages than black women (tables 9 and 20).[3] It cannot be argued that black parents kept youngsters out of the work force so that they could attend school while Hispanic parents removed their children from the educational system and sent them into the labor market (tables 15 and 21).[4] The number of Hispanic children who were workers is not sufficient to account for the low school attendance of Mexican Americans. Although school attendance was high among blacks, more black children were also out of school than were in the labor force. School attendance, therefore, was not necessarily a factor in a youth's decision to refrain from entering the labor market.

[3]The census data do not permit a similar analysis of workers under the age of 15, however, only 205 female workers ages 10 through 14 were reported in 1930.

[4]For a discussion of the relationship between the family economy and the education of children among the Irish, German, and native white populations of late-nineteenth century Philadelphia, see Claudia Goldin, "Household and Market Production of Families in a Late 19th Century American City," *Explorations in Economic History* 16 (1979):111–31.

Elizabeth Pleck found that children's education and mothers' labor-force participation in black families were not linked in a single, direct fashion at the turn of the century. Elizabeth Pleck, "A Mother's Wages: Income Earning among Married Italian and Black Women, 1896–1911," in Nancy F. Cott and Elizabeth H. Pleck, eds., *A Heritage of Her Own: Toward a New Social History of American Women* (New York, 1979), pp. 378–79, 387. Pleck also found that black wives were more likely than Italian wives to pursue paid work in their own homes. Data on school attendance appear in table 15.

Work rates by age and marital status show that marriage affected black and Hispanic women's decisions to seek employment in opposite ways (tables 22 and 23). In the youngest category of black workers (ages fifteen through nineteen), marriage encouraged women to seek work, while single teenagers were less likely to work than were married teens. For young Mexican-American women, however, marriage was a signal to cease paid work and return to home responsibilities. Marriage also discouraged employment among young native Anglos, though the impact was less pronounced than among Hispanic girls. No married teenage Anglo immigrant was a worker.

Work patterns demonstrate that women fulfilled different roles in the family economic unit according to ethnicity or race. Mexican-American women were most likely to be employed as working daughters, a temporary stage that ended with marriage. The importance of a daughter's earnings to the family may be reflected in the older age at marriage of Hispanic women as opposed to that of black women.

Foreign-born Anglo women occupied a place in the family similar to that of Hispanic women in that single girls aged fifteen through nineteen years were somewhat more likely to work than were native-born Anglo teenagers, and marriage marked a more nearly certain withdrawal from the labor force. Of all San Antonio women, however, foreign-born Anglos were the least likely to marry at all. Consequently, proportionally more Anglo immigrants than other women passed directly from the status of working daughters to working adults. For these women the greatest changes in the family economic unit were the losses or departures of parents and siblings.

Native-born Anglo girls rarely worked during their early teens, but labor-force participation picked up rapidly after age seventeen, when secondary schooling was completed. The economically superior position of Anglo families permitted young girls to remain at home longer. In 1930 there were a number of white-collar jobs requiring a high-school diploma into which Anglo girls entered directly after graduation. Telephone operators in particular comprised a working sector dominated by Anglos between the ages of eighteen and twenty-four (table 27). Native-born Anglo women who married did not feel the degree of pressure to refrain from employment that characterized immigrant or Mexican-American families. As long as they remained childless, native Anglo wives might persist in the labor force. The Depression encouraged married Anglos to work, and in numerical terms they were more successful in finding jobs than were mi-

Patricia Wilson at work, ca. 1935. The expanding clerical sector drew Anglo high school graduates into the work force, while black and Mexican-American women faced declining job opportunities.
(*San Antonio Light* Collection, University of Texas Institute of Texan Cultures, San Antonio.)

nority women. Nevertheless, proportionally more black than Anglo or Hispanic wives were in the work force in 1940 as well as in 1930.

In contrast to Anglos and Hispanics, black women entered the work force as individuals whose age or marital status had separated them from the parental economic unit. The black female's life cycle rarely included youthful employment as long as she did not marry. Virtually the only labor market for black females was domestic work, and in this area prospective employers discriminated against the youngest applicants. As long as she remained single and out of the labor market, there was little pressure for the black youth to leave school, as the late school-leaving age of black girls confirms. On the other hand, because such daughters were nonproductive members of the family unit, there was no economic incentive for black par-

Black girls receiving instruction in mattress making at a San Antonio high school. There was no demand for this skill in the local economy. With few opportunities for employment, most black children remained at school through age seventeen. (Delores Linton, San Antonio. Copy from University of Texas Institute of Texan Cultures, San Antonio.)

ents to keep them in the household. Early marriage relieved black parents of some of their burdens and propelled the teenage wife into the work force.

Once she had married or had nearly reached majority as a single person, a black woman embarked upon long-term involvement in the work force. The employment imperative felt by black women reflected not only the relative poverty of black families but also the relative absence of children in the household. If she had children, the black wife would probably stay at home as long as her husband brought in wages; otherwise, she would continue to work. Whether or not she had children, a black wife was usually a paid worker by the time she reached her late twenties, and she remained in the work force at least until the age of fifty-five years.

For all ethnic and racial groups critical decisions regarding work occurred between the ages of eighteen and twenty (tables 21 and 22). For all groups labor-force participation among single women accelerated rapidly after age eighteen, and the vast majority of all single women twenty years old or older were workers. Black women were the only population group who were highly likely to combine marriage and employment. Black women were also distinguished from all other females by the length of their stay in the work force. Among black women ages forty-five through fifty-four, three-fifths were in the labor force in 1930, while approximately one-fifth of other women of the same ages were workers. Similarly, one-half of black women ages fifty-five through sixty-four and one-fourth of black women ages sixty-five through seventy-four were workers, while for other women participation levels were less than one-fifth and less than one-tenth, respectively.

The apparent relationship between fertility or family size and female work-force participation among the four groupings in 1930 confirms that the presence of young children discouraged female labor-force participation. In San Antonio the highest levels of work-force participation were among black women, who had the fewest children under the age of ten, and the lowest participatory rate was for Hispanic women, who had the highest fertility. In 1930 nearly three-fourths of all black families had no children under age ten, while less than half of Hispanic families had no young children (tables 9 and 10).

In 1940 the U.S. Census Bureau estimated a number of characteristics of family structure from sample statistics. The estimates include breakdowns of women's work rates by numbers and ages of children. The figures suggest that the presence of young children under the age of ten had a greater influence in removing black than white (Anglo and Hispanic) wives from work outside the home. Whether or not they had young children, black wives were more likely than white wives to be in the labor market, but the difference between the work rate of wives with young children and rate of wives without young children was much greater for blacks than for whites. In both racial categories the majority of mothers of young children in male-headed households stayed at home.

In 1930 and in 1940 proportionally more ever-married black working women than other female workers were household heads (table 8). In 1940 separation from spouses encouraged women in all groups to enter the labor market, as was true in 1930. For women without spouses in the household, the presence of young children did not necessarily discourage work-force participation. On the basis of the bureau's estimates of 1940, the presence of young children in the home discouraged single black mothers from working but encouraged employment among single white mothers.

If female labor-force participation and fertility were related in a simple and direct fashion, a consistent pattern of absence from the work force of ever-married women with young children ought to be demonstrable for all ethnic groupings. While there are ecological problems with the data available, the aggregate data do not suggest a simple relationship between the absence of young children and the presence of ever-married women in the labor market. If black and Hispanic women only are considered, a relationship appears to exist. Single women of both groups were in the work force in large numbers, ever-married Hispanic women, who had many young children, were rarely in the work force, and ever-married black women, who had few children, most likely were workers. Ever-married native Anglo women, who had lower fertility than Hispanics but higher fertility than blacks, had an ever-married participation rate only slightly higher than that of Hispanics. Foreign-born Anglos had relatively few young children but the lowest work rates of all. Although the presence of young children discouraged black wives from working, they were more likely to work than were white wives with young children.

San Antonio was a major center of industrial homework in the 1930s. Women with young children could then have accommodated themselves to the realities of poverty and family responsibilities through the pursuit of employment carried on in their own homes. Available data on the employment of homeworkers do not suggest that paid homework was a significant factor in the employment options of the mothers of young children or that Hispanic mothers were more likely to be homeworkers than were black mothers. Data collected by the U.S. Women's Bureau in 1932 offer a corrective to the 1930 census count of homeworkers.[5] The Women's Bureau found that a number of women in one household frequently worked together on home sewing. Since only one person went to the shop to deliver and receive goods and to collect wages, many who participated in the work may not have reported themselves as workers.

For all women loss of spouse through death or divorce encouraged entry or reentry into the labor market. In 1930, however, only black wid-

[5]Records of the Women's Bureau, Materials Relating to Bulletin no. 126.

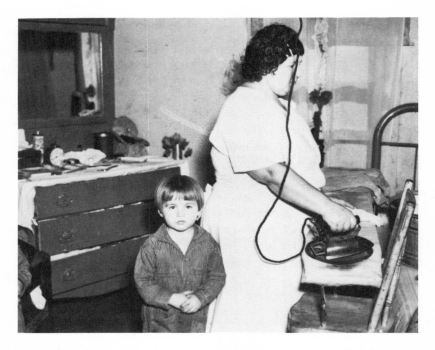

A home laundress watches her children while ironing. Anglo and black women earned money by taking in laundry, while most Mexican-American homeworkers engaged in pecan shelling or garment making.
(Copy from University of Texas Institute of Texan Cultures, San Antonio.)

owed and divorced females had higher work rates than single women. Despite their persistence in seeking work, many black women found that relief agencies as well as the Depression prevented them from finding jobs. As one woman wrote to President Roosevelt:

My name is Lula Gordon. I am a Negro woman. I am on the relief. I have three children. I have no husband and no job. I have worked hard ever since I was old enough. I am willing to do any kind of work because I have to support myself and my children. I was under the impression that the Government or the W.P.A. would give the Physical fit relief clients work. I have been praying for that time to come. A lady, Elizabeth Ramsie, almost in my condition, told me she was going to try and get some work, I went with her. We went to the Court House here in San Antonio, we talked to a Mrs. Beckmon. Mrs. Beckmon told me to phone a Mrs. Coyle because she wanted some one to clean house and cook for ($5) five dollars a week. Mrs. Beckmon said if I did not take the job in the Private home I would be cut off from everything all together. I told her I was afraid to accept the job in the private home because I have registered for a government job and when it opens up I want to take it. She said that she was taking people off of the relief and I have to take the job in the private home or none. I ask her if I take the job would I be transferred when the W.P.A. jobs open. She said there was no such thing as that. She was giving me a job and if I wanted work take the job and if I did not I wouldn't get that and nothing else. I have read in the paper that the Government is not going to put any one to work in private homes, that is why I was afraid to accept the job. I had to accept the job because I have to have work to live, but Mrs. Coyle was talking to someone looking for work when I phoned her. She told me if she need me she would let me know. If she does not need me what will I do? If she does need me is that the kind of work the government is giving the women. I need work and I will do anything the government gives me to do. . . . Will you please give me some work.[6]

The question of how many women workers were entirely self-supporting and how many were participants in a family economy cannot be answered definitely, but some indication of the scale of differences among ethnic groupings can be gleaned from available census data. In 1930 the incidence of female-headed families was highest among blacks; 28 percent of black families were headed by women, while among all other groups between 17 and 19 percent of families were headed by women. A rough estimate of the numbers and percentages of workers who were contributing workers can be calculated by subtracting the number of female family heads from the number of total workers.[7] Not all women who headed families were in the work force, but the Depression made it increasingly difficult for family heads to refrain from entering the labor market even though employment was difficult to obtain. Since the category of family heads included single persons living alone, who most likely had to work, and since most female family heads with dependents can be presumed to have been workers, the subtraction of female family heads from total number of female workers produces a minimal estimate of the number of women who pooled their incomes with one or more family members. The results add a dimension to women's work-force decisions that is not revealed in the statistics on marital status alone. Only among foreign-born Anglos were the majority of women in the labor market not members of a household with more than one worker. In contrast, among black women contributory workers, or workers who were members of a family group with more than one worker, were most prevalent. Black families were more likely to uti-

[6]Records of the Work Projects Administration. RG 69, Texas, file 690.

[7]The term "contributory worker" is used here to distinguish a worker who combines his or her earnings with other family members' wages as opposed to a sole worker who provides the total family income.

lize the labor of wives or daughters to supplement male income, while Hispanic families, who were overall the poorest group in the city, were least
inclined to send women into the work force as additional workers.

The census provides data on the number of workers per family that
permit further clarification of the role of contributory workers. Subtraction
of the estimates of female contributory workers from the total number of
workers who were not family heads produces an estimate of male roles as
contributory workers. The figures, both reported and estimated, indicate
that the American dream, the patriarchal one-worker nuclear family was
not a reality for a large portion of the San Antonio population. If all one-
worker families had been male-headed, these families would have constituted just under 60 percent of the city's families (tables 24 and 25).[8] On the
other hand, if one-worker families had included all female-headed families, only 41 percent of San Antonio families in 1930 would have received
all their earnings from one male worker. While an exact enumeration of the
number of families in which the father went off to work while the mother
and children stayed at home or in school cannot be obtained, in roughly
half of all San Antonio families a different economic pattern prevailed
in 1930.

The figures on workers per family suggest that men, not women, were
the vast majority of contributory or "secondary" workers and that for both
men and women market labor was more often undertaken as part of a family group than as a sole supporter. San Antonio did not vary widely from
other major Texas cities in the structure of family economic units. In
Dallas and Houston as well, contributory workers outnumbered sole workers. The data on widowed and divorced women workers and female heads
demonstrate the weakness of the assumption that women were "secondary" or "supplementary" workers. The Texas data on contributory workers suggest that, if the notion of a "supplementary" worker has any valid-
ity at all, it must be applied to a significant proportion of male as well as
female workers. In comparison with Houston and Dallas, San Antonio had
an unusually large number of families with no workers. That these families
were disproportionately concentrated among Anglos, who were substantially more prosperous than blacks or Mexican Americans, suggests that
pensioned or otherwise retired persons constituted an important component of such families.

[8]The data on workers per family do not identify the sex of the family head. The two
extremes of possibility are presented here.

The estimates on contributory workers also indicate significant differences in economic structure among families by ethnicity. Only 50 percent of black families had no contributory workers, as opposed to 71 percent of native-born Anglo families. The figures also indicate that proportionally more black and Mexican-American families than others contained more than two workers. In view of the fact that income among blacks and Hispanics was considerably lower than that among Anglos, the differences are not surprising. In light of family size, however, the similar size of black and Mexican family work units is puzzling. Both the child-woman ratio and the data on family size indicate that black women had the fewest children and the smallest families of all groups in the city and that Hispanic women had the largest families. However, the percentages of families who had at least one child at home under the age of twenty-one but no children under ten was nearly the same in both groups. The availability of youthful workers, therefore, was essentially equal in the two minority groups.

A sample of 1,004 women workers drawn from the city directory of 1934 yielded information on household structure that conflicted somewhat with the census returns (table 34). Of women in the sample 46 percent were the only adults in their households. An additional 17.4 percent were listed as workers in households with adult males present but not working. In contrast, the 1930 census indicated that only 39.7 percent of San Antonio's women workers were on their own or were heads of families. While male pride or mere oversight by directory compilers may have resulted in the failure to list occupations of wives and daughters, the high incidence of women who supported male family members is surprising nevertheless. Given the sample bias in favor of women alone, it is probable that the circumstance of women supporting husbands, fathers, and grown children was even more widespread than indicated in the sample.

Consistent with Mexican cultural proscriptions against an independent life-style among women, the Spanish-named women workers were more likely to live in households of two or more adults than others in the sample and less likely to live alone. Although Spanish-named women were less likely to be on their own than other women, they were equally likely to be the sole workers in the family. Contrary to the patriarchal focus of the Mexican family, Hispanic women in the sample were more likely than other women to be the working heads of families that included adult males. Undoubtedly this situation reflects the high unemployment rate among Mexican-American males and the possibility that many males followed the crops and were not recorded as workers in the city. Contemporary impressionistic accounts of the Depression in San Antonio note the erowding of several generations into single households on the Mexican West Side,[9] but Mexican-American households did not contain significantly more workers per family than other households.

Between 1930 and 1940 both the percentage of families with no workers and the percentage of families with one worker increased. The change in family work patterns suggests, first, that the Depression forced some people to leave the work force regardless of their status as breadwinners. Older workers, who had extreme difficulty landing new jobs, probably account for a large portion of the rise in nonworker families. The increase in no-worker and one-worker families suggests that, although some wives replaced their sons and daughters in the work force during the Depression, the traditional ideal of the father as the single provider was more nearly the norm in 1940 than in 1930. Between 1930 and 1940 the number of female family heads increased from 10,293 to an estimated 17,420, or from 8.5 percent to 10.7 percent of all families. This change could then have accounted for some but not all of the increase in no-worker or single-worker families, but female-headed families were more likely than male-headed families to include child wage earners. Of children ages fourteen to seventeen who were workers in 1940, the majority were members of female-headed families.[10]

In view of the poverty of the Mexican-American community, Hispanic women should have entered the work force at levels comparable to those of black women, but clearly they did not. One option for the homemaker, even if she was pressed by cultural prescriptions or the presence of young children to remain in the home, would have been homework, but there were significantly more black homemakers reported in the census than Mexican-American homemakers who pursued paid work within their own homes. Mexican-American wives were reluctant to seek paid labor of any kind. Given the small number of lodgers in Hispanic families, income from this source also would have been negligible. The data on workers per family and family size tell a simple and stark fact: Mexican Americans supported larger families on the income of fewer workers than black families.

[9]Records of the Women's Bureau, Materials Relating to Bulletin no. 126.
[10]According to 1940 estimates, 23.1 percent of female-headed families that included persons ages 14 through 17 contained one or more youthful workers, while the percentage was 15.7 in male-headed families.

Many Hispanic families did have more than one worker, and a large number of additional family workers were female. The vast majority of these female workers were single, however, as opposed to ever-married. Hispanic families as well as Anglo immigrant families preferred to send daughters rather than wives to work.

As women passed through the Depression in San Antonio, their families were the focus of their experiences and their concerns. Most young girls entered the work force before marriage to contribute some part of their earnings to the parental family. Their brothers were expected to do likewise. Marriage altered roles and responsibilities, and ethnicity was a strong indicator of the work and family cycle that a young woman entered upon marriage. Increasingly between 1930 and 1940 married women entered or remained in the work force, but mothers of young children almost never worked outside the home. Black women with young children were more likely to be workers than were other women with young children. Not surprisingly, black women who had young dependents were the most likely to find employment that they could perform in their homes. In this respect the income needs and the structure of black families reinforced one aspect of female occupational segregation by race. Hispanic women and black women married young, which signaled the exit of Mexican-American but not black women from the paid work force. Hispanic mothers had the heaviest child-care responsibilities and the longest periods of child-bearing of all San Antonio women, circumstances that interacted with cultural prescriptions to keep them at home. The rise in the labor-force participation rates among women during the Depression, a rise in which San Antonio conformed to the national trend, was accounted for almost exclusively by the presence of Anglo wives in the labor market. Although fertility declined during the Depression, the decline was temporary, while the increase in married work rates was long term. Furthermore, the fertility decline of the Depression was not precipitous enough to account for the work behavior of women in the 1930s. Clearly other factors influenced women's entrance into the labor market.

The family economy of all ethnic and racial groups was changing during the 1930s as child and teenage workers were pushed out of the work force. Their lost wages were not usually replaced by their mothers' decisions to accept employment. Wives in the labor market in 1940 were predominantly young women who were either childless or the mothers of children too young to work, as were the working wives of 1930. In Anglo families more and more wives were going out to work. Families had to adapt to the changes that were taking place in the work lives of women, but changes in family structure and composition complemented rather than caused the movement of Anglo wives into the labor market. That movement is most fully explained by the broadening employment opportunities for Anglo women, opportunities that grew despite the Depression.

[5]

Adapting: Occupational Segregation and Unemployment

The Depression didn't affect me because we were all on the same level then.

—Janie Reeves, domestic worker

Well, there are no girls in Geo Huntress' office this morning but Julia Haas and a Mrs. Riley who came down but was not supposed to.

—May Eckles, clerical worker

Dora Reyes, 131 Monterey St., and Trinidad Martinez, 15, said they were gassed on the picket line.

—Testimony in the 1938 pecan shellers' strike[1]

FOR most of her adult life Janie Reeves worked as a domestic in San Antonio. During the 1930s she lived in the homes of the people who employed her. Her employers were military personnel, and when an employer was transferred to another post, she found a position with another family without great difficulty. Life during the Depression passed much the same as it had during the 1920s and as it would during the 1940s. She had plenty to eat and a roof over her head, but she had little money to spend. May Eckles watched nervously through the Depression as her fellow clerical workers in the abstract office and surrounding offices were laid off and as her salary was cut time after time. She grew anxious about taxes, mortgage payments, and food costs, but she found ways to postpone payments and to generate a little extra income. Trinidad Martinez's family sent her to work in the pecan-shelling sheds while she was a child. In 1938, at the age of fifteen she united with fellow shellers in striking against a pay cut. On the picket line she joined Mexican-American girls as young as eleven years who were tear-gassed or beaten by police in the biggest strike of the decade.[2]

[1]Anonymous interview, May 26, 1979; Eckles diary, March 7, 1933; *San Antonio Light*, February 24, 1938.
[2]*San Antonio Light*, February 22–24, 1938.

Janie, May, and Trinidad experienced the Depression in very different ways, each with singular joys, fears, and problems. The three women demonstrated the intensity of occupational segregation in San Antonio and the degree to which the reality of employment conditions defined female experiences during the Depression. Janie, being black, had virtually no alternative to domestic work, but many black women were not as fortunate as Janie in remaining employed throughout the leanest years. As an Anglo, May had access to a vast pool of white-collar jobs that was closed to blacks and Hispanics, but as a woman she had almost no chance of advancing beyond the clerical ranks into a management position. Trinidad was representative of many Hispanic workers in moving into the work force at a young age. Hispanic women might choose domestic jobs, but most found employment in the city's factories. As industrial workers Mexican-American women were more likely than other women to participate in strikes and other organized protests against Depression conditions.

A small group of San Antonio women achieved economic affluence, social prestige, or both through their careers. Their achievements stand in glaring contrast to the prospects of most other women, though they were not especially noteworthy in comparison to the wealth and influence of their male counterparts. In 1930, 5 dentists, 25 physicians and surgeons, 7 attorneys, and 13 college professors comprised the city's female professional elite, whereas 1,041 San Antonio men pursued these occupations. In San Antonio the most prominent women were generally not career women but the wives and daughters of the male commercial elite. Two exceptions were Emma Tenayuca and Rebecca Taylor, labor leaders with opposing views whom San Antonians remember today for their persistence in attacking worker poverty in Depression San Antonio.

Although most San Antonio women were not wage earners, the city economy relied heavily on the paid labor of women. San Antonio during the 1930s was a commercial center whose shops and offices were primarily staffed by women. Tourism was a significant but seasonal industry in which hundreds of women found work for a few months each year. Fort Sam Houston, then the nation's largest army base, is adjacent to the San Antonio city limits. While Fort Sam Houston was not a direct employer of a large number of women, it was the area's largest single employer and significantly influenced social and economic conditions. Three other military installations in Bexar County augmented the role of the federal government in the local economy. The military personnel at Fort Sam and smaller installations supported restaurants and other service industries that were a major source of employment for women. There were also several light but labor-intensive industries such as food canning, pecan shelling, garment manufacturing, and cigar rolling that employed large numbers of women at low wages. The Depression destroyed many of San Antonio's smaller manufacturing and service industries and displaced thousands of workers. The tobacco and food-processing industries, which had been major employers of women in 1930, never recalled their pre-Depression workers, and hundreds of women workers found other occupations or left the work force.[3]

As was true elsewhere in urban America, the vast majority of black women worked in domestic and service occupations. San Antonio blacks were more strictly segregated into domestic work than were other black women in southern cities. Unlike the urban Southeast, in San Antonio the black female population was smaller than the number of domestic-service jobs available, and competition among black women for service work was therefore less intense than elsewhere. San Antonio had a number of European immigrant women, however, who did accept jobs in the domestic sector. Hispanic women also competed with blacks for some domestic jobs. Clearly the availability of Hispanic and other women to fill manufacturing jobs worked against occupational diversification for black women. Both the stereotype of the black domestic worker and competition for jobs outside the domestic or service areas intensified the occupational segregation of black women in San Antonio.[4]

Although some Mexican-American women pursued domestic occupations, the vast majority sought work in the food-processing, garment, or tobacco industries (tables 26 and 30). Whereas 91 percent of black women engaged in domestic and service work, 79 percent of Hispanic women

---

[3]T. R. Fehrenbach, *The San Antonio Story*, pp. 159–77; Green Peyton, *San Antonio: City in the Sun*, pp. 1–28; Charles Ramsdell, *San Antonio: A Historical and Pictorial Guide*, pp. 213–23; Mary Olivia Handy, *History of Ft. Sam Houston*.

[4]In 1930, 91.2 percent of black women workers in San Antonio were employed in domestic and service occupations. In Atlanta and New Orleans, cities with proportionally larger black populations, the concentrations of black females in the domestic sector were 90.1 percent and 83.7 percent, respectively. Within the service sector San Antonio's black women were also more concentrated in private household service than were black women in the other two cities. Black women in San Antonio lost proportionally fewer jobs during the Depression than did black women in the other two cities. Julia Kirk Blackwelder, "Women in the Work Force: Atlanta, New Orleans, and San Antonio, 1930 to 1940," *Journal of Urban History* 4 (May, 1978):337–55.

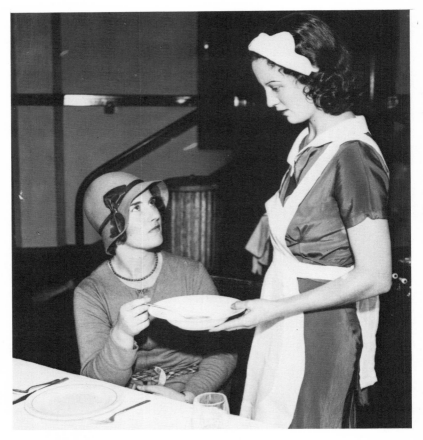

Mrs. William Tobin Thornton being served by Ruth Morris in a YWCA household-efficiency class, January 22, 1933. Although Anglo women clearly preferred to work outside the domestic-service area, the YWCA sponsored a project to train unemployed Anglo women for housekeeping employment.
(*San Antonio Light* Collection, University of Texas Institute of Texan Cultures, San Antonio.)

found employment in industrial occupations. Anglo women dominated both clerical and trade jobs in the city. In comparison with black women, Hispanic women fared well in commercial occupations, but most of these women worked in stores and small cafés that served the Hispanic community. Foreign-born Anglo women were better represented in domestic jobs than were native-born Anglos, but they also had a higher percentage employed in the professions.

As San Antonio moved through the Depression, some occupations felt the brunt of the economic contraction more heavily than others (tables 26, 28, and 30). Unemployment rose most dramatically in manufacturing. Hispanic women, concentrated in San Antonio's small factories, were hit hardest by the manufacturing decline. Anglo women, conversely, found better employment prospects in 1940 than they had in 1930 as the clerical sector continued to grow despite the Depression. Although black women in San Antonio did not lose as many jobs as did black women in other cities, such as Atlanta and New Orleans, they lost jobs while white women held their own in domestic and service jobs.

Although men and women in San Antonio were highly concentrated in specific jobs by gender and ethnicity, there was relatively little segregation between native-born and foreign-born Anglos (table 31). The lack of nativity-based occupational divisions among Anglos confirms the castelike distinctions among Anglos, blacks, and Mexican Americans as primary determinants of socioeconomic status. Overall, jobs were more strictly segregated by sex than by ethnicity, suggesting that "racial" discrimination functioned within two separate labor markets for men and for women.

The pattern of occupational segregation demonstrates that Anglos, whether native- or foreign-born, whether male or female, whether employers or employees, exercised an ability to separate themselves from the jobs of black and Hispanic persons. In contrast, blacks and Hispanics revealed either little desire or little success in protecting their occupational areas from incursion by others. Black and Hispanic men showed little power to define their work as inappropriate for women workers of the two underclasses. Women, whether by their own occupational choices or by employers' hiring decisions, were more highly segregated by ethnicity than were male workers. It might be argued that society viewed "racial" mingling as more threatening to women than to men, but it was also true that women's work in some occupations had been stereotyped by employers as particularly suited to particular "racial" skills or aptitudes.[5]

If the ability to choose a job among one's own kind is an expression of sociopolitical power, the San Antonio work force manifested a power structure in which Anglo males were most successful in segregating themselves from other workers. Anglo females were more successful in protecting their jobs against competition from black and Mexican-American women than were blacks and Mexican-American women in eliminating

[5]For information on job labeling, see appendix A.

competition among themselves. The two minority groups, blacks and Hispanics, displayed relatively little power to separate themselves simultaneously by gender and ethnicity. Mexican-American and black males and Mexican-American and black females were all members of very similar occupational structures. The inability of the underclasses to establish occupational distance from all other ethnic- and gender-specific groups identifies them as the targets rather than the sources of discrimination. The highest degrees of dissimilarity in work existed between black females and Anglo or Mexican-American men, but black males experienced considerable job competition from both Mexican-American males and black women. Anglo male power thus operated to protect Anglo male workers from competition by all groups. Similarly, Anglo employers protected Anglo female workers against displacement.

Although black women predominated in domestic jobs, expressed employer preferences suggest that black women acquired these jobs by default when Anglo or Hispanic women failed to meet the demand for domestic workers. Mexican-American women, married or single, were reluctant to enter domestic work, a trend that continues into the contemporary period.[6] In the classified-advertising sections of the daily newspapers San Antonians revealed their sensitivity to race and ethnicity. In domestic work, where employees have a close association with their employers and their families, ethnic or racial preferences were most pronounced. San Antonio residents advertised for a "white housekeeper," a "clean German girl," an "experienced white or Mexican girl," and occasionally a "colored woman." The advertisements carried delimiters of age and marital status as well. Although prospective employers sometimes wished to employ young Anglo or Mexican "girls," maturity was preferred in black employees and frequently in Anglos and Hispanics as well. One such advertisement requested a "middle-aged colored woman for cooking and general housekeeping."[7] A hotel in San Antonio sought to employ a "middle-aged woman positively alone."[8]

Women seeking domestic work through the newspapers were sensitive to local prejudices. In placing advertisements, they included information that would allow readers to screen out categories they would not employ.

[6]Leo Grebler, Joan W. Moore, and Ralph C. Guzman, *The Mexican-American People: The Nation's Second Largest Minority*, p. 212.

[7]*San Antonio Express*, January 12, 1932.

[8]*San Antonio Express*, June 10, 1932.

Women looking for work identified themselves as American, German, Polish, Bohemian, Mexican, or colored and as "experienced," "middle-aged," "refined," "alone," or "with children."

Black women in Depression San Antonio understood that domestic work was their lot. On the one hand, they understood the necessity of protecting the jobs they could find. On the other hand, employment discrimination did not prevent them from educating themselves for a brighter future. Blacks pursued secondary education despite their expectations that it would have little utility in their immediate work lives. Anna Graves went to San Antonio from Seguin in 1932 to live with an aunt and uncle so that she could take advantage of the additional year of schooling offered blacks in San Antonio.[9] She learned typing in school, though she knew at the time that black women would be employed only as cooks or maids. After high school Anna married and moved to San Marcos, but when a cousin fell ill, she returned briefly to San Antonio to protect her cousin's job as a domestic by working in her place. After World War II she again returned to San Antonio and became the first black clerical worker at Kelly Field.

Mexican-American females, closed out of white-collar jobs by discrimination or lack of education and underrepresented in domestic work by discrimination or their own preferences, found positions in manufacturing and food processing their best employment options. The low income of Mexican-American males and the excess of labor during the late twenties and the thirties made it possible for employers to hire young Mexican-American women for manufacturing and shelling at lower wages than those paid black or Anglo women.

It could be argued that many of San Antonio's Mexican Americans were recent immigrants from poor regions who lacked sufficient knowledge of English and the occupational skills to hold sales, office, or professional positions. A closer look at the breakdown of workers in the less-skilled category, however, reveals an even more startling pattern of occupational segregation that cannot be explained by lack of skill. Hispanic women dominated jobs as seamstresses and pecan shellers, while other women held numerical advantages as servants and waitresses. Domestic service has traditionally been viewed as the least desirable "legitimate" job for women, but pecan shelling and hand sewing were the lowest-paying jobs in San Antonio. Local observers as well as federal agents reported

---

[9]Anonymous interview, May 16, 1978.

incomes averaging under one dollar a day for shellers and hand sewers.[10] Robert Landolt observed that employers preferred Hispanics for the needle trades on the grounds that

Mexican American women were found characteristically to have the dexterity and temperament for being adept at both hand and machine needlework. Their ability to work well on highly repetitious jobs was attributed to their Indian ancestry. Their particular proficiency in the skills of garment making was attributed to the centuries-old practice of the Catholic nuns teaching Mexican and Indian women to sew, and the emphasis on excellence in needlework was handed down from mother to daughter.[11]

The geographic distribution of female workers followed the general configuration of population density (tables 35–38). Women workers, like the rest of the city's population, were more highly concentrated in the area west of the Central Business District with a slightly lower concentration east of that district. These were the two areas of the city with the largest Mexican-American neighborhood (west San Antonio) and the largest black community (east San Antonio). A third band of workers stretched directly northward from downtown in an area less densely settled and dominated by Anglo-Americans. These three distinct zones of workers reveal interesting occupational differentiations.

Professionals were most strongly represented in the North Side (Anglo) zone and most poorly represented in west San Antonio (Mexican-American). Domestic and service workers were well distributed among the three zones, a situation reflecting the high incidence of domestic workers who lived in or near the households of North Side employers. In east San Antonio the largest category of women workers was domestic and service workers. On the West Side over half of all female workers were pecan shellers or factory operatives. The West Side, which included the poorest area of San Antonio, had a surprisingly large number of managers, business owners, and semiprofessionals. These women are accounted for by the unusually large numbers of small café operators and street vendors in Mexican sections of San Antonio. The northern zone had a disproportionate share of sales and clerical workers, a not surprising situation since Anglo women, who predominated in north San Antonio, held considerable

[10]Seldon C. Menefee and Orin C. Cassmore, *The Pecan Shellers of San Antonio*, pp. 23–26; Harold A. Shapiro, "The Workers of San Antonio, Texas, 1900–1940" (Ph.D. diss., University of Texas, 1952), pp. 118–23.

[11]Robert G. Landolt, *The Mexican American Workers of San Antonio, Texas: The Chicano Heritage*, pp. 184–85.

Annie Charo, a skilled embroiderer at age six, March 1927. Annie began sewing when she was two years old. Needle skills passed down by Mexican women from one generation to the next encouraged the growth of garment making in San Antonio.
(*San Antonio Light* Collection, University of Texas Institute of Texan Cultures, San Antonio.)

advantage over Mexican-American and black women in obtaining pink- or white-collar jobs. In contrast, factory operatives lived overwhelmingly in west San Antonio, and pecan shellers were entirely restricted to that area. The concentration of workers dropped sharply outside the three zones, the remaining female workers living out from the city in a northwesterly direction and on the South Side. On the Northwest Side the proportion of professionals increased significantly, paralleling the expected geographic distribution of male professionals.

Particular facets of female occupational segregation in San Antonio have been causally related to residential segregation. Low-paying female industrial work in San Antonio, a condition unsurpassed in other twentieth-century American cities,[12] could not have flourished without excess labor. Also, however, it could not have existed without high population density. At pay of four to six cents an hour, workers had to walk to work. All the sewing shops, cigar factories, and pecan plants were established on the overcrowded West Side after a large community of Mexican immigrants gathered there. Consequently black and Anglo women were unlikely to be drawn into these industries. Residential segregation was one of the several factors that reinforced occupational segregation by gender and ethnicity and that consequently influenced individual women in their decisions to enter or to forego entering the labor market.

As the development of hand industries in west San Antonio in the late 1920s illustrates, the local economy and the labor force were interactive, each having some dependence on the other. Between 1920 and 1930 the number of female San Antonio workers in sewing, food processing, and cigar making increased from 2,695 to 4,480. Since few shops employed as many as 100 women, the increase meant the establishment of many new concerns. Investors in the city based decisions to expand operations partly on their knowledge of the existing labor pool, but the creation of new job opportunities also drew new workers into the job market. Occupational segregation by gender and ethnicity in Depression San Antonio was so intense that virtually six separate labor markets functioned, one for each ethnic group of men and of women. At the bottom of the occupational ladder and between the two underclasses segregation was less strict than at the top and between Anglos and others, but at all levels segregation circumscribed opportunities for prospective workers.

Work-force participation by women was determined by the interaction among the factors of family income, number and ages of children, cultural attitudes toward women's paid work, and the ethnic-specific female occupational structure. In reaching a decision to seek work, a woman judged her prospects of getting a certain type of job as a black, Anglo, or Hispanic female and weighed those prospects against economic and family circumstances that were also highly differentiated by ethnicity. Employers, who were well aware of the constraints under which women in each of the three ethnic groups behaved, organized their industrial or commercial enterprises to conform to existing patterns of ethnic and gender segregation and

[12]T. R. Picnot, "The Socio-Economic Status of Low Income Groups of San Antonio" (mimeographed copy of address, n.d.), p. 9.

to the particular conditions that brought women of the desired ethnic group into the work force. As the kinds of available employment changed, women of one ethnic group might be leaving the work force because job opportunities for their group were dwindling while women of another ethnic group were being drawn into the labor market. The discouraged-worker effect, the decision to stop job hunting after an extended period of unemployment, might then be driving black women out of the work force at the same time that Anglo women were seeking work in greater numbers.[13]

Employment patterns in San Antonio demonstrate that cultural definitions can withstand tremendous economic pressures and that occupational segregation itself influences both the age at which women seek work and their decisions to enter or withdraw from the work force after marriage. Despite the severity of the Depression and their history of poverty, Mexican-American families kept wives and mothers at home and sent out sons and daughters in search of work. For the Mexican-American family it was not a question of weighing the value of low-paying market work against the housewife's value in child rearing and home maintenance. Paid homework, which might be entered into without the necessity of choosing market labor over unremunerated home labor, was a more frequent choice of black than of Mexican-American homemakers. In 1930, 475 Hispanic and 537 black homemakers reportedly engaged in paid work at home (table 7). Mexican-American girls as young as twelve years of age might enter pecan shelling, but there were no comparable jobs to draw young black girls into the work force. Anglos concentrated in white-collar occupations that demanded a high-school diploma, and they were consequently unlikely to enter the labor market before age eighteen.

In summary, San Antonio in the pre–World War II period demonstrated an occupational structure that was highly segregated by gender and ethnicity. Occupational segregation was a powerful determinant of rates of female labor-force participation. The persistence of occupational segregation in a time of intense economic crisis indicated that the citizens of San Antonio paid a high price to maintain traditional practices of discrimination. Employers were restrained from replacing less efficient with more efficient workers or more expensive with less expensive workers because of their own prejudices or those of the community in which they lived. Although the fruits of discrimination included uniformly lower wages for

[13]Jacob Mincer, "Labor Force Participation of Married Women: A Study of the Labor Supply," in H. Gregg Lewis, ed., *Aspects of Labor Economics*, pp. 63–106.

women than for men, discrimination also protected some jobs for women at the expense of men. Similarly, Anglo women had the better jobs among female workers, but the domination of black and Hispanic women in domestic and industrial labor made it difficult for Anglo women to fill the lower-paying positions even if Depression conditions led them in that direction. The differences in the age structure and the marital status of women workers in the three ethnic groups also reflect the considerations that families gave to the occupational structure in reaching decisions about the nature of the family as an economic unit.

The vast majority of San Antonio women in the Depression labor force engaged in "women's work," occupations clearly marked as jobs fit for female rather than male efforts. As factory operatives in light industries, as laundresses and servants, as teachers and nurses, San Antonio women filled roles that had comprised women's sphere since the nineteenth century. The positions of telephone operators, store clerks, typists, secretaries, and laundry operatives were no less dominated by women, though female prominence in these areas followed from technological advances or attitudinal changes occurring in the twentieth century. The significant facts of women's jobs were that in San Antonio as elsewhere in the nation occupational segregation was the rule, and women were concentrated in the lowest-paying ranks of the occupational structure. Domestic and personal-service work was the largest area of female employment in 1930, and the most common single occupation reported to census takers was that of servant. Nearly two-fifths of all women workers were in the service sector, and slightly less than one-fifth were servants.

At the time of the 1930 census, taken in April, 1930, unemployment had not reached serious proportions in most sectors of the work force. A second unemployment census, taken in January, 1931, showed higher levels of unemployment, but it was widely regarded as an undercount (tables 41 through 43).[14] According to local observers, unemployment in San Antonio reached its depths sometime between 1932 and the end of 1934, but city leaders based their estimates of the rise and fall of unemployment on the demands for relief services. Federal reports of 1935 reveal that Mexican Americans constituted more than half the families certified for relief despite the considerable discrimination against Hispanics and despite the fact that Mexican Americans comprised only one-third to two-fifths of the

[14]Valerie Kincade Oppenheimer, *The Female Labor Force in the United States*, pp. 1–6.

population. Black families were overrepresented in the relief population, similarly indicating that they were also disproportionately burdened by unemployment. Since the relief census was taken closer to the depths of the Depression than were the unemployment censuses, it better suggests the extent of suffering caused by unemployment in San Antonio than do the other counts of the unemployed. The census of 1930 reported 6,797 experienced workers unemployed or laid off during the final week of March. Five years later 12,752 workers were certified relief clients.

In 1937, when a federal census of unemployment and partial employment was taken, 13,845 workers reported themselves as totally unemployed, a figure twice as large as the number of out of work in 1930. In addition, 5,725 persons were employed on publicly or privately funded relief jobs, and 7,726 workers were employed only part time. By 1940 the number of unemployed had decreased to 10,780, and the number of emergency workers had declined as well, but a large number of discouraged workers had left the work force, artificially inflating the unemployment decline (table 44).

High unemployment among black women during the 1930s resulted from a constriction of the job market for domestic workers, a long-term trend in occupational change that was greatly intensified by the Depression. Racial prejudices prevented black women from entering other occupations, even within the broad category of service jobs, as their two most important occupations (servant and laundress) dwindled in prominence. On the other hand, the acceptability of black women as domestic workers was high enough that they were no more likely to lose their jobs than were white domestic workers. On the contrary, white female domestic workers were somewhat more likely to be unemployed in 1940 than were black women in domestic work. White women, however, had been much more successful in other service occupations, such as hairdressing and waitressing, which expanded as domestic work declined.

Although the information regarding Mexican-American women is less concrete, it appears that they were similarly the victims of interaction between occupational segregation and structural changes in the economy. In 1940 the highest level of unemployment among women occurred among factory operatives and kindred workers. In the garment, cigar, candy, and food-processing industries, where Hispanic women predominated, the number of workers in these industries declined from 3,577 in 1930 to 2,285 in 1940; of the latter figure 365 were unemployed. The second major area of Hispanic female employment in 1930 was domestic work, an area also hard hit by the Depression. Mexican-American women had somewhat more flexibility within the segregated job market than black females, but all the occupations in which Hispanic women were well represented in 1930 underwent extreme contraction over the decade. The high level of unemployment among factory operatives in 1940 suggests that Mexican-American women were largely unsuccessful in making a transition to the expanding sales and clerical sectors.

Both the unemployment rates by ethnicity and specific areas of high unemployment confirm that structural changes in the San Antonio economy, aggravated by the Depression, altered employment opportunities in such a way as to drive blacks and Hispanics out of the work force while drawing increasing numbers of Anglo women into it. After the Depression few of the jobs lost by minority women were restored, and the losses were more severe for black than for Hispanic women. As the economy recovered, other areas of employment expanded. The garment industry grew stronger during the post–World War II period than it had been before the war, and Mexican-American women, who had been displaced from cigar making, home sewing, and pecan shelling, could move into these factories. Hispanic women also made some headway in entering white-collar occupations. For black women, however, the decline was more serious; very few new areas of employment had opened as late as 1960, and representation outside domestic work remained small (table 33). Consequently, the work rate of black women in San Antonio was lower in 1960 than it had been in 1930. In contrast, Hispanic female work rates were about equal in 1930 and 1960, though the Mexican-American population had grown much faster than the city's black population.

Although employment did not contract in the broad category of service occupations in San Antonio during the 1930s, the economy did not absorb new workers in this area, and jobs for domestic as opposed to other service workers declined. In 1940, two-fifths of all unemployed women were domestic or other service workers. Since these were virtually the only occupations open to black women, there was little incentive for them to enter or remain in the work force. Hispanic women, who are not separated from other white women in the 1940 census, appear to have suffered the greatest losses in employment. Hispanic women were concentrated in manufacturing occupations, where the biggest reductions occurred. Overall, Mexican Americans had more occupational choices than blacks had, but discrimination and inferior education closed most white-collar positions to them. For these reasons it appears that the place of Hispanic women in the work force declined over the decade, the gains in employment going primarily to Anglo women.

[6]

Home and Shop: Wages and Working Conditions

If they have $5.00 they stay out till they spend it. You can't make a Mexican work a whole week if they have money enough to live on.

—Operator, San Antonio shelling firm, 1932[1]

FOR many black and Hispanic women in San Antonio, employment carried the burden and the insult of working for less than a dollar a day. Employers frequently rationalized that the low wages paid Hispanics reflected the humble aspirations of Mexican-American workers. One pecan dealer who employed many Hispanics estimated that San Antonio recorded the lowest wages of any major city in the United States, commenting that low pay is likely to persist "where ignorance is bliss."[2] The attitudes of San Antonio's employers toward their workers suggest the economic implications of occupational segregation.

The statistics of occupational segregation clearly articulate the inferior position of black and Mexican-American women, and the consequences of their low status emerge clearly from data on wages and working conditions in Texas gathered by the Women's Bureau in 1932. Although industrial workers usually earn more than domestic workers, the Women's Bureau documented that thousands of women, mostly Mexican-American, worked at industrial tasks at home eight to twelve hours a day for less than the Depression pay of three dollars a week that May Eckles's maid, Maria, received. Factory-employed industrial workers fared better than homeworkers, but the Women's Bureau found their incomes also to be below those of industrial women elsewhere in the nation and their working conditions deplorable.

The Women's Bureau survey of Texas workers in 1932 documented many aspects of occupational discrimination that went beyond job labels. The bureau found that "Mexican women were receiving very much lower

[1]Interview with George Azar and Miss Azar, Records of the Women's Bureau, Materials Realting to Bulletin no. 126.

[2]Interview with A. Pomerantz, manager, Southern Pecan Shelling Co., ibid.

wages than white women, even when working side by side in the same occupation and establishment."[3] The bureau also uncovered finite details of occupational segregation that the census does not reflect. Within the garment industry both Anglo and Hispanic women were employed, but in factories that made infants' and children's wear no Anglos were on the payrolls (three of the four manufacturers of youth garments investigated by the bureau were San Antonio firms). The bureau reported sizable differentials statewide in the pay scales of Anglo as opposed to those of black and Hispanic women. In commercial laundries, the only industrial employers of large numbers of black women, Hispanic workers had lower average earnings than black workers. In the women's-clothing industry, however, the wages of Hispanic workers were higher than those of Anglos. During one week in 1932 median Anglo wages for selected industries ranged from a low of $4.15 in nut-shelling firms to a high of $12.45 in department stores as opposed to a range of $2.65 and $9.00 for Hispanics and $2.65 and $7.25 for blacks.

The history of the development of industrial employment of women in San Antonio amplifies the meaning of occupational segregation. Black women, generally considered unsatisfactory labor for most industrial jobs, were denied access to most of the industrial employment that opened in the 1920s. The availability of Mexican-American women, deemed ideal industrial workers, prompted the establishment of new factories and shelling plants. Black women, despite their segregation in domestic occupations, were a scarce commodity in the labor market relative to Mexican-American women, and their Depression wages did not fall below those of Mexican-American handworkers. In commercial laundries, where the work was compatible with "domestic talents," black women found employment opportunities and were wage-competitive with Anglo and Mexican-American women.

In San Antonio, described by a local labor paper as a "pest hole of low paid labor," social and economic conditions interacted to encourage the growth of paid homework before and during the Depression. Deploring the exploitative aspects of home labor, the paper's editor complained: "The New Deal glorified the fact that the sweat shop of the home had been abolished. The sweat shop in the homes still continues in this city, and if any-

[3]Mary Loretta Sullivan and Bertha Blair, *Women in Texas Industries*, Women's Bureau, Bulletin no. 126, p. 5.

thing is on the increase." [4] There were two major areas of industrial employment for the city's homeworkers, hand sewing and pecan shelling, with approximately 4,000 persons deriving income in each of these areas during the mid-1930s. In 1937 it was estimated that 15,000 to 20,000 families in and around San Antonio existed on industrial homework.[5] Although the sewing trades were exclusively female, men as well as women worked as pecan shellers. The vast majority of industrial homeworkers were Mexican Americans, a situation that reflected discrimination, the dislocation of Hispanic agricultural workers, and the geographic segregation of Mexican Americans on San Antonio's West Side.

The labor shortages during World War I and the decline of immigration from Europe encouraged mechanization in many sectors of the American economy. For farmers in the Southwest, however, wartime labor shortages were offset by a dramatic rise in immigration from Mexico, and manual labor persisted there as the backbone of production. Throughout the 1920s, Mexico provided what seemed an endless stream of workers for migrant agricultural work. The extremity of depression conditions in Mexico in the twenties guaranteed that Mexican immigrants would undercut Anglo or black workers in unskilled labor. The eagerness of Mexicans to cross the border likewise guaranteed that Mexican Americans could not withhold their labor to bargain for higher wages. Although thousands of immigrants crossed and recrossed the border in search of work, most of them believed that they were better off in the United States despite the seasonal nature of work in the fields. Thousands of low-paid, temporarily unemployed migrant families wintered in San Antonio and encouraged the expansion of nonmechanized industrial work in the city at a time when the national economy was moving away from hand labor. Similar developments occurred in Texas border towns as well, though on a smaller scale.

The expansion of homework in Depression San Antonio ran counter to announced federal goals, and local labor's disenchantment with the New Deal proceeded from the contrast between goals and achievements. During the Depression federal policies on homework were both unenforced and inconsistent. The Women's Bureau had made the elimination of industrial homework one of its major goals during the 1920s, and at the beginning of the Depression officials of the bureau asserted that most such jobs had been

[4]*San Antonio Weekly Dispatch*, July 20, 1934.
[5]*San Antonio Weekly Dispatch*, January 15, 1937.

terminated. The wage and standards codes of the National Recovery Administration also contained provisions against homework. On May 15, 1934, however, President Roosevelt gave executive approval for the continuance of homework by persons who were unable to work outside the home because of physical infirmities, persons whose presence was required in the home for the care of invalids not suffering from contagious diseases, and homeworkers aged fifty years or older who could not adapt to factory labor. Individuals who wished to pursue homework were required to secure certification from a state agency designated by the U.S. Department of Labor.[6]

Federal and state studies published early in the Depression indicated that even before the NRA codes were adopted homework had fallen off as part of the general business depression. Because the executive dispensation for particular classes of homework also carried requirements that pay and hours equal that of factory labor in the same industry, there was no overwhelming incentive for employers to replace factory labor with homework. NRA codes were not uniformly or universally observed, however. The U.S. Department of Labor reported that homeworkers were paid less than living wages and worked excessively long hours despite the NRA codes and the exemption program. Although the total number of homeworkers in the nation decreased, in certain industries the Depression brought a dramatic shift to homework. For example, a Pennsylvania study revealed a transition to homework between 1933 and 1935 in the men's-neckwear industry.[7]

In San Antonio employers flagrantly violated NRA regulations, and homework conditions in the late 1930s mirrored the situation that the NRA had tried to eradicate. In addition to an equal wage level for homeworkers, the NRA provisions required certification that workers were free of contagious diseases and maintained sanitary surroundings. It was precisely the failure of the San Antonio Health Department to enforce these standards that led to a local ban on industrial homework in 1940. In San Antonio only one pecan-shelling firm accepted the 1933–34 NRA code, and it went out of business shortly thereafter. The NRA codes were unenforceable be-

[6]*Monthly Labor Review* 40 (1935):595–98, 651–52.

[7]"Homework and Sweatshops," *Handbook of Labor Statistics: 1936 Edition*, U.S. Bureau of Labor Statistics, Bulletin no. 615 (Washington, D.C., 1936), pp. 196–204; Bertha M. Nienberg, *A Policy Insuring Value to the Woman Buyers and a Livelihood to Apparel Makers*, Women's Bureau, Bulletin no. 146 (Washington, D.C., 1936), pp. 18–201.

cause compliance was voluntary; moreover, government officials never appointed an authority to oversee the code for the shelling industry. Similarly, factory-employed garment workers in San Antonio were unaffected by the NRA code, as were the homeworkers. The code stipulated that "all materials and findings must be supplied by the employer and delivered and returned without expense to the worker. No deductions may be made for spoiled work. The homeworker must pledge himself not to allow other persons to assist in any part of the homework. The assignment of more work than it is possible to complete in the applicable code hours is prohibited." [8] When interviewed by representatives of the Women's Bureau in 1932, San Antonio workers consistently complained about the continuance of the exploitative conditions that the NRA forbade.

Both the pecan industry and the needle trades in San Antonio illustrate that abundant cheap labor attracts capital investment during a period of economic expansion. In 1920, when the major influx of Mexican labor to San Antonio was in its early stages, there was relatively little employment in garment manufacturing or food processing. By 1930 employment in food processing had more than doubled among men and had quadrupled among women. Employment of female workers in garment factories had more than doubled. The number of nonfactory seamstresses had increased significantly, while the number of males employed in tailoring, a trade requiring specific skills virtually unknown to Mexican male immigrants, had increased only slightly. Food processing was a small industry in 1920, but it had become the city's largest industry by 1930. The census figures document dramatic increases but overlook many homeworkers in sewing and many seasonal workers in the shelling business both in plants and at home.

Although the abundance of cheap Mexican labor encouraged both home shelling and home sewing, the pattern of growth in the two industries was somewhat different. Pecans are native to East Texas, and there was some commercial shelling in San Antonio before World War I. By the early 1920s machinery to crack the nuts and separate the shells from the meats had been developed, leading to an expansion of the pecan trade in San Antonio. By 1926, however, the large number of Mexican immigrants in the city had depressed the wages of unskilled labor to the point that hand labor

[8]"National Recovery Administration, Press Release no. 9861, January 28, 1935; *Monthly Labor Review* 40 (July, 1934):44; ibid. (March, 1935):651–52; *San Antonio Weekly Dispatch*, August 18, 25, 1933; January 19, 1934; May 25, 1934; September 28, 1934.

was cheaper than machine shelling.[9] Owners of shelling plants stopped investing in machinery and gradually replaced the shelling machines with hand labor. In Saint Louis, the other major pecan-shelling center in the United States, the reconversion to hand labor did not occur. Because hand shelling required less capital outlay than mechanized plants, cheap labor was also an inducement to expansion of the industry. The development of the contract system of shelling, which could be initiated with even less capital than hand-shelling plants, further enlarged the industry in San Antonio and its hinterland. Contractors furnished pecans to individuals or families, who were paid $0.06 to $0.08 a pound to shell the nuts at home. A single worker in the 1920s might average $6.00 to $7.00 a week in such labor, either at home or in the shelling plants. By the late 1930s wages had fallen as low as $0.04 a pound, and work was available less regularly. Whole families working together could not earn enough for the barest subsistence. Weekly shelling incomes of adult workers fell to an average of $2.50.[10]

Mexican Americans in San Antonio initially entered into pecan shelling and provided an attractive labor supply for shellers because the work was seasonal and could be taken up after the agricultural harvest. Shelling plants were concentrated on the West Side, where Mexican-American residence centered and population density was highest. Since not many Anglos or blacks lived in the area, few had much knowledge of the shelling industry, and fewer still sought employment in it. As the contract system was adopted, pecan shelling became less centralized, with individual contractors delivering and collecting pecans at points distant from the West Side and frequently outside Bexar County as well, but the dominance of Mexican-American workers in shelling persisted.

During the 1920s some shelling was conducted throughout the year, but most of it was done from October through May, providing opportuni-

[9]Selden Menefee and Orin C. Cassmore, *The Pecan Shellers of San Antonio*, p. 16; "Working Conditions of Pecan Shellers in San Antonio," *Monthly Labor Review* 45 (March, 1939):549–50.

[10]Ibid. Pecan shelling was one of the few jobs in which the Depression broke down rather than reinforced gender segregation, but again it demonstrates that the least powerful members of the society were least able to enforce a preference for gender or ethnic segregation. Although picking and sorting were primarily done by women, many Hispanic men entered the work during the thirties as jobs of last resort. As labor activist Alberta Snid remembered, during the Depression her father was driven to shelling because he was unable to find any other work.

ties for steady employment for many agricultural workers who wintered in San Antonio. With the onset of the Depression opportunities for migrant employment dwindled, enlarging the importance of income from shelling. Simultaneously the price of pecans fell, driving some shellers out of business and compelling others to cut wages. The use of the contract system, which cut overhead by eliminating the costs of maintaining a plant, became more attractive as prices declined. An El Paso shelling-plant operator stated in 1932 that he had cut wages 20 percent but that he could no longer maintain even the lower wage level because of falling prices. He told a Women's Bureau agent that he planned to close his plant and sell unshelled pecans to home shellers and buy back the meats because he saw no other way to compete with San Antonio shellers who were driving down rates and prices through this arrangement. The plant owner said that he had complained to the federal government about the situation and had received a reply that the prohibition of homework was a state matter.[11]

A strike by factory-employed shellers in 1934 dramatized the plight of pecan workers. The striking workers sought the support of home shellers and endeavored to prevent contractors' distribution of pecans to homeworkers. While the strike of 1934 and the more protracted and violent strike of 1938 closed down several plants, they were ineffective in interfering with home shelling and encouraged plant owners to adopt the contract system.

The children's-wear and handkerchief industries were not seasonal to the same extent as shelling. The growth of the garment industry in San Antonio and elsewhere in Texas depended on cheap labor made available through the interaction of circumstances. Garment workers, unlike shellers, did not follow the crops and generally had not done so in the past, though their male relatives may have done so. San Antonio had an abundance of Mexican-American women who preferred not to take domestic work or to follow the crops. The women had learned or were learning from family members the skills of the garment sweatshop. Mexican-American women seeking work were excluded from sales and clerical jobs because of inadequate education and ethnic prejudices. Coming from among the city's poorest families, Mexican-American garment workers accepted wages below the overall substandard wages paid other San Antonians. Conse-

[11]Interview with T. Azar, Records of the Women's Bureau, Materials Relating to Bulletin no. 126.

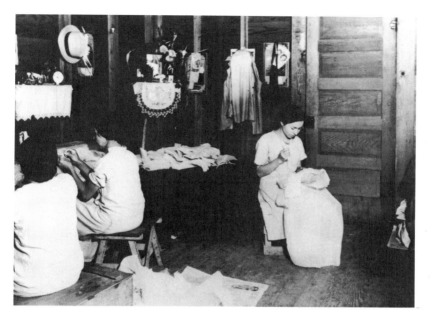

Mexican-American homeworkers, 1932. Investigators of the U.S. Women's Bureau noted the fine quality of sewing and the low pay of San Antonio workers. (National Archives, Washington, D.C.)

quently, Mexican-American women comprised a capable labor pool that was wage-competitive with hand sewers in any other American city.

The farming-out of garment sewing from pieces cut in New York City, either to homeworkers or to workshops was not unique to Texas. Connecticut, New Jersey, and Pennsylvania jobbers received such work from the New York garment district before and during the Depression. One explanation for the growth of homework was the passage in the 1920s of New York State laws governing hours and conditions of female and child labor that were stricter than laws in other states. Sending the work as far as Texas clearly reflected the lower wage levels among Mexican-American workers. An Anglo handworker interviewed by the Women's Bureau stated that the Mexican women set the pace for speed and quality of work and that it was up to the Anglos to keep up or look for other work.[12]

Much of the sewing and embroidering done by San Antonio's hand-

[12] "Homework and Sweatshops"; homeworker interview no. 77, Records of the Women's Bureau, Materials Relating to Bulletin no. 126.

workers was extremely exacting. In addition to the fine stitching required for handkerchiefs and infants' clothing, the women often smocked, appliqued, and embroidered garments. The Women's Bureau reported that "the articles usually were of so fine and delicate a texture that the utmost care was required in handling so as to preserve their freshness and daintiness."[13]

Like the pay for pecan shelling, pay for hand sewing was extremely low. One worker reported that she was paid forty-two cents for twelve hours' work on a single dress that sold for eight dollars in an eastern shop. The Women's Bureau obtained wage information on 100 homeworkers in San Antonio, 53 of whom reported hourly earnings under five cents. Outside Texas wages reported by homeworkers were markedly higher. A Women's Bureau study documented wages for 1936 in New Jersey and Pennsylvania as ranging from five to eleven cents an hour for inexperienced homeworkers, while the most skilled needleworkers averaged twenty-one cents an hour.[14]

Some San Antonio homeworkers described the exploitation they felt in their jobs. One woman said that her employer had started as a garment cutter himself but that he and his family now had a "big factory, own big cars, have a beautiful home, and pay the workers very little. Their factories get bigger and bigger and they pay us less and less. We make very little and work so much."[15] To such complaints employers responded that they did not exploit workers more than they themselves were exploited. One San Antonio businessman, who contracted hand-embroidered garments for a New York firm, objected to the low rates paid workers after the home office instituted a number of cuts in 1931 and 1932. The New York office countered that San Antonio "must compete with cheap Puerto Rican labor or lose the contract."[16] From July, 1931, through June, 1932, Puerto Rican handwork rates ranged from $2.67 to $2.77 a week per worker, and more than 12 million women's and children's garments and 1.5 million handkerchiefs entered the continental United States from Puerto Rico.[17]

Although garment factories were a major component of San An-

[13]Sullivan and Blair, *Women in Texas Industries*, p. 72.

[14]Nienberg, *A Policy Insuring Value*, pp. 17–18.

[15]Homeworker interview no. 88, Records of the Women's Bureau, Materials Relating to Bulletin no. 126.

[16]Typescript report on homeworkers, ibid. Unless otherwise indicated, all the data on wages and working conditions in Texas presented in this chapter can be found in the typescript report.

[17]Ibid.

tonio's economy, most children's garments and handkerchiefs were produced by hand labor. Some of the companies, such as the Texas Infant
Dress Company and the Randolph-Kohlman Company, were locally owned
concerns that operated factories to supplement the labor of homeworkers.
Other companies, such as the Juvenile Manufacturing Company, were
branches of New York firms that sent bundles of cut fabric to San Antonio
and other Texas cities for distribution to the workers. Women who worked
for this second category of firm frequently complained of long delays in
receiving their wages because requisitions for payment came from New York
after the San Antonio office had certified the amount of work completed.

Employers supplied materials for workers, including patterns, cut
fabric, and thread. Workers returned the finished garments or handkerchiefs to the contractors, who paid only for those products that were completed to their satisfaction. The work was then pressed at the shops and sent
on to buyers or the home offices. Although the work was precut, the designs or smocking patterns were not stamped on the materials. The worker
had to be extremely skillful to get the exact amount of tautness in smocking or drawn work that the employer desired and had to have a well-
practiced knowledge of embroidery to copy the intricate designs from the
patterns.

Since all homeworkers, except a privileged few who sewed designers'
samples, were required to call for and deliver their work, the vast majority
of workers lived near the manufacturers' offices or plants. Wage levels
were so low that they could not afford carfare for the weekly trips that most
of the women made to the plants. Employers originally located plants on
the West Side because they calculated their profits on employing skilled
Mexican women for whom few employment alternatives existed. The
Women's Bureau survey of 1932 revealed that the West Side location of the
industry discouraged both black and Anglo women from seeking work
there.

Incomes reported by handworkers in the Women's Bureau study
ranged from $1.10 to $3.30 a week. Workers reported that one employer
had cut rates from $1.50 per dozen garments to $1.10 per dozen, and that
similar wage cuts had been adopted by other employers. Despite the in-
credibly low wages, one worker claimed that San Antonio concerns sent
some handwork to Laredo, where wages were even lower. A Laredo
woman who acted as a contractor for a San Antonio firm was fined after
being arrested a second time for smuggling work into Mexico, where

women could be hired at one-fourth the prevailing wage in Laredo. This tale is illustrative of the power of employers to exploit Mexican-American workers in San Antonio. Many workers were aware of conditions in Mexico and border communities and knew that there were people earning even less than they. The fear of "voluntary" deportation to Mexico was an ever-present concern to Mexican Americans in the 1930s, when the repatriation movement flourished. Individuals were anxious not to make themselves conspicuous to employers as complainers or troublemakers. The experience of workers in San Antonio, even at wage levels well below subsistence, was that employers could pick and choose among workers because of the abundance of labor. Although pecan shelling was done by family work units, home sewers for the most part worked alone. A surprising number of the women interviewed were the sole support of their families or had the wages of only another occasional worker in the family to supplement their earnings.[18]

The Women's Bureau interviewed 100 San Antonio homeworkers in the needle trades, 84 Mexican Americans and 16 Anglos (no black women were employed by clothing contractors). The women ranged in age from sixteen to sixty-five years, most being over thirty. The vast majority of the women were married or had been married, which supports the conclusion that homework appealed primarily to women who were homebound because of child-care or other household responsibilities. All the single homeworkers were Mexican Americans, which may reflect either the Mexican preference for keeping daughters at home whenever possible or the relative lack of alternative employment options for Mexican-American women. One Hispanic woman commented that her daughter had been working as a maid for three dollars a week but that she quit because she could "make that much at home without killing herself." A young Mexican-American girl commented that sewing paid poorly but that housework was the only other job that she could get and that she "would not feel right staying in another house" (tables 37 and 40).[19] One worker questioned the interviewer about the Women's Bureau's intentions because the "foreman of [the] factory told her that the Labor Department women were

[18]Of 115 homeworkers interviewed in San Antonio and Laredo, 42 (36.5 percent) were numbers of families that had no family member working outside the home full time. Sullivan and Blair, *Women in Texas Industries*, p. 77.

[19]Homeworker interviews nos. 5, 71, 34, Records of the Women's Bureau, Materials Relating to Bulletin no. 126.

going around trying to get information to be used in discontinuing homework for Mexicans." Another worker said that factory wages were no better and that workers were fired for talking on the job.[20]

The conditions under which women entered and continued homework
differed significantly for Anglos and Mexican Americans. A number of the
Hispanic women reported that they had learned needlework from other
homeworkers in their families, but none of the Anglo women commented
on having acquired their skills in this way, and none of the Anglos had relatives who assisted them in fine sewing. Many of the Mexican-American
women had done such work for several years, while the Anglos were
mostly newcomers who had taken up handwork because of sudden changes
in their economic circumstances. One Anglo told the interviewer that she
had previously been a seamstress and milliner but that home sewing was
the only work she could get at present. Another Anglo had taken up homework after her husband and daughter lost their jobs. The family got by temporarily by moving in with her mother and sharing expenses with a brother
who also lived at home. Unlike virtually all the Hispanic women, the Anglos did not walk to the factory but drove or rode the bus to the plant to
deliver and collect their work.

From calculations based on the estimated wages that workers reported
to the interviewers, the *average* wage was approximately $2.20 a week for
a few hours of work a day part of the week to a sixty-hour week. The highest wage reported by any of the workers was $5.53, and the lowest was
$0.83. In contrast, the study found the *median* wage of workers in four San
Antonio garment factories to be $5.70 a week. Of one worker who claimed
to earn only $1.00 a week as the sole supporter of children and an unem-
ployed spouse, the interviewer noted, "Mystery to agent how they live."[21]
Many families like this one got by from day to day only through the charity
of friends and relatives. Only two of the workers stated that they had received any relief assistance. Other families survived through the combined
efforts of two or more homeworkers. While some reported that the work
was steadily available, others found sewing work only periodically.

The workers had fairly clear ideas about the rates offered by various
San Antonio employers, and the most consistent comment was that the
rates had been cut 50 percent since the onset of the Depression. A char-

[20]Homeworker interviews nos. 27, 101, ibid.
[21]Homeworker interview no. 36, ibid.

acteristic comment was that a garment maker "used to earn more and didn't work so hard." [22] Despite the cuts the sewers kept on with their jobs out of desperation. They believed that they would be fired if they complained, and many had had no other work experience.

Although some of the women were not at their sewing tasks full time, most claimed to work more than eight hours a day at least six days a week. Full-time workers complained of exhaustion, muscle cramps, and eyestrain. A nineteen-year-old girl said that because of the demanding nature of the sewing she could no longer maintain the long hours that she had worked in earlier years.

Almost all the women told the bureau's investigators that homework income was critical to family survival. Of San Antonio homeworkers interviewed, 46 had spouses in the household, but only 15 of the husbands were full-time workers. Twenty of the husbands were unemployed, and the remaining 16 had part-time or occasional jobs. Most homeworkers pooled their incomes with other family members, though not necessarily persons in the immediate family, to survive. In 46 of the 100 cases investigated in San Antonio, however, homework of one or more women in the family was the only source of income. Sixty-five of the women lived in households that included adult children, adult siblings, or more distant relatives or friends. Despite the heavy responsibilities and apparently below-starvation wages, only 2 of the 100 women had succeeded in obtaining public or private relief.

Not all Mexican-American homeworkers came from the lowest socioeconomic brackets. Homework in the needle trades did not violate Mexican cultural notions of proper female behavior, and some middle-class families permitted their women to seek such work. One young Hispanic girl told a Women's Bureau interviewer that her father supported her comfortably and that she did sewing for spending money. A spinster from a prominent Hispanic family engaged in homework during the Depression because she wanted to be of some assistance to the family in getting by the hard times, but family members finally convinced her that spending long hours with the needle for pennies was not worth wearing out her shoes walking back and forth to the office. [23]

In 1932 the Women's Bureau found that, overall, women in Texas industries worked for the lowest wages in the nation. Anglo women working

[22]Homeworker interview no. 25, ibid.
[23]Homeworker interview no. 23, ibid; interview with Carmen Perry, May 22, 1979.

as shop clerks and telephone operators experienced cuts in their modest wages during the Depression, but their wages remained two to three times those of homeworkers, and their working conditions were comfortable in comparison with factory standards. The Women's Bureau concluded that throughout Texas "Mexican women were receiving very much lower wages than white women, even when working side by side in the same occupation and establishment." [24] In industries employing women of all three ethnic groups, black and Mexican-American women were wage-competitive with each other but not usually with Anglo women. Although some black women included in the Texas survey were employed in food-processing and cloth-bag factories, nearly three-fourths of the black women were laundry workers. In the last industry black women earned higher wages than Mexican-American women and achieved nearly as high wages as Anglos.

The bureau reported on various industries in San Antonio that employed women of all three ethnic groups in a single establishment, but the reports do not make clear the extent to which tasks were segregated within a single plant. Administrative employees, almost always Anglos, were not included in the industrial survey. In all the establishments wage cuts had been instituted between 1930 and 1932. In laundries, shelling plants, and other industries women's meager wages were further eroded by company policies requiring employees to wear uniforms purchased at their own expense.

The Women's Bureau documented that working conditions were poor in most factories employing women. As a rule conditions were worst in the lowest-paying industries. Working conditions were usually better in the larger firms than in the smaller ones, but in all industries the absence of lunchrooms and dressing rooms, improper seating for workers, and inadequate and unsanitary restrooms were pervasive problems. Cluttered workrooms and improper ventilation were common.

A notable exception to the generalization that conditions were preferable in large firms was the Finck Cigar Company, which employed more than three hundred women, even after an employee cutback in 1931. Conditions including damp and stuffy workrooms and deductions from wages for uniforms and for towel rental were among the grievances that led Finck workers to strike in 1934. Clearly some employers understood that hard times permitted pushing workers to the very limits of their tolerance of

[24]Sullivan and Blair, *Women in Texas Industries*, p. 5.

poor working conditions and low wages. A Finck spokesman revealed in 1932 that he expected labor trouble from his workers, an expectation that was met by a strike in 1933 and the longer strike of 1934. Finck had negotiated with an outside firm interested in purchasing the plant and mechanizing cigar rolling. The firm that offered to buy out Finck planned to improve the facilities and lease them back to Finck to operate. Finck administrators understood that their options were to remain open with hand labor as long as capital improvements and wage raises could be avoided or to sell out. Although Finck lasted through the 1930s with handworkers, its determination not to bend to pressure for improvements was demonstrated when the management removed the Blue Eagle insignia from the plant after refusing to comply with NRA demands for wage increases and factory improvements.[25]

Each industry presented particular environmental problems. In laundries heat and humidity were the workers' primary enemies. Workroom temperatures during the Woman's Bureau survey in April ranged from 86° to well over 100°; in contrast, wrappers in meat-packing plants regularly worked in temperatures below 50°. In one laundry the bureau investigator found laundry checkers and markers working in standing water. In another laundry women stood on wooden platforms caked with soap to avoid the wet floors. Laundry workers generally put in fifty-four hours a week in these unpleasant surroundings. Laundry work also carried dangers of industrial accidents. Sofia Jaquez, an ironer at a commercial laundry-and-dry-cleaning establishment, caught her arm in a hot mangle. It took several minutes for coworkers to free her from the machine, which had broken her wrist and severely burned her arm.[26]

Overall, work in the pecan-shelling plants was the least desirable, partly because the firms were the most marginal establishments in San Antonio. Basically all that was involved in establishing a shelling plant was the purchase of unshelled pecans and the rental of a room furnished with tables and benches. In many of the pecan sheds workers provided their own tools, consisting of hammers and picks. Shelling was divided into two central tasks, cracking and picking. Cracking, which paid by the hour, was the job of breaking the shells. Cracking was generally done by men, who earned more than the predominantly female pickers. Pickers separated the

[25]Interview with O. H. Finck, Records of the Women's Bureau, Materials Relating to Bulletin no. 126; *San Antonio Weekly Dispatch*, September 28, 1934.
[26]*San Antonio Light*, February 9, 1938.

Workers at Southern Pecan Shelling Company, San Antonio, February 13, 1938. Poverty and residential segregation interacted to draw Mexican-American women into dominance in pecan-shelling work. The painstaking labor paid the lowest wages of any industry in Depression America.
(*San Antonio Light* Collection, University of Texas Institute of Texan Cultures, San Antonio.)

nuts from the shells and the complete halves from broken pieces. Pickers were paid by the pound of shelled nuts, with separate rates for halves and pieces. In addition to the tediousness of the work, pickers' fingers became swollen and sometimes infected from the continuous handling of the broken shells. In many plants pickers crowded together along worktables in dark, unheated, improperly ventilated rooms. Oil and broken shells that covered the workroom floor were an additional hazard to workers.

The Fair Labor Standards Act eventually guaranteed a living wage for shellers and garment workers, but in the process most jobs in both industries were eliminated. The initial response of employers to the legislation was avoidance, accomplished partly through the replacement of plant labor with homework. A technique adopted by some pecan plant owners as well as home-shelling contractors was to sell the unshelled nuts to workers and buy back the meats, asserting that the shellers were independent businessmen, not employees, and that the Fair Labor Standards Act did not apply. Although most plant owners did not choose to convert to home shelling, the number of home shellers reportedly increased in 1938 and continued to increase in areas surrounding the city through 1939.[27] The reintroduction of machine shelling was well under way before the end of 1939, but home shellers were still operating in the city in 1940.

The Women's Bureau's investigation of conditions in pecan shelling and garment making rallied organized labor, women's groups, and a number of public officials behind a movement to eliminate homework. In September, 1936, L. P. Bishop, head of the San Antonio Health Department, appeared before the city council to request passage of an ordinance that would appropriate funds for the department to enforce sanitation standards in the shelling industry. Bishop testified that the department destroyed any pecans that it knew had been shelled in homes but that most of the pecans escaped the department's notice.[28] Although the city had initiated a system of issuing health cards to food handlers and food processors in May of the same year, it was beyond the department's capacity to administer physical examinations to San Antonio's many thousands of food workers. The examinations were perfunctory, and home shellers were ignored.

After the release of the findings of the Women's Bureau, the San Antonio Trades Council newspaper, the *Weekly Dispatch*, began its own investigation of homework conditions in the city and printed several articles about homework written by representatives of women's clubs in Texas. In December, William B. Arnold, the editor of the *Dispatch*, reported that he had interviewed a number of home sewers and that he

found in one instance the worker sitting along the side of the bed where her husband was lying (he had a case of tuberculosis) sewing infants' garments and the garments spread out on the bed.

In another hole in the wall two women were sewing garments and by the side of one were piled several pieces of goods and a small mangy dog was sleeping on them.[29]

In the following February, Representative William Carssaw of Bexar County introduced a bill in the Texas Legislature to regulate homework in

[27]Menefee and Cassmore, *The Pecan Shellers of San Antonio*, pp. 19–22; "Working Conditions of Pecan Shellers in San Antonio," pp. 549–50.
[28]*San Antonio Weekly Dispatch*, September 26, 1936.
[29]*San Antonio Weekly Dispatch*, December 4, 1936.

the garment industry. The initial goal of Carssaw, the *Dispatch*, and the women's groups was to establish a system of issuing health cards to workers and to require sterilization of the finished products. Clearly the predicament of thousands of exploited workers was not the central concern. In the succeeding months the *Dispatch* carried a series of articles supporting Carssaw's bill and carrying scare headlines about disease-infected products. Carssaw's bill was defeated, however.

The movement to control pecan shelling gained a renewed following some years later. In 1938 the inadequacies of the food-handler certification system became the target of a muckraking article in *Focus* magazine. *Focus* warned its national audience of the danger to health in consuming shelled pecans from Texas.[30] In 1940 the San Antonio City Council adopted an ordinance forbidding both the home shelling of pecans and the sale of garments manufactured by homeworkers.[31] The institution of a ban rather than a set of controls on homework was enforceable, and homework declined precipitously after 1940. Enforcement of the Fair Labor Standards Act against shellers had begun between 1938 and 1940, encouraging a reconversion to machine shelling. Puerto Rican workers had already undercut the pitifully low wages of Texas home needleworkers. By 1940 there was little reason for managers in either the pecan-shelling or the garment industries to oppose a ban on homework.

The history of San Antonio's home shellers and hand sewers illustrates both the grimmest consequences of the economics of discrimination and the vested interests of potential employers of labor in maintaining occupational segregation. The abundance of locally noncompetitive workers in San Antonio encouraged employment expansion, but the expansion was calculated on minimal capital investment or the replacement of capital with labor.

The relationship of the San Antonio shelling industry and the garment industry to the same industries elsewhere in Texas, the continental United States, and Puerto Rico demonstrates that geography or the proximity to markets or supplies offered a labor pool little protection from competition. At the local level, however, various factors, including prejudice, ethnic work preferences, and the location of industries, effectively prevented one

[30] "Disease and Politics in Your Food: The Case of San Antonio," *Focus*, April, 1938, p. 3.
[31] *San Antonio Weekly Dispatch*, April 26, 1940.

ethnic group from competing with another for jobs. For the Mexican-American worker in San Antonio an absence of competition locally and intense competition regionally or nationally spelled disaster.

As the Depression deepened, the trend to increasing labor intensity continued, for there appeared to be no level below which the wage of shellers and garment workers could not fall. The move away from machinery had been completed in the 1920s, and the expansion in shelling employment brought an increase in output despite falling prices. The Fair Labor Standards Act destroyed San Antonio's competitive edge over other garment and pecan producers. Consequently, handworkers were replaced by sewing-machine operators and shelling machines. For the garment industry the change meant that hand embroidery would be given to foreign producers and the homework industry might be replaced by the sweatshop. The guaranteed wage meant fewer jobs for Mexican-American women because it destroyed their competitive edge in the national labor market without affecting the pattern of discrimination that excluded them from clerical and sales jobs. After the Depression ended, many handworkers moved into garment factories, but these women remained economically disadvantaged compared with Anglo workers because occupational segregation persisted, a continued influx of labor into San Antonio held wages down, and the legal or illegal garment sweatshops in border towns on both sides of the Rio Grande competed with manufacturers in San Antonio.

The women who moved from homework to the garment factories during World War II gained significant improvements in wages, but the discriminatory patterns of the Depression years persisted. Pecan and garment homeworkers in San Antonio may well have been the lowest-paid industrial workers in Depression America, and their situation reflected the prevalence of cheap labor and poor working conditions throughout Texas. In San Antonio and elsewhere in Texas factory women had somewhat higher wages than homeworkers, but they endured uncomfortable and sometimes dangerous working conditions. Women who shelled pecans in plants were no better off than were homeworkers.

[7]

Unemployment Relief and Emergency Job Programs

Many of us were desperate, the unhappy victims of circumstances over which we had no control. Patriotism was dying in our hearts and was being replaced by rebellion. It is unalterably true that shabbiness and hunger are the foes of self-respect. With our homes broken, our children scattered, our souls torn with anguish and desperation, we were ready for any scheme that might promise in the slightest measure relief from a situation that had become intolerable.

Some of us had lost our homes which were nearly paid for, had sold our furniture, piece by piece, our jewelry, and even most of our clothes, hoping against hope that something in the way of a job would materialize before the last cent was gone.

Just when all seemed lost and maddened by grief and fear we were ready for anything, this Adult Educational Program came, providing us with a means of livelihood, a ladder up which we could climb again to patriotism and self-respect.

—Stella Boone and Ethel Stringer, WPA teachers, Sidney Lanier School[1]

THE WPA educational programs in San Antonio offered hope and economic assistance to scores of teachers, but the programs reflected local racial and ethnic prejudices as well. The vast majority of students and teachers were Anglo, but Mexican-American residents enrolled in some courses alongside Anglos and in other courses for Spanish-speakers. Adult classes in English, citizenship, and trade skills were offered through the "Americanization" program at the Sidney Lanier School, a Hispanic secondary school. Anglo and Hispanic women in San Antonio's education projects studied business and clerical subjects with the goal of gaining white-collar jobs. They also enrolled in such classes as furniture making that were created primarily to teach housewives to "make do" with home furnishings that could be constructed from scrap materials. Graduates of the home-improvement courses were expected to pass on their newly learned skills to female friends and neighbors. Under the WPA Anglo and Hispanic women were also employed in domestic work in the Housekeeping Aid Projects,

[1]Letter to Mrs. Franklin Delano Roosevelt, May 6, 1936, Records of the Works Projects Administration.

programs to assist in home and child care when parents were ill or otherwise incapable of managing by themselves. The Housekeeping Aid Projects were totally separate from the Household Workers Project, the only educational program for black women, which taught them to be "capable domestics." The jobs performed by the two categories of workers were essentially the same, though housekeeping aides worked under the supervision of home economists and registered nurses.[2]

The first large public relief project for San Antonio women was a federally funded canning plant, which employed 900 women in the summer of 1934. Project administrators expected to double the plant payroll by the end of the year, but in January, 1935, only 450 women were employed.[3] The second large project was a WPA sewing room. The first sewing room opened with 278 employees in October, 1935, and within a year sewing projects had expanded to employ 2,300 persons. The sewing rooms were the largest WPA projects for women, though various other programs employed lesser numbers of blue- and white-collar female workers. Women with clerical or administrative skills worked on all programs sponsored by the Federal Emergency Relief Administration and the WPA within and outside the Division of Women's Work, but more than half of all female WPA administrators in San Antonio worked with the sewing projects as supervisors or in some other administrative capacity.

While public works programs generally discriminated against women in a variety of ways, WPA projects offered a few women an unprecedented opportunity to develop and apply executive skills as project and agency administrators. In Texas as elsewhere women headed the offices and nearly all the projects of the Division of Women's Work. A second category of white-collar jobs for women under emergency work programs was recordkeeping, both as administrative functions of public agencies and in special projects such as the Historical Records Survey and local projects to organize city ordinances and criminal records. Women in San Antonio served in various publicly funded positions as clinical aides, hospital workers, school cafeteria workers, and nursery-school workers. Librarians, editors, writers, artists, and musicians found work in the WPA professional programs. Women appeared regularly in WPA musical and theatrical performances in San Antonio and participated in arts programs under both the

[2]"WPA Projects in San Antonio" (mimeographed report), May 17, 1940, ibid.
[3]*San Antonio Express*, August 1, 1934; January 14, 1935. Relief statistics appear in appendix B, tables 42, 43, and 45.

Beatrice Denmark, representative of the National Youth Administration, inspecting a San Antonio sewing room in which Mexican-American women predominated, February, 1937.
(*San Antonio Light* Collection, University of Texas Institute of Texan Cultures, San Antonio.)

WPA and the National Youth Administration. Early in 1936 the San Antonio WPA office reported that 1,280 women and 2,739 men were employed in local professional projects.[4]

In a city like San Antonio, where the Depression reached so broadly and deeply, the FERA and the WPA provided the margin of survival for many women and their families, though there was always more demand for work than either agency could begin to meet. Public works projects were late in coming to San Antonio, and women had an especially long wait for their meager share of emergency employment. Before the arrival of federal public assistance the legions of hungry and unemployed resi-

[4]Noneye Johnson to Ellen S. Woodward, May 1, 1936, Records of the Works Projects Administration.

dents had few places to turn for help. Since neither San Antonio nor Bexar County dispensed local public relief funds, the unemployed could turn only to private charities during the early years of the Depression. The Salvation Army, the Junior League, the International Institute, Catholic and Protestant churches and convents, settlement houses, and other organizations helped feed and clothe destitute local residents and transients. The Bexar County Red Cross provided food, clothing, and shelter, and their relief expenditures increased 300 percent from 1928 through 1931. As San Antonian Veda Butler recalled, the relief commodities dispensed by the Salvation Army to the East Side black community were insufficient and barely edible, but people waited in line for hours for these handouts because of their desperate need.[5]

There were virtually no Anglo-financed private social services other than the Salvation Army to which blacks could turn in times of need. However, a history of steady employment and the strong economic base of black churches provided the black community with some weapons to fight the ravages of the Depression. The Mexican-American community lacked the overall economic strength to see its members through hard times. A few private charities dispensed food and clothing on the West Side, but they could do little to mitigate the widespread starvation and disease. The concentration of poverty in San Antonio and its consequences are revealed in health statistics of the Depression years. In 1937, after public relief had alleviated some of the city's health problems, Mexican Americans suffered a death rate from tuberculosis of 310 per 100,000, blacks 138 per 100,000, and Anglos 56 per 100,000, giving San Antonio the worst record of any major American city. The infant death rate was 144 per 1,000 live births among Hispanics, 105 among blacks, and 51 among Anglos. For Mexican Americans housing conditions were as severe a threat as starvation. The high incidence of infant diarrhea and enteritis among Hispanic children testified to environmental dangers. Hundreds of mothers watched helplessly each year as their young children sickened and died.[6]

Throughout the Depression local politicians and relief administrators discriminated against blacks and Hispanics. Racism was at the heart of the resistance to locally funded public relief, but early in the Depression, San Antonio leaders moved to improve the dispersal of private relief assistance. At the end of 1931, Mayor C. M. Chambers announced the forma-

[5]Interview with Mrs. Veda Butler, May 28, 1979.
[6]San Antonio Department of Health, *Annual Report* (1937).

West Side women receiving soup from John Lopez of the International Institute, March 4, 1937. The institute was a private agency that extended relief to Mexican Americans.
(*San Antonio Light* Collection, University of Texas Institute of Texan Cultures, San Antonio.)

tion of the Central Unemployment Relief Committee (CURC), which was authorized to collect private funds for relief efforts and to certify workers for the few public jobs funded by a recent bond issue. Encouraging charity was as far as either the city or the county would go in ameliorating local problems. The CURC exemplified Anglo antagonism to Hispanics in announcing that no aliens would be hired for jobs funded through contributions to the committee. The committee began providing make-work the following January, but the funds and foodstuffs the CURC could distribute made little impact, and by March the funds had been exhausted. During its three months of operation CURC distributed about $55,000 in money and food among the unemployed. The committee reported that "about 5,000 heads of families have registered with the committee and it is estimated that an additional 1,000 white families, who having been placed in such circumstances for the first time in their experience, due to a sense of humiliation and pride, have not registered."[7]

Throughout 1932 stories of tragedy and suffering abounded. The *San Antonio Express* reported "five motherless children, living with a sick father in an old storebuilding, had no bed clothes and practically nothing to eat. Such instances of dire need are encountered frequently enough in normal times, but unemployment conditions have multiplied them."[8] Private charities were unable to meet the demand for assistance during the same months that CURC offered relief. The Milk and Ice Fund, which had been established to provide a supply of sanitary milk to needy San Antonio children, assumed broader relief responsibilities early in the Depression. At the beginning of 1932 the fund warned that it could not continue its efforts through the remainder of the year without additional contributions, and in 1935 all fund activities terminated. The failure of public agencies to allocate general relief funds handicapped the city and county utilization of outside assistance. The Federal Farm Board's donation of 300,000 pounds of wheat flour nearly went unused because many families had no stoves and no funds were available to bake bread from the flour. The San Antonio Federation of Women's Clubs raised funds to bake 10,000 loaves of bread, and the rest of the flour was distributed to the needy.[9]

After CURC ceased operations in March, 1932, the San Antonio Chapter of the Loyal Legion surveyed homes and businesses to gain promises of odd jobs and temporary employment for displaced workers. A few companies adopted a "share-work" plan under which employees took off one day a week without pay. The company then hired unemployed workers for one-day jobs. Later in 1932 CURC was reorganized to coordinate private relief activities, since San Antonio had no community chest. The commission reported that as of December less than 10 percent of its fund goal had been pledged.[10]

Despite the obvious inadequacy of private funds to meet the local emergency, some civic leaders continued to oppose public relief. Commenting on President Hoover's plea in 1932 that relief administrators

[7]*San Antonio Express*, February 21, March 22, 1932. The activities of the CURC are discussed in Mary Maverick McMillan Fisher, "San Antonio I: The Hoover Era," in Robert C. Cotner, ed., *Texas Cities and the Great Depression*, pp. 53–68.

[8]*San Antonio Express*, January 22, 1932.

[9]*San Antonio Express*, May 9, 1932.

[10]*San Antonio Express*, November 7, December 7, 1932.

"make sure that no American this winter will go hungry or cold," the *San Antonio Express* argued that "Responsibility for that achievement rests, first of all, upon the individual citizen, who cannot evade his 'God-imposed obligation to look after his neighbor.' When that debt shall have been discharged, it will be time to appeal for government assistance, through the Reconstruction Finance Corporation." [11] In fact, some RFC funds had already flowed into Bexar County, and in the fall of 1932 the city sought a $300,000 loan from the new corporation. The chamber of commerce estimated that twice that amount would be needed to sustain the unemployed through the winter. [12]

RFC funds, administered by tax collector Maury Maverick, built the veterans' camp that supplemented the camp constructed by the Veterans of Foreign Wars. The CURC, also with the help of an RFC loan, constructed a shelter and soup kitchen for transients. In May, 1933, the federal government temporarily suspended all RFC fund payments in Texas until the state legislature ratified a constitutional amendment authorizing state matching of relief funds. The CURC offered occasional make-work in exchange for commodities and direct payments through 1933. The committee maintained a relief roll of 13,000 to 17,000 cases through the year despite the advent of the Civilian Conservation Corps. When the suspension of RFC funds forced a brief shutdown of CURC activities in May, the unemployed mobilized work gangs and sought relief work directly from employers. Others rioted at CURC headquarters. Suspension of the RFC fund dramatized the severity of the local crisis, and there was little hesitation thereafter in applying for federal funds. [13]

Both the city and the county benefited from expenditures of the NRA, the CWA, and the WPA. Local government first became directly involved in relief in June, 1933, when Harry Hopkins, director of the Federal Emergency Relief Administration, ordered that all relief funds must be administered by public agencies. The CURC had to be reorganized as a public board, and in the process it became a countywide committee under the guidance of the Texas State Relief Commission. In early August the committee, now federally funded, began making cash disbursements to relief

[11] *San Antonio Express*, November 7, 1932.
[12] *San Antonio Express*, October 9, 18, 1932.
[13] Fisher, "San Antonio I," pp. 66–68; Lyndon Gayle Knippa, "San Antonio II: The New Deal," in Cotner, ed., *Texas Cities*, pp. 69–72.

Betty Reid, fifty-three, and her son Thomas, fourteen, carrying home the last supply of groceries given out by the Central Unemployment Relief Committee before it closed for lack of funds in May, 1933.
(*San Antonio Light* Collection, University of Texas Institute of Texan Cultures, San Antonio.)

clients. On August 5 more than one thousand persons lined up outside the Bexar County Courthouse to receive their payments of $4.50 per household head in exchange for two days' labor on relief projects.[14]

Relief administrators heavily criticized cash payments as encouraging workers to refuse the jobs that were available. A. W. Greene, manager of the U.S. Employment Service office in San Antonio, asserted that he had

[14]*San Antonio Light*, August 6, 1933.

been unable to meet requests for cotton pickers because of the cash payments. Greene insisted that hundreds of pickers, who had left San Antonio for the fields, turned back to the city when they learned that relief cash would be dispersed. A few days after Greene's statement to the press, police were called in to disperse a crowd that had besieged the farm-employment office on the West Side. The *San Antonio Light* reported that the crowd was composed of job applicants who had rushed to find picking jobs after hearing that all local work projects and cash relief payments would be suspended.[15]

In September the relief committee, now known as the Bexar County Board of Welfare and Unemployment, replaced one central office with nine neighborhood relief offices. While bringing services closer to the clients, the decentralization also effectively segregated Anglo, black, and Mexican-American clients from each other. State and federal evidence of mismanagement of relief funds in Bexar County forced a second reorganization of the relief board in the late fall of 1933. Local work funds were cut back in February, 1934, when the CWA closed down. Relief rolls again rose to more than 17,000 families. The termination of work relief prompted disorder at the Mexican-American welfare office on the West Side.[16]

The WPA and the NYA provided the major sources of help for the unemployed from 1935 through 1939. With the beginnings of the WPA in 1935, the relief board was again reorganized, with responsibilities only for relief of unemployables. By the end of 1936 federal funds for the relief of unemployables had come to an end, and direct relief again became the burden of private agencies. The city finally agreed to provide administrative assistance for the distribution of the available relief commodities, but neither the city nor the county would assume direct responsibility for relief in the final years of the Depression. City and county officials had maintained that code and charter provisions forbade the expenditure of local public funds for relief efforts, but other Texas communities had successfully circumvented similar charter complications. Not until 1940, when the Depression was lifting, did San Antonio move to amend the city charter to provide for public welfare expenditures.[17]

•   Federally funded relief provided the margin of survival for thousands

[15]*San Antonio Light*, August 10, 1933.
[16]Knippa, "San Antonio II," pp. 75–81.
[17]Ibid., pp. 83–90; *San Antonio Weekly Dispatch*, November 22, 1940.

of San Antonians, but there were never sufficient resources to meet the needs of all who qualified for assistance, and per capita relief expenditures in the city were low. In New Orleans, a city also hard-hit, monthly emergency relief expenditures under the FERA averaged $29.68 for a family of four, while in San Antonio the average was $15.74.[18] Women workers in San Antonio, whether family heads or supplementary workers, faced special obstacles in obtaining emergency jobs.

Despite the establishment of women's divisions and the prominence of women in some New Deal agencies, women were second-class citizens under most work and relief programs. Under the operating procedures of the WPA and other agencies, job preference was given to male family heads. Separated or widowed female family heads received first-priority ratings only if there were no adult male children in the household. A married woman whose husband was present in the home achieved first-priority certification only if her husband was disabled. An applicant of second-priority status stood no reasonable chance of employment in public works. Although the NYA created jobs for youthful female workers who had been denied employment in the CCC, boys received preference over girls in NYA placement.

Overall, men dominated the better-paying emergency jobs. Among women the superior status of Anglos is revealed in statistics showing that a disproportionate number of women's jobs went to whites rather than blacks and no black or Hispanic women were prominent in the administration of federal programs for women in San Antonio. The general pattern of discrimination against women in the allocation of public or private relief jobs throughout the Depression also emerges in direct relief statistics. While needy men were given jobs, needy women were frequently extended only commodities. While men received most of the relief jobs in San Antonio, women comprised most of the direct relief clients.

As scholarly studies of the New Deal alphabet agencies have documented, the federal government accepted and reinforced southern laws and traditions of segregation in the administration of relief and public works programs.[19] In San Antonio separate relief projects were maintained for

[18] "Emergency Relief, May, 1935" (mimeographed report), Records of the Works Projects Administration.

[19] William E. Leuchtenberg, *Franklin D. Roosevelt and the New Deal*, pp. 185–87; Harvard Sitkoff, *A New Deal for Blacks: The Emergence of Civil Rights as a National Issue*, vol. 1, *The Depression Decade*, pp. 47–57, 69–70; John B. Kirby, *Black Americans in the Roosevelt Era: Liberalism and Race*, pp. 273, 276–77.

blacks and whites. Mexican Americans and Anglos were not adminis-
tratively segregated from each other in the work programs of the FERA or
the WPA, but Anglo and Mexican-American clients rarely crossed paths in
applying for relief commodities or emergency jobs. A relief office on
the West Side served most of the Mexican-American clients, channeling
Mexican-American men and women into unskilled work and reserving the
few white-collar positions for Anglos. Similarly, federal and local relief
agencies respected the tradition of occupational segregation by gender.
The establishment of the women's division under both the FERA and the
WPA generated segregation by sex in federal emergency job programs
throughout the nation.

Particularly in San Antonio relief administrators regarded women as
temporary workers whose primary role was in the home. Relief programs
were structured to equip female clients with domestic skills that they could
utilize after the Depression had passed. Relief programs developed around
the assumption that additional women had been propelled into the labor
market by declining male employment and that these women would retire
to the home when the work of fathers and husbands returned to normal.
Administrators recognized that some women would always be in the work
force, and these workers were rigorously segregated into "appropriate"
occupations. As the Texas relief director reported in 1935, "We believe our
projects for women, in addition to keeping them from the despair of idle-
ness, provide the more lasting benefit of permanently equipping these
women to meet responsibilities in the home and to accept industrial opportunities as they develop." [20]

Federal New Deal administrators demanded local support before they
approved individual works projects. The refusal of San Antonio and Bexar
County to appropriate relief funds presented a special problem in obtaining
federal relief. Local support had to be obtained through private donations,
usually of building use and supplies, or the allocation to federal projects of
employees already on city or county payrolls and the use of space in city
or county properties. Mary Taylor, director of women's work in Texas,
complained to her supervisor: "By way of illustration, I should like to cite
the case of San Antonio, Bexar County. They have been most niggardly in
their appropriations for recreational purposes. I refused to entertain their
project applications as long as they were asking us to provide assistance in

[20]Adam R. Johnson, Texas relief commissioner, quoted in *Texas Relief Commission
News Bulletin*, January 22, 1935, Records of the Works Projects Administration.

25 parks whereas they were paying only one full time recreational supervisor." [21] Even after these initial barriers were overcome, lack of equipment
and supplies frequently delayed or interrupted approved projects. The relief canning plant was forced to shut down for a period in 1935 because
beef shipments failed to arrive. Shortages of machines and materials in the
sewing rooms caused especially severe problems because the sewing projects employed the most women.

Although sewing projects were created primarily as an appropriate alternative to direct relief for female family heads, Texas officials recognized
the value of the workers' efforts in providing relief commodities. In 1935
the director of the WPA women's work division in San Antonio wrote the
Washington office seeking continued support for sewing rooms:

> There is a most widespread and pressing need for garments for indigents, both
> for the unemployable of the Texas Relief Commission and also for those who are
> really employable but who have not yet been put to work. We feel that in operating
> these sewing rooms we can not only occupy our women profitably but can also do
> something of great value, particularly in clothing the school children of relief fam-
> ilies, many of whom cannot attend school until such clothing is provided.[22]

Texas officials frowned on any works project that employed women at
tasks that they perceived as nontraditional. Although Texas women had
worked as migrant agricultural laborers for generations, the state WPA
head vetoed projects that required heavy outdoor labor. The WPA employed women on grounds improvements in several southern cities, but the
Texas office refused to approve a similar project in the state, and the WPA
in Texas also objected to federal funding of laundry work for women,
though women were already extensively employed in commercial laundries throughout the state. Women's projects of the CWA, the FERA, and
the WPA in Texas were largely confined to sewing, food processing, and
domestic service or health care.

Programs for black women functioned on the assumption that the destiny of the black woman was domestic work. In an economic environment
in which opportunities for the employment of domestic workers in homes
were declining, the FERA and the WPA reinforced occupational segregation and participated in a discriminatory educational system that denied
black women the skills to compete for the few areas of female employment
that expanded during the Depression. In 1937, Mary Katherine Dickson, a

[21]Mary Taylor to Ellen S. Woodward, September 12, 1935, ibid.
[22]Mary Taylor to Ellen S. Woodward, October 1, 1935, ibid.

Catalina Felan, employed on a WPA project to clean schools and school equipment during summer holidays, June, 1939.
(*San Antonio Light* Collection, University of Texas Institute of Texan Cultures, San Antonio.)

local administrator, pointed out that a black church in San Antonio had been conducting a training program for black domestic workers and argued the need for such a program through the WPA adult-education program. Dickson reasoned that domestic training was the most suitable education for black women because "between 75% and 85% of persons employed in household service are black." [23] In elaborating on her justification, Dickson

[23] "Proposal for Training Negro Adults," November 17, 1937, ibid.

revealed her personal perspective that the best interests of blacks and whites would be served by educating black women to function in an inferior place:

> In fact, the majority of housewives in San Antonio have a very real servant problem on their hands and, at present, no means of solving it satisfactorily. A black picture confronts us, and we have, as a result, economic and social instability, friction, and maladjustment. The public school system here, as elsewhere, has provided, in the past, essentially the same curriculum for the negroes as for the whites, in spite of the fact that their environments, their economic expectations, and their places in the social scale are mostly different. Most of the negroes never get to the high school level with the result that the large mass of them is illiterate.[24]

The proposal went forward to federal officials in Washington with a supporting letter from Maury Maverick, the new congressman from San Antonio, whose election campaign had been marked by racist undercurrents. Maverick worked for household-worker projects through the following year. After an initial period of funding in 1938, Maverick cited the regional significance of the WPA Household Workers Training Project, noting that it was "the first attempt by the government to actually train these people for the jobs they are now performing. In the South . . . the field of labor for Negroes is restricted."[25] Black women had a more difficult time than others in securing certification for WPA jobs. WPA supervisors and employees of the county employment office told black women that they should seek employment in private homes. As Lula Gordon complained to Eleanor Roosevelt, black women were forced into accepting domestic jobs, though such work often proved of short duration. Their employment in this manner might remove them from immediate consideration for any WPA jobs opening up, but if they refused the work, they would be taken off the WPA roles altogether.

In seeking federal approval and funding of women's work projects, local administrators frequently revealed their racial, ethnic, or sex-role biases. In 1936 the San Antonio office successfully proposed the creation of a program to train black domestic workers, stating that "the Object of this Vocational Training School is to teach fundamental principles of service, courtesy, honesty, cleanliness, and efficiency as applied in the gen-

[24]Ibid. In the late 1930s the Texas Department of Education withdrew accreditation from San Antonio's black secondary school because of its inferior program. Throughout the 1930s only ten years of public schooling were available to the city's blacks.

[25]Maury Maverick to Aubrey Williams, October 20, 1938, Records of the Works Projects Administration.

eral household activities; and to fit them for duties which are in keeping with their mentality." [26] Justifiably, relief administrators in San Antonio were concerned about the possibility of charges of racial or ethnic discrimination, especially in the black community, which was better organized politically than the Hispanic West Side. Mary Taylor, the local WPA women's work supervisor, sought to head off such charges in the face of budget cuts by publicizing programs for San Antonio blacks that had continued to function. In 1936 she wrote to her regional supervisor:

As you know I had given considerable thought to developing good Negro projects—for obvious reasons! As soon as quota reduction was announced I asked Mr. Drought if he would approve my having a series of articles on such projects prepared and sent to the big Negro newspaper in Pennsylvania. I thought it might forestall criticism as to racial discrimination. [27]

WPA officials in San Antonio faced charges of racism not only because they did discriminate against blacks but also because San Antonio blacks had articulate spokesmen and organizations working on their behalf. Blacks in San Antonio suffered discrimination under the WPA that was unequaled in other parts of the state. Although Anglo and Hispanic garment workers were almost entirely segregated from each other in the private sector, no administrative decisions by the FERA or the WPA mandated separate public sewing rooms for the two groups. Nevertheless, officials assigned black women exclusively to separate projects. J. E. Thompson, a black San Antonio clergyman, supervised one project for black women in the city. In 1939, Thompson, who had conducted a private domestic-worker training program at the church he pastored, was fired as coordinator of the Household Workers Training Project. The National Association for the Advancement of Colored People and other groups unsuccessfully protested the dismissal. WPA administrators in San Antonio argued that blacks would not respect the authority of a member of their own race, though black supervisors had been successfully employed elsewhere. [28]

[26] "San Antonio Training School for Domestic Activities Proposal," March 10, 1936, Records of the Works Projects Administration.

[27] Mary Taylor to Blanche M. Ralston, May 6, 1936, Records of the Works Projects Administration.

[28] Maury Maverick to Aubrey Williams, November 17, 1937; Gus W. Thomasson to A. Marco Smith, n.d.; Mary K. Taylor to Florence Kerr, June 20, 1939; Mary Katherine Dickson, "Proposal for the Training of Negro Adults," 1937, Records of the Works Projects Administration.

The WPA office in San Antonio sought to assist nonworking as well as working women. The WPA attempted to help the housewife cope with a tightened budget by improving her home-management skills. A program to train housekeeping demonstrators and a center for homemaking involved Anglo, black, and Mexican-American women. One woman employed in the home-demonstration program complained to Ellen Woodward, the national women's work coordinator, that the WPA did not pay her a living wage for her efforts. The WPA also conducted the housekeeping-aides program, in which women were trained to be visiting housekeepers in homes where mothers were ill or confined after childbirth. The aide project, which put Anglo women to work in private homes, drew considerable criticism. The aides complained that the work was dirty and exhausting. Their situation was taken up by the Texas Protective League, which complained to Washington that the aides were no more than slaves sent to work in the homes of the affluent. The league protested that the women, who were paid six dollars a week by the WPA, were considered servants by the women they assisted and that the WPA officials threatened to fire them if they criticized working conditions.[29]

WPA officials took a broader view of the occupational possibilities of Mexican-American women than of black women. The adult-education program of Sidney Lanier School, which enrolled more than three hundred Hispanic men and women, had Americanization as a unifying goal but presented various training and educational programs. Women were offered training in nutrition and home and child care. Clerical skills were another area of study, and some graduates of the school obtained employment as stenographers and bookkeepers. However, the majority of Hispanic WPA clients found jobs in sewing rooms and did not enter WPA classes.

Discrimination on the basis of marital status added to the liabilities of gender and ethnic origin that many women bore as they sought employment in Depression San Antonio. As Lois Scharf has documented with regard to the nation as a whole, the work rate among married women increased dramatically, but the increase occurred despite the disapproval of husbands, societal pressure, and some legal measures taken to deprive wives of employment.[30] The Depression elicited unprecedented public

[29]James O. Rail to Harry Hopkins, May 5, 1936, Records of the Works Projects Administration.

[30]Lois Scharf, *To Work and to Wed: Female Employment, Feminism, and the Great Depression*, Contributions in Women's Studies, no. 15, pp. 85, 107.

pressure to drive women, particularly married women, from the work force. It did not matter that men were unlikely to prepare for or accept jobs as teachers, nurses, or secretaries; society demanded that married females withdraw from the work force. In 1931 the American Federation of Labor adopted a position endorsing discrimination in hiring against women whose husbands earned a decent wage.[31] Depression divorce, the agreement of marital partners to terminate their marriage so that each could remain employed, was publicized by the press, though there is no persuasive evidence that the course was widely adopted. A society columnist for the *San Antonio Express* forecast that Depression divorce would win acceptance only among those "who would hail it as a good excuse for living apart."[32]

Nationally the unfounded fears that women competed with men for a limited number of employment openings and that they displaced employed male workers was translated into a law prohibiting a husband and wife from simultaneous employment by the federal government. Section 213 of the Economy Act of 1932 did not specify which partner in a marriage would be hired or continued on the federal payroll, but since wives almost universally had less earning power than husbands, it was women who gave up federal jobs. Only a few states adopted similar legislation during the 1930s. Most states left the matter of working wives to local governments. At the local level female public employees were most visible in the schools, and married women teachers were the most common targets of discrimination.[33]

Depression San Antonio was a city without a strong voice for women's rights. Although women in Atlanta, Georgia, and some other cities successfully fought policies preventing the employment of married female teachers, the dismissal of married women from the San Antonio schools met little opposition. In August, 1931, the San Antonio school board announced that married women would receive low priority in the hiring of new teachers. In June, 1932, all previously hired married women whose husbands earned a minimum of two thousand dollars a year were terminated.[34] In 1931 offices in the Bexar County Courthouse began dismissing married women, a practice apparently opposed only by the victims. May Eckles noted in her diary: "There has been a mess stirred up in Jack Burke's office over cutting out the married women and Mrs. Achs is sure

[31]*San Antonio Weekly Dispatch*, October 29, 1931.
[32]*San Antonio Express*, February 21, 1932.
[33]Scharf, *To Work and to Wed*, pp. 65–85.
[34]Fisher, "San Antonio I," pp. 59–60.

on the warpath, she says she is going to give Mr. Burke a piece of her mind at four o'clock this afternoon." [35] Eckles registered her lack of sympathy with her coworkers when she noted, "Well all the married women are missing this morning and I aint sorry, for I certainly am not in favor of married women working unless they have to, there are too many unmarried ones without jobs." It did not trouble Eckles that there were three adult workers in her household while other households were being reduced to one or possibly no workers. [36]

San Antonio's union voice was unsympathetic to the plight of the married female workers. William B. Arnold, editor of the pro-labor *San Antonio Weekly Dispatch*, accepted the fallacious argument that the firing of married women would create jobs for men, and he also argued that home and family suffered when wives went out to work. In 1939 he wrote:

> The wife is inescapably the builder of the home and the guardian of its children. These duties are necessarily neglected by working wives. Probably no laws could or should be enacted to bar married women from jobs. But business and industry, by agreement, could establish rules under which married women would be employed in exceptional cases, the first of which would be that the husband was not able to provide a living for the family. We want no dictators telling women what to do; but the country cannot ignore the deterioration of the home, due to the pressure of married women in industry. [37]

In drafting emergency employment programs for women, Texas relief officials were wary of drawing in married women. Texas officials balked at setting up household-worker projects in the state if second-priority female workers—women living with employed or employable fathers, husbands, or sons—were to be recruited. A Texas administrator reported that several organizations in San Antonio would donate space for conducting WPA training programs as long as no woman with an outside source of income was certified for entrance, because "the general feeling in this part of the country is that her husband and father should earn the livelihood for the family." [38]

Although married women were discriminated against by the school board and had difficulty obtaining emergency jobs, personal influence in

[35]Eckles diary, November 18, 1931 (see chapter 1 above).
[36]Eckles diary, November 19, 1931.
[37]*San Antonio Weekly Dispatch*, July 14, 1939.
[38]Mary Taylor to Anna Marie Driscoll, March 6, 1936, Records of the Works Projects Administration.

local administrative offices could break down the barriers that had been erected against their hiring. Anglo women, of course, were much more likely to have pull in city and county offices than were black and Hispanic women. Throughout the New Deal era citizens complained to officials in Washington about the hiring of the wives of local administrators on relief payrolls. In 1933 an investigation by the Texas Senate of the Bexar County Board of Welfare and Employment involved accusations that wives of city and county employees were receiving emergency work wages while other San Antonians went hungry. The secretary of the welfare board presented evidence substantiating the complaints to the senate.[39] Subsequent reorganization of the board eliminated the advantages that some wives had had, but complaints that privileged women received jobs to the detriment of the needy continued throughout the remainder of the Depression.

Women workers understood that their only competitors for emergency work were other women. The most likely critics of working women were unemployed women. Late in the Depression a widow with two dependents wrote Eleanor Roosevelt that her WPA salary had been cut while wives with no real need had experienced no reduction:

I have been on the W.P.A. at a salarie of $57.60 per month for the past few years. Recently I was cut to a $40.00 a month salarie. Instead of cutting the women who had other income and husbands to support them, they have cut the widow women with children and no other income. If the W.P.A. had made this cut after an investigation to prove that people did not need their jobs, it would have been different, but they are taking the jobs away from the little people, while they have increased their own salaries. Why? Because the little fellow had no pull. It is not efficiency or education or refinement or need that counts in San Antonio, it is pull. I have none. . . . I could give you the names of W.P.A. women that have their own homes, cars, and working sons and husbands. They have their beer and cigarettes and all the luxuries of life, while others that do not do these things have a mear existence.[40]

Throughout the New Deal era women in supervisory positions were special targets of accusations that they did not need jobs or that they had obtained their positions through personal connections. Both the men and the women most likely to have influence were persons with white-collar skills. When supervisory positions on women's projects were filled, different criteria of selection were applied from those used in selecting women

[39]Knippa, "San Antonio II," pp. 75–77.
[40]Mrs. Lucille L. Jones to Mrs. Franklin Roosevelt, May 11, 1939, Records of the Works Projects Administration.

to perform the sewing, canning, cleaning, or inventorying that the projects involved. Mary Taylor wrote to Ellen Woodward that in the matter of supervisory personnel her office had not "made it a point to employ only needy people" [41] but that when there were two equally qualified candidates the candidate with greater need was given preference.

In San Antonio as elsewhere in the nation, the administration of both public and private relief entailed endless bureaucratic red tape. Caseworkers were viewed with suspicion; almost all of them were Anglos and few were bilingual, though Mexican Americans comprised more than half the relief population. When Ruth Kolling was appointed to oversee local relief operations, she was characterized by the Bexar County Protective League as well seasoned in "the kind of charity where a poor woman is asked a bunch of impertinent questions and given a bunch of carrots and a bunch of beets and told not to eat it all at once." [42]

Adela Navarro was the first Hispanic appointed as a caseworker in San Antonio, and it was more than a year before a second was hired. Often frustrated by official procedures or policies, she found ways to circumvent the rules when it seemed necessary. She refused to report to her superior that among her cases was a couple living together out of wedlock because she knew that they would be stricken from relief rolls if the information was divulged. However, said Navarro, someone was "so damn mean" that the information reached the relief office despite her silence on the issue. When her supervisor asked whether she knew that a particular couple were not married, she answered that she did not consider it her place to sit in moral judgment and that what she did know was that the people were hungry, and she could get them food. Satisfied with her response, the supervisor no longer interfered with her case reports. [43]

Although public and private relief work was inconsistently administered and always inadequate to meet women's needs, clear patterns of preference and discrimination characterized the programs. Women were regarded merely as temporary and secondary workers who needed help getting by in hard times. The content of training programs generally militated against occupational advancement for women and was frequently

[41]Mary Taylor to Ellen S. Woodward, May 13, 1936, Records of the Works Projects Administration.

[42]*San Antonio Light*, August 12, 1933.

[43]Interview with Adela Navarro, May 29, 1979.

unsuited to the local economy. Although black women were perceived as permanent workers, they received the fewest opportunities for training. Mexican-American women fared better than blacks in the variety óf public works that employed them, but many Hispanics were turned away from relief and employment offices because of their alien status.

[8]

Women and the Labor Movement

It is easier to organize those who make more. [Infants'-wear workers] are intimidated until they don't know whether their souls belong to them or not.

—Myrle Zappone, garment worker and ILGWU organizer[1]

SAN ANTONIO'S women workers engaged in a number of major strikes during the Depression. Mexican-American women were especially prominent in labor protest. After 1934 the Congress of Industrial Organizations provided critical economic and organizational resources for female workers. While the American Federation of Labor refrained from strike support, throughout the Depression the San Antonio Trades Council gave moral encouragement and modest financial support to striking AFL locals. The *San Antonio Weekly Dispatch*, edited and published first by William L. Hoefgen and after 1935 by William B. Arnold, informed members about the council's union activities and featured national labor news. Throughout the Depression women were most active as members not of AFL unions but of union wives' auxiliaries. As the 1930s progressed, the number of women organized into AFL unions in San Antonio increased, but at the end of the decade there was only a handful of AFL unions in which women predominated or were well represented.

In the early years of the Depression it was the women's auxiliaries rather than the unions themselves that dealt most directly with the realities of rising unemployment. Union wives solicited funds from working families for the relief of unemployed union members and organized fund-raising activities. In 1931 the *Weekly Dispatch* carried a plea from one group that "in their work of charity among needy families of printers, the ladies of the Typographical Auxiliary have found that with cooler weather approaching, contributions of clothing from members to help these cases will be a factor in helping to alleviate suffering from this source."[2] The women also held a

---

[1]Interview with Myrle Zappone, October 5, 1936, Workers Alliance File, Labor Movement in Texas Collection, Barker Texas History Collection, University of Texas at Austin.
[2]*San Antonio Weekly Dispatch*, October 29, 1931.

public barbecue to replenish their relief fund. The ladies' auxiliary of the painters' union used the proceeds of their fund-raising event to pay the union dues of unemployed painters.

Although the AFL did not make a conscientious effort to organize women until the CIO threatened their stronghold in the early 1930s, the San Antonio Trades Council was not as hostile to women in the labor movement as were other local organizations. The prominence of women workers in a number of trades made them a presence to be reckoned with if men were also to be organized. Because tourism was a major industry in San Antonio, the city had an unsually large number of restaurants and cafés. The AFL had unionized some of these workplaces, though few food-service workers were union members. Among the unionized cafeteria and culinary workers women had strong representation. The strongest women's local affiliated with the San Antonio Trades Council in the early 1930s was Garment Workers Local No. 176. Unlike other groups of female workers in San Antonio, this organization did not go on strike during the Depression, though its members suffered layoffs and cutbacks in 1931 and 1932.

The CIO, which in 1934 began aggressive campaigns to organize San Antonio's women, including garment workers, did not obtain significant gains for women workers in the strikes in which it participated. By 1940 women who had joined the International Ladies' Garment Workers Union under CIO leadership had switched their allegiance to the AFL.[3] The only other large women's group to affiliate with the San Antonio Trades Council during the 1930s was the Office Workers Union. In the mid-1930s, the trades council tried to induce the San Antonio Teachers Association to join their ranks, but the teachers' organization declined membership in the council. Also outside the umbrella of the trades council was the National Federation of Telephone Workers local. The Wagner Act, which passed in 1937, forced the abolition of management-sponsored employee organizations at Southwestern Bell Company in San Antonio. The telephone operators, who were all female, cooperated with other Southwestern Bell employees to form a new body under the National Federation of Telephone Workers.[4]

Although the AFL and the San Antonio Trades Council did little for women in San Antonio before or during the Depression, women were

[3]*San Antonio Weekly Dispatch*, June 7, 1940.
[4]Grady Lee Mullenix, "A History of the Texas State Federation of Labor" (Ph.D. diss., University of Texas, 1955), p. 321.

Finck Cigar Company workers striking for better conditions, August 11, 1933.
(*San Antonio Light* Collection, University of Texas Institute of Texan Cultures, San Antonio.)

highly visible on the local strike scene. More women than men participated in protests against low wages and poor working conditions in San Antonio during the Depression. The first major strike of the 1930s was the Finck Cigar Company strike in August, 1933, in which an estimated four hundred women walked off their jobs as cigar rollers and tobacco strippers. It was the first of several strikes against the company. Like most other strikes of the period the Finck strike was initiated by a group of discontented workers who turned to unionization after their protest was under way. The Finck strike was also representative of all the major strikes in San Antonio in the 1930s in that the workers involved were among the poorest paid in the city and Mexican-American women dominated the work force.

The Finck strikers were led by Mrs. W. H. Ernst, a Mexican American, who was fired by Finck for attempting to organize her fellow workers. The strikers who picketed Finck during August were peaceful and disciplined, but they were also determined to prevent strikebreakers from entering the plant. On August 17 pickets succeeded in turning away two plant foremen and persuading twenty workers who were not participating in the strike not to enter the shop. The next day three women workers were escorted into the plant by San Antonio police, and the strikers exchanged only taunts with those crossing the picket line. The strike ended within the month when Finck reported that it had signed a wage-and-hour agreement with the National Recovery Administration guaranteeing a forty-hour week. The women returned to work even though the NRA had accepted a wage scale at Finck of $0.175 an hour for strippers and $0.225 an hour for rollers, a scale of $0.075 to $0.125 below the national cigar makers' code of $0.30 an hour. Workers had walked out initially in response to the company's announcement that cigar rollers, who were employed on piecework rates, would be penalized three good cigars for every cigar that was improperly rolled. In the strike settlement the penalty was reduced to two for one.

Throughout the strike the women held mass meetings to organize and publicize their cause, and they sponsored benefit events to sustain themselves during the strike. When the strike ended, the *Dispatch* was displeased that, "so far as organized labor is concerned, the strikers refused to accept any of its overtures to unionize the strikers."[5] The *Dispatch* had earlier complained, however, that "representatives of the International Cigarmakers Union came to San Antonio to talk about organizing after the strike began"[6] and the workers had already selected their leaders, raised strike funds, and articulated their demands without ICU assistance.

In the strikes that followed the Finck strike of 1933, women workers became even more militant, the strikes were more protracted, and the police made more determined efforts to keep the factories open. Subsequent strikes produced fewer results on paper than did the Finck strike, but the victory was illusory, since Finck failed to live up to its commitment to the NRA, and the leaders of the strike were not permitted to return to their jobs.

Early in 1934 the organized workers in the Finck plant struck again. The cigar makers, now affiliated with the San Antonio Trades council, stayed out through March. The *Dispatch* displayed none of the traditional antagonism to Mexican Americans in urging that "the Cigarmakers Benefit Dance . . . should be attended by every member of organized labor and show their interest in the gallant fight that these girls are making against unbearable industrial conditions."[7] During the strike the Regional Labor Board, which reported to the National Recovery Administration, con-

[5]*San Antonio Weekly Dispatch*, May 25, 1933.
[6]*San Antonio Weekly Dispatch*, August 18, 1933.
[7]*San Antonio Weekly Dispatch*, March 23, 1934.

ducted hearings on wages and working conditions at Finck. Workers testified that the Finck plant failed to repair leaky pipes above work areas, that
unsanitary conditions prevailed, and that workers were not provided with
adequate restroom facilities. In addition to authorizing a plant cleanup, the
RLB ordered Finck to reinstate one hundred women who had been fired for
union activities. While the workers remained on strike, the company appealed the RLB ruling. When the National Compliance Administration
upheld the board's ruling, Finck abrogated its agreement with the NRA,
returning its NRA Blue Eagle insignia. A Finck spokesman stated: "They
want us to take these people back, and as we see them, they are Reds. . . .
Before we'll put them back to work, we'll close up." [8]

Finck succeeded in undermining the effectiveness of the Cigarmakers
Union, keeping the plant open without rehiring union workers as it had
been ordered to do by the NRA. However, when the company raised the
penalty for defective cigars to four for one, the women again walked out.
Although she had never been rehired by Finck, Mrs. Ernst again assumed
leadership of the strike, and the union regained some of its former strength.
In the meantime local conditions had changed dramatically with the adoption of a fierce antistrike stance by San Antonio's chief of police, Owen
Kilday, who was reputedly head of the Bexar County Democratic machine.
County Sheriff Albert West cooperated with Kilday in undermining the
strike's effectiveness. The police and the sheriff's deputies threatened both
citizen and alien strikers with deportation. The *Dispatch* reported that
"threats and intimidation have been plentiful. Some of the workers have
been charged with being aliens, and deputies in contacting some of them
have threatened them with deportation unless they go back to work." [9]

Unlike the previous two strikes, there were violent outbreaks in the
Finck strike in March, 1935, when Kilday acted on his determination to
keep the plant open despite pickets. At the outset of the strike pickets attacked scab workers who tried to enter the plant, ripping their clothes from
them. It was reported that when the police arrived on March 16 to escort
additional workers into the plant, disorder broke out in which clothes were
torn, hair was pulled, and strikebreakers were pelted with lumps of coal.
The *Dispatch*, however, reported that violence flared when police tried to
force women into the plant against their will. Before the end of the day
twenty-one demonstrators including Mrs. Ernst were arrested. On March

[8] *San Antonio Weekly Dispatch*, September 28, 1934.
[9] *San Antonio Weekly Dispatch*, March 22, 1935.

24 another confrontation between strikers and police-protected strike-breakers resulted in the arrests of twenty-five strikers and thirty-six male supporters.

The grievances of workers were never met, and the strike was eventually broken through the employment of nonunion women. All charges against strikers arrested in the March disturbances were finally dismissed in April. However, a conciliator from the U.S. Department of Labor failed to achieve arbitration or redress of workers' claims that Finck exploited workers by requiring physical examinations by a company doctor for which each worker was charged three dollars, that the company did not actually pay workers the weekly wage of ten to twelve dollars that it had reported to federal officials, and that the company had a policy of lending money to its employees at an interest rate of 8 percent a week.

The *Dispatch* charged that the public was insensitive to the plight of the cigar workers because they were Mexican Americans and that the chamber of commerce had used its influence to secure exceptions from the NRA codes for Finck. The *Dispatch* protested:

Had it been any other class of workers but the lowly, trusting Mexicans, public indignation against the inhuman and slavish conditions pursued in the Finck Cigar Factory would long since have been corrected. But determination to keep the Mexicans in an inferior status, more readily susceptible to exploitation by our philanthropic and Christian employers of this city of Texas liberty, contributes to this indifference and neglect of a unit of our citizenry.[10]

Labor organizers made protracted efforts to build unions among San Antonio's female garment workers, most of whom were also Mexican American. In 1934, Emily Jordon, representing the United Garment Workers Union, went to San Antonio to organize women workers. Garment Workers Local No. 421 was installed as a Trades Council affiliate in March of that year. Jordon remained in the city through July, continuing to recruit members for the fledgling organization. Although the United Garment Workers continued to function throughout the Depression, it was overshadowed in the mid-1930s by the ILGWU, which had begun its campaign in San Antonio in 1933. Credit for the ILGWU activities in San Antonio belongs principally to Rebecca Taylor, a native of San Antonio, who was recruited as a bilingual organizer by the ILGWU and who assisted San Antonio workers in several trades. The ILGWU made a major policy decision in the early 1930s to invest heavily in time and union funds in organizing

[10]Ibid.

the garment workers of San Antonio. The decision was based on the union's realization that organized garment workers in the Northeast were incapable of competing with the pitifully low wages of Texas workers. An initial grass-roots organizational drive among garment workers was held in 1933 and helped bring both the plight of San Antonio workers and the competitive advantage of San Antonio manufacturers to the attention of the ILGWU. The local joined the ILGWU, but participating workers soon experienced retaliatory action from employers. According to Meyer Perlstein, an ILGWU official, the International was not able to give San Antonio workers the crucial support needed at the time, and in December, 1934, he reported that "the only thing that is left of that local at present is the charter." [11]

Perlstein's comments came after the ILGWU had made a commitment to San Antonio as a major target. From this important juncture the union committed funds and energies to the effort in San Antonio, well aware of the difficulties peculiar to organizing workers in the Southwest. As Perlstein noted:

The problem of organization in these cities is very complicated because of the nationality question, and also because the Mexican border is open for immigration, and at any time that the Mexicans who reside in this country want to organize or ask for any improvement, they are let out and new Mexicans brought in to take their place. [12]

The presence of a virtually endless supply of labor, whether from Mexico or from among Mexican Americans elsewhere in Texas, coupled with ethnic discrimination proved the major stumbling block to the organization of the garment industry as well as other industries like pecan shelling in which Mexican-American labor predominated. In Rebecca Taylor's view the situation ultimately spelled defeat for unionization of the garment industry, keeping San Antonio one of the nation's least-organized and lowest-paying labor centers into the 1970s. [13]

After Perlstein's visit in 1934, the efforts of the Ladies' Garment Workers were led by Taylor, who became the union's educational director. During her years of union activity in San Antonio, Taylor garnered considerable respect among civic leaders as well as union sympathizers. She was not infrequently consulted by public officials and the press regarding labor

[11]*San Antonio Weekly Dispatch*, December 21, 1934.
[12]Ibid.
[13]Interview with Rebecca Taylor, May 30, 1979.

problems outside her area of activity with the garment workers. Taylor made slow but steady headway during 1935. The Trades Council was supportive of ILGWU efforts, and the *Dispatch* urged its members to support the union's first fund-raising event, a dance to be held at the Labor Temple, assuring readers that "among the membership are included some of the most comely of the feminine sex to be found anywhere. They are good seamstresses besides." [14]

Although she gained new union members in the first few months of her work, Taylor found the recruiting difficult. Dutiful Mexican-American wives and daughters would not participate without their husbands' or fathers' approval. If she tried to reach a worker at home, a skeptical husband might say that his wife was not at home or that the woman she sought did not live there. At this time the ILGWU experienced encouragement rather than competition from the United Garment Workers. In mid-March, 1935, the two groups cosponsored a rally to sell workers on the idea of cooperative activity. The *Dispatch* reported, however, that despite the work of Taylor, Emily Jordon, and others "very little headway has been made due to the indifference of the workers." [15]

Although Taylor taught union members the basics of labor philosophy and union tactics and presented the union's position to the public, Myrle Zappone was the central figure in achieving union affiliation and loyalty among the city's Mexican-American garment workers. Unlike Taylor, Zappone came to the union movement on her own initiative after several years of employment in women's wear plants. Zappone first worked with Emily Jordon and the United Garment Workers but came over to the ILGWU when Meyer Perlstein offered to put her on the payroll as an organizer. Working together in 1934 and 1935, Zappone and Taylor organized the A. B. Franks and the Halff garment factories, and the vast majority of workers in both plants signed membership cards. Both victories turned sour when the Franks factory, which was already in financial difficulties, closed its doors after the plant was unionized. Halff circumvented negotiations with the ILGWU by changing to the manufacture of men's shirts after the firm had been unionized. [16]

Garment workers participated in a number of strikes in the 1930s, but, like the cigar workers, they gained no real improvements from their efforts.

[14] *San Antonio Weekly Dispatch*, March 1, 1935.
[15] *San Antonio Weekly Dispatch*, March 15, 1935.
[16] Interview with Myrle Zappone, October 5, 1936.

In 1936 members of the ILGWU struck the Dorothy Frocks company. After
a violent confrontation between company officials escorting strikebreakers
and male and female demonstrators, Chief of Police Kilday "announced he
would take personal charge of the strike detail." [17] The following day police
escorted nonstriking workers to their jobs. The pickets held fast, after
which the company obtained an injunction restraining strikers from interfering with normal business operation. The court acted after strikers had
prevented workers arriving by cab from entering the factory. The strikers'
appeal against the injunction was denied. Although the ILGWU was not
associated with the AFL, the Trades Council offered encouragement to the
strikers, sponsoring a mass meeting at the San Antonio Labor Temple to
protest the injunction.

Perlstein returned to the city to supervise the strike, also offering encouragement to striking beauticians of the Frost Brothers Beauty Shop.
After Perlstein's arrival tensions continued to mount. When Dorothy Frocks
contracted some of its work to a smaller San Antonio firm, Esser Manufacturing Company, to prevent a work stoppage, strikers attacked Esser workers. One worker later charged that her dress had been torn off by Dorothy
Frocks strikers. In clarifying the injunction, a local judge ruled that the
strikers could allow three of their number to picket without banners in front
of the plant as long as the names of the pickets were provided to company
management.

Fourteen garment workers were arrested and brought to trial for violating the terms of the injunction. The women received fines of $100 to
$250 and jail sentences of one to ten days. The strike ended when Dorothy
Frocks announced the closing of its San Antonio plant in October, 1936,
and the opening of a new plant in Dallas. In December, however, Dorothy
Frocks announced that it would reopen its San Antonio shop and signed an
ILGWU contract to pay wages of $0.40 to $0.63 an hour. The contract was
an important victory for Taylor and the union, but employment by Dorothy
Frocks in San Antonio never again reached the prestrike level. [18]

The Dorothy Frocks strike was a particularly important contest for the
ILGWU because a strong grass-roots organization had been established in
the San Antonio plant and in the early 1930s the plant owner had expressed
willingness to negotiate with the union. Dorothy Frocks paid the highest

[17] *San Antonio Light*, May 17, 1936.
[18] *San Antonio Weekly Dispatch*, December 4, 1936.

garment makers' wages in the city, and the union hoped that its workers could lead the way for others. However, the owner of Dorothy Frocks died in 1935, and his widow took over direction of the business. The plant closed down for three months before the strike in 1936, and when it reopened, the management fired and blacklisted several union members. The refusal of the new plant managers to talk with union representatives about the firings precipitated the strike. The removal of the plant to Dallas destroyed the momentum of the ILGWU's efforts in San Antonio, though workers negotiated a contract with Dorothy Frocks when the firm returned. After the failure of the strike in the fall of 1936, the ILGWU concentrated its efforts on the infants'- and children's-wear workers, who generally earned less than womenswear workers. At the end of 1936 two separate locals, one of women's garment workers and one of infants' and children's garment workers, were functioning.[19]

From 1937 through 1940 the ILGWU gained significant headway in San Antonio. The victories of the late 1930s as well as the sustained campaign of the Dorothy Frocks strike were secured through the continuous flow of funds from the International. In 1937 a strike led by Myrle Zappone at another factory, Shirlee Frocks, brought the ILGWU its first victory in San Antonio. Factory workers and homeworkers cooperated in this campaign against a children's-wear manufacturer, and the strike was won despite the support of the company's position by the mayor and the police commissioner. With Zappone coordinating the strikers and Rebecca Taylor negotiating and articulating the positions of the workers to the public, the Shirlee Frocks workers obtained a contract providing a wage of $0.20 an hour and a forty-hour week, a contract that doubled the pay of most of the workers. ILGWU's efforts to improve wages at the Texas Infants' Dress Company early in 1938 were less successful, but later in the year a contract guaranteeing a $0.20 minimum wage and a union shop was obtained at the Juvenile Manufacturing Company, a large employer of factory labor and homeworkers. At the end of the decade the ILGWU claimed more than one thousand members.[20]

Mexican-American women were also deeply involved in strikes in the

[19]Interview with Myrle Zappone, October 5, 1936; interview with Rebecca Taylor, May 30, 1979.

[20]Melissa Hield, "Union Minded: 'Women in the Texas ILGWU, 1933–50,'" in Richard Croxdale and Melissa Hield, *Women in the Texas Workforce: Yesterday and Today*, pp. 9–10.

Two workers hiding their faces from photographers as they cross the Shirlee Frocks picket line, 1937.
(*San Antonio Light* Collection, University of Texas Institute of Texan Cultures, San Antonio.)

pecan-shelling industry in 1934, 1935, and 1938. The shelling industry was particularly vulnerable to worker protests because it employed more workers and paid lower wages than any other industry in San Antonio. In July, 1934, the newly organized Pecan Shelling Workers Union struck after employers announced a wage cut. The strikers demanded the restoration of the former piece rates of $0.06 a pound for pecan halves and $0.04 a pound for broken pieces, from the recently instituted rates of $0.045 and $0.035, respectively. The San Antonio Police Department cooperated with the industry's attempts to keep the shelling plants open and provided protection for strikebreakers who entered the plants. Strikers failed to gain endorsement of their walkout from a fledgling AFL shellers' local. By July 31, however, in the second week of the strike, an estimated two thousand strikers in a work force of eight thousand had virtually closed down the city's shelling plants. Police turned their attention to keeping order and protecting company property. Some weeks later the strike collapsed with no gains for the workers. In March, 1935, pecan workers again struck the plants, but this similarly unsuccessful strike affected only a few plants.

The longest and bitterest strike of the Depression was the shellers' strike of 1938. It was the only strike of the decade that was characterized by charges of political radicalism against strike leaders. Many of these charges emanated from the CIO's participation in organizing shellers and coordinating the strike. The *Weekly Dispatch* had announced the arrival of CIO organizers in the city in April, 1937, and had assured members of the San Antonio Trades Council that the AFL would concentrate on recruiting pecan shellers and laundry workers who were likely CIO targets. On February 1, 1938, the Texas Pecan Shelling Workers Union, affiliated with the CIO, declared a strike in San Antonio. The striking workers received an endorsement from Emma Tenayuca, a local Hispanic labor sympathizer and an avowed Communist. Tenayuca immediately assumed a leadership role among the striking workers, to whom she was well known. Tenayuca's prominence on the strike front confirmed the public's association of the CIO and Communists. Not until Tenayuca was convinced by CIO officials that her leadership compromised the strikers' chances of a favorable settlement did negotiations proceed. In April an arbitration board achieved agreement on a seven-month contract with a wage increase of $0.005 a pound. Most of the workers had already returned to work in mid-March, when both sides agreed to submit to arbitration; however, production halted again in October when management fought compliance with the Fair

Strikers detained by the police during the pecan shellers' strike in 1938. The youthfulness of the strikers reflects the reliance of Mexican-American families on their daughters' wages.
(*San Antonio Light* Collection, University of Texas Institute of Texan Cultures, San Antonio.)

Labor Standards Act. In December the U.S. Department of Labor Regional Labor Board denied the request of major operators for a six-month delay in meeting the $0.25-an-hour minimum wage. Subsequently small operators closed their businesses, the larger firms converted to machine shelling, and the demand for workers fell to between two and three thousand.

In the meantime many strikers had been arrested, some were threatened with deportation, and charges of police brutality abounded. On March 2 police dispersed crowds of demonstrators with tear gas. A union spokesman charged that arresting officers treated women particularly harshly, overcrowding patrol wagons and jail cells. On March 4 county officials announced that one striker would be deported and that the citizenship status of all others arrested in the strike was under investigation.

Some of the pickets were held in jail until March 18, when the union agreed to arbitration and the companies and county officials agreed to drop all charges against the pickets.[21] Most of the arrested demonstrators had been charged with disobeying a county-court injunction against pickets carrying signs. When strike leaders and the American Civil Liberties Union countered the arrests with a request for an injunction restraining police from indiscriminate arrests, harassment of strikers, and the use of tear gas, a local judge denied the request. James V. Allred, governor of Texas, reportedly contributed $400 to help fund an appeal bond in an effort to gain a reversal of the judge's decision.

Hearings on conditions prevailing in San Antonio shelling plants, which were scheduled before the strike began and were conducted by the Texas Industrial Commission, took place in the tense environment of the strike. The investigation documented both the deplorable wages and working conditions in the shops and the strike-related police brutality. A young Hispanic woman, who testified that she had struck for higher wages, told investigators that she began shelling work when she was eight years old. She, her sister, and her mother working together were able to earn a total of $5.00 a week at prestrike rates. She charged that the arresting officer clubbed her in the stomach while she was on the picket line. Another Hispanic girl, aged seventeen, testified that she had been employed for the past six years at a shelling plant, where she earned $1.50 to $2.00 a week.

The strike of 1938 was one of the largest in San Antonio to that time. Nearly all of the 6,000 strikers joined the union, and approximately 3,000 paid their dues. New members were required to pay a $0.50 initiation fee and dues of $0.20 a month while out of work, a considerable sum for workers who had earned only about $2.50 a week.[22] Unlike earlier strikers, these workers had organized relief efforts. Three soup kitchens operated during the strike until one was closed by a hostile public administration through a health-department condemnation.[23] When the strike was in its fourth day, Cassie Jane Winfree, a representative of the Women's International League for Peace and Freedom, reported that she and other women had fed 1,763 persons affected by the strike. She asked Mayor C. K. Quinn to issue her a permit to solicit food and funds after the chief of police ordered her to stop collecting without a permit. Collection and preparation of

[21]*San Antonio Weekly Dispatch*, March 18, 1938.
[22]*San Antonio Light*, February 7, 1938.
[23]*San Antonio Light*, February 11, 1938.

food were major contributions to the strike effort by both striking and non-striking women.[24]

Although the ctiy's newspapers and merchants demonstrated some sympathy for the strikers, the mayor and especially Chief of Policy Kilday were virulently hostile. After hearing of the strikers' plight from Winfree and her associates, Mayor Quinn visited the pecan factories to urge the strikers to desert their "communistic leaders" and submit to arbitration. Although Quinn offered to arbitrate the strike himself, he warned that he would not permit "any Communists" or persons "not residents of San Antonio" to participate in the strike.[25] Quinn's comments were directed toward both Donald Henderson, a CIO organizer who had arrived to direct the strike, and Emma Tenayuca, the Mexican community's homegrown Communist. Some days later Chief Kilday warned that Communists led by Tenayuca would seize control of the city's 12,000 shellers and their families if the strike was not crushed.[26] He had earlier charged that there were about 500 Communists in San Antonio, mostly recruited from the Mexican community.

The president of the conservative League of United Latin American Citizens, eager to defuse spiraling charges of strikers' radicalism, assured a *Light* reporter that Henderson's leadership would be eliminated. In fact, a few weeks into the strike the CIO decided that Henderson was so strongly associated with radicalism in the public mind that another leader would have to represent the union at the arbitration table. In his determination to break the strike, Kilday had banned picketing on the third day of the strike and then had begun arresting demonstrators. On the tenth day of the strike tear gas was used to break up a crowd of strikers. The same tactic was employed the following day, and many of the strikers were arrested. Although the Bexar County court system was so backlogged that most cases were dismissed before they came to trial, the first of the arrested demonstrators went to court just ten days after their arrest. Nine pickets, several of whom were women, were convicted of blocking the sidewalk and fined.[27]

Emma Tenayuca was the strike sympathizer whom Chief Kilday was most intent on discrediting and eliminating from the scene. Tenayuca was

[24]*San Antonio Light*, February 4, 1938.
[25]*San Antonio Light*, February 9, 1938.
[26]*San Antonio Light*, February 12, 1938.
[27]*San Antonio Light*, February 13, 1938.

arrested on a vagrancy charge the first day of the strike but released shortly thereafter. Chief Kilday warned, "If she gets out of line, I'll arrest her again." He explained that he did not intend to "let any reds get mixed up in this strike." Tenayuca's communism was self-proclaimed, and some prominent friends of organized labor perceived that her presence spelled disaster. Rebecca Taylor was outspoken from the first. The *Light* quoted Taylor as stating:

Some of the workers walked out and held a meeting. Emma Tenayuca Brooks got wind of it and came over and took charge of the meeting. The CIO was pushed into the background.

The situation is that 10,000 pecan workers are being jeopardized by Emma and Homer Brooks, Willie Garcia, and three other Communists. While the garment workers are in sympathy with the strikers, still we question the wisdom of having persons with police records and well-known communistic affiliations placed over the heads of local union officials.[28]

In the end Taylor's view prevailed. Although Tenayuca was enthusiastically supported by strikers and was endorsed by *La Prensa*, San Antonio's Spanish newspaper, the CIO considered her visibility the kiss of death, though the union did not charge that she had attempted to usurp its leadership.

During the 1930s, Emma Tenayuca and Rebecca Taylor emerged as the leading personalities of the San Antonio labor movement. Both women had strong roots in San Antonio, but their backgrounds were distinctly different and their roles in the labor movement frequently found them in conflict with one another.

Rebecca Taylor's father managed the Mexican interests of an American petroleum firm until the nationalization of oil holdings in Mexico. Taylor's family owned land in Mexico, and they stayed on for a time as ranchers after her father left the oil business but later returned to San Antonio. Rebecca went to boarding school in Virginia and to college in Boston. She graduated in the early 1930s and went home to San Antonio, where she found a job teaching night classes in a vocational school. Early in 1934 she received a call from an ILGWU representative, who asked whether she would be interested in a position with the union in San Antonio. Taylor had had no previous interest in the local labor situation but had come to the notice of the union because she was educated and bi-

[28] *San Antonio Light*, February 1, 1938.

Rebecca Taylor, of the International Ladies Garment Workers Union, conferring with Maxwell Burkett, attorney for workers in the 1938 strike against the Texas Infant Dress Company.
(*San Antonio Light* Collection, University of Texas Institute of Texan Cultures, San Antonio.)

lingual. Taylor accepted the ILGWU's job offer primarily because she was not particularly happy in her teaching position, but her move to the IL-GWU marked the beginning of a twenty-five-year career in the labor movement. Throughout her years in union work in San Antonio she was recognized as a conservative influence in contrast not only to Tenayuca but to other labor voices as well. Her conservatism, as well as her mild and considerate manner, earned her respect. More important, they earned her the audience of the political and business establishment of San Antonio, where the direct and inflammatory Tenayuca continually met hostility. Taylor, however, never won the loyalty and affection of Hispanic workers that Tenayuca inspired. Myrle Zappone, a garment worker who had become an ILGWU organizer in 1934, worked with Taylor in the late 1930s. She recalled that Taylor, an Anglo, was seen by the Hispanic workers as an outsider and that they were always somewhat skeptical about her commitment to them. They long recalled that during the Dorothy Frocks strike Zappone was jailed repeatedly but Taylor was not.[29]

Emma Tenayuca lived with her grandfather while completing high school in San Antonio. She distinguished herself as a student but experienced ethnic discrimination that confirmed her desire to work for the betterment of San Antonio's Mexican Americans. Tenayuca's grandfather introduced her to socialism, and in her early-adult years she championed communism. Despite her fine high school record, Tenayuca did not continue her education beyond the secondary level. After graduating in 1934, she went to work as an elevator operator and began developing her ties with local labor leaders, the Mexican-American community, and the Communist party in Texas. Her career as a spokesman for Mexican-American workers was relatively short. She was elected to a position of leadership in 1936, and by 1939 public outrage at her professed communism had forced her retirement. Although Tenayuca continued to live in San Antonio, she was not visible in politics or the labor movement after the 1930s.

Tenayuca's devotion to communism stemmed from her desire to free Hispanics from the exploitation they suffered in local labor markets. At first she sought a remedy for poor working conditions by organizing Hispanics into a union affiliated with the AFL and the San Antonio Trades Council. In 1936 she joined with Mrs. Ernst in efforts to bring all Mexican-American workers together in a single organization.[30] Tenayuca was an energetic leader and a fiery speaker, but she, Mrs. Ernst, and others failed to build an organization among the workers after an initial meeting filled the Labor Temple to overflowing. Although at the meeting Tenayuca was elected to lead organizing among the women, her subsequent efforts were toward building a Communist base among men as well as women. When the Workers Alliance, founded by Tenayuca, built headquarters on the West Side, it was attacked and vandalized by city police.

Tenayuca was a favorite target of Kilday, San Antonio's virulently anti-Communist chief of police, and Tenayuca was periodically arrested and released during the 1930s. Kilday first publicly denounced Tenayuca after she led a 1937 sit-in of unemployed Hispanics at city hall in protest against relief policies. Mayor Quinn, however, authorized the hiring of two additional caseworkers to process relief requests after Tenayuca and her

[29]Interview with Rebecca Taylor, October 7, 1936; Workers Alliance File, Barker Texas History Collection; interview with Myrle Zappone, October 5, 1936.
[30]*San Antonio Weekly Dispatch*, March 12, 1936.

supporters presented their grievances. Three days later Tenayuca and her
followers again stormed Mayor Quinn's office in protest against harassment of the demonstrators. Tenayuca charged that one demonstrator, Juan
M. Zacarias, had been wrongfully arrested at the earlier demonstration.
Demonstrators also complained that sympathizers who appeared at Zacarias's trial were arrested, turned over to immigration officers, and beaten.[31]
In April, 1937, members and supporters of the Workers Alliance held a
third sit-in after the mayor refused to issue a permit for the group to hold a
May Day parade. On the mayor's order Chief Kilday used the threat of
force to evict the demonstrators from city hall. After the demonstration
Kilday maintained a police guard at alliance headquarters, "alert for possible danger."[32] On May Day the alliance held a rally at a West Side park in
lieu of the parade.

At the beginning of the shellers' strike of 1938, Tenayuca was "held
for investigation" but released thirty hours later. During the first phases of
the strike Tenayuca and the Workers Alliance wrestled with the CIO for
control of the workers. Initially a spokesman for the CIO announced that
the union had not endorsed the strike, saying that "it's just a bunch of radi-
cals who walked out under the leadership of Emma Tenayuca Brooks and
Homer Brooks."[33] Rebecca Taylor, however, asserted that the workers had
called a strike and that Tenayuca and her fellow Communists had quickly
moved in and jeopardized CIO leadership. Taylor reported that CIO official
Donald Henderson would ensure that Tenayuca and the others were removed from the forefront. During the next few days, however, it became
clear Tenayuca had a following among the shellers. While the *Weekly Dispatch* was highly critical of Tenayuca's role in the strike, *La Prensa* lis-
tened to Tenayuca and condemned the harassment she received from the
Anglo press and the police. On the second day of the strike Tenayuca con-
ceded that her official leadership of the strike would undermine its chances
for success, and she agreed to take a back seat. While recognizing that she
was neither a sheller nor a CIO official, the workers indicated their respect
for her leadership by electing Tenayuca honorary strike leader. During the
second week of the strike, however, Henderson announced that the "radi-

[31] *San Antonio Light*, February 16, 19, 1937.
[32] *San Antonio Light*, April 28, 1937.
[33] *San Antonio Light*, February 2, 1938. Tenayuca married fellow-Communist Homer
Brooks in the mid-1930s. Although she continued using her maiden name, others frequently
added Brooks. Her husband had run for governor of Texas on the Communist ticket.

Emma Tenayuca leading members of the Workers Alliance in a demonstration at
city hall in 1937.
(*San Antonio Light* Collection, University of Texas Institute of Texan Cultures, San
Antonio.)

cal element" had been eliminated, and Tenayuca was less visible for the
remainder of the campaign.[34] She continued to support the strike from the
headquarters of the Workers Alliance, principally through verbal encouragement and assistance in feeding the strikers. After the arbitration board
had announced a wage package for the shellers, police raided alliance
headquarters, seized Communist literature, and arrested a number of alliance workers. Five of the nine persons arrested were Mexican citizens,
and federal immigration authorities sought their deportation.[35]

In 1939, Tenayuca made plans to hold a Communist rally in San

[34]*San Antonio Light*, February 8, 1938.
[35]*San Antonio Light*, April 15, 16, 1938.

Antonio. She obtained a city permit to stage the speeches at the recently completed American Legion Municipal Auditorium. Angry Legionnaires besieged Mayor Maury Maverick and asked him to revoke Tenayuca's permit. Maverick, defending the constitutional right of free speech, refused to buckle under the pressure. On the night of the rally mobs surrounded the auditorium, where barely 150 persons had dared appear for the program. After stoning the building and breaking the windows, the mob entered the auditorium and defaced the interior. Tenayuca, the other speakers, and those who had come to listen escaped safely, but the Workers Alliance never recovered from the riot. Mayor Maverick was hanged in effigy, charged with Communist sympathies, and held responsible for the disorder. It was later charged that "Emma's Reds" were the principal cause of Maverick's defeat in the next mayoral election. Tenayuca subsequently retired from her public role of political activist.

As union members, as activists within AFL auxiliaries, and as labor sympathizers, women were prominent and dedicated contributors to the labor movement in Depression San Antonio. Auxiliary members encouraged public support for unions through union-label campaigns and helped ease the burdens of unemployment for union members through fund-raising activities. Women were the major actors in San Antonio strikes from 1933 through 1938. During the Depression strikes were concentrated in the city's lowest-paying industries: cigar making, pecan shelling, and garment making. In these three industries Mexican-American women predominated, and consequently they were the driving force behind strikes and the formation of new labor organizations.

Some of San Antonio's working women were organized in locals of garment, beauty-shop, restaurant, and other workers' unions associated with the San Antonio Federation of Trades, but the vast majority of female industrial workers and those receiving the lowest pay and enduring the poorest working conditions were unorganized at the onset of the Depression. The early activities of Myrle Zappone and Mrs. Ernst were indications of grass-roots support among the city's industrial women. The San Antonio Federation brought Emily Jordon to the city in 1934 to organize locals in the garment industry, but the efforts of Jordon and the Trades Council had little lasting impact. The ILGWU, whose organizational efforts in San Antonio were headed by Rebecca Taylor and Zappone, was substantially more successful in building locals among the garment workers. There were internal squabbles among ILGWU members in San Antonio, but these difficulties did not prevent organizing, and ILGWU members presented a united front during the Dorothy Frocks strike. As the garment workers' reservations about Taylor suggested, internal tensions frequently followed from ethnic divisions, but Anglo and Hispanic women learned to work together in their unions. Friction between Anglo and Hispanic women was minimized by the realities of occupational segregation. In the garment, cigar, and pecan plants, where organization was undertaken during the 1930s, Hispanic women predominated so heavily that Anglo dissent had little effect. Similarly, the issue of racial segregation did not arise in these locals because black women had virtually no access to such jobs. The only industry in which black women had gained a foothold was the laundry industry, in which shop-by-shop segregation remained largely intact. Anglo and Hispanic workers could thus organize their individual workplaces without addressing the problems of black laundry workers.

On the whole the union movement made little headway among women in Depression San Antonio and secured few victories, though the ILGWU was an important exception. The failures of the AFL and the CIO to build strong organizations resulted from the extremely high odds against which organizers fought. Labor was so abundant in San Antonio that shop-by-shop strikes could not be effective. Many San Antonio firms existed on the edge of failure, and a rise in labor costs or a strike could force them to close. In addition, San Antonio, through the chamber of commerce and other businessmen's organizations, had long and successfully resisted unionization in almost all areas but the construction trades. Outside the Hispanic community there was almost no support for the supposedly radical ideology of the CIO. The violence that greeted Emma Tenayuca in her last public appearance in 1939 not only was indicative of San Antonio's virulent anticommunism but also reflected basic antagonism toward the city's poorest Hispanic workers. In the view of Rebecca Taylor the Fair Labor Standards Act also hurt the union cause. The large majority of industrial women in San Antonio earned less than the $0.25 an hour minimum wage set by the Fair Labor Standards Act. Those women who remained on the job after the cutbacks and closings of 1938 concluded that it was the government rather than unions, which demanded dues, to which the workers should look for help. In subsequent decades the problems that had plagued union organizers and officials in the 1930s continued to hamper the union movement.

[9]

Crime: The Role of Women

We are not going to let some lawyers run the corporation court for the benefit of these women. We will protect their constitutional rights but we don't see any reason to let them out of jail 15 minutes after they are put in just because some lawyer signs a bond for them.

—Mayor Maury Maverick, announcing "war on prostitutes," July 10, 1939[1]

DURING its long history as a military and trading center, San Antonio developed a reputation for a high crime rate and a tolerance of vice. As mayor, Maury Maverick was no more systematic or successful in suppressing prostitution and other forms of vice than were the less-determined public officials who preceded him. Throughout the 1920s and the 1930s prostitution flourished in the city, uninhibited by its illegality. The prevalence of prostitution, and the reality that the city quasi-legalized its existence through an inadequate though official prostitute-registration program, reflected both the absence of dedicated civic leadership and the indifference of San Antonio citizens. Maverick was the first progressive to occupy the office of mayor, but he did little to alter the situation. In a city where crime and politics had a long association and the local court system was grossly overburdened, the problems of law enforcement could not be solved by administrators besieged by the needs of the unemployed and the hungry.

San Antonio had both a hospitable environment for the criminal and peculiar socioeconomic characteristics that encouraged particular criminal activities among women. As one San Antonian described the general attitude toward crime in his hometown:

Crime and rackets of all varieties increase annually here as criminals flock in from places where the law is sterner. The word has got around in jails and hobo jungles the country over that San Antonio is a "red-hot" town where it is easy for a smart crook to get by.[2]

[1]*San Antonio Light*, July 10, 1939.
[2]Ralph Maitland, "San Antonio: The Shame of Texas," *Forum* 102 (August, 1939):51.

An editorial in the *San Antonio Express* in 1935 warned that "San Antonio again—as repeatedly before—requires an anti-crime cleanup." [3]

In the atmosphere of the time the women of San Antonio entered the Depression with various income possibilities that do not emerge in employment figures and occupational censuses. Vice was so widespread that prostitution, gambling, and traffic in alcohol and other drugs cannot be overlooked as "industries" affected in some way by the Depression. Contemporary accounts of prostitution during the Depression reveal that economic conditions increased competition among prostitutes and that many of the women lived at the very edge of survival. Other forms of vice were not depressed in the same way by the downturn. Women who derived income from bootlegging continued to find markets for their goods. Although bootlegging and prostitution were the primary illegal sources of income for women, they also participated in other criminal activities.

Aside from prostitution, most crimes committed by women were minor thefts that reflected the desperate economic conditions. Women commonly came before county courts on charges of theft under five dollars, theft under fifty dollars, and theft of a cow, pig, or chicken. While these crimes were the most numerous, the pattern of their occurrence through the Depression cannot be traced.[4] Felony records, however, reveal that criminal activities, like legitimate occupations, were segregated by gender and ethnicity.

Prostitution was unquestionably the most prevalent female crime. Only a small percentage of offenses resulted in arrest, usually on vagrancy charges, and fewer cases ended in conviction. Officials of the San Antonio Department of Health and local welfare workers estimated that about 2,000 prostitutes lived in San Antonio. At the time of his 1939 campaign to suppress prostitution, Mayor Maverick reported that approximately 1,600

---

[3] *San Antonio Express*, February 1, 1935.

[4] For the purposes of this chapter, crime is defined as any act except a traffic offense that violated local, state, or federal criminal statutes. A minor crime or misdemeanor was any offense for which the maximum sentence was less than one year and which was tried in corporation or county courts. Major crimes or felonies carried possible sentences of one year or more and were tried in the Texas District Court or the United States District Court. Bexar County has apparently retained a record of all county-court proceedings. The records are stored in cartons in the courthouse annex but are not shelved in any order. My conclusion about the nature of female misdemeanors during the Depression years are based on counts of offenses by type that were appealed from corporation courts and appear in docket books in the annex.

prostitutes were registered with the health department and that an equal number of unregistered prostitutes were living in the city.[5] The large market for prostitution also encouraged white slavery. In 1932, Pedro Sanchez and Edward Ramirez were charged in federal court with bringing two young girls to Bexar County from Arkansas for the purposes of prostitution.[6] Sanchez's wife was charged with conspiring to aid in the crime. Conviction under the Mann Act was difficult to obtain, however, and the small number of cases that came into federal court in Bexar County during the 1930s did not result in a single conviction.

San Antonio's red-light zone, known as the "District," became a prosperous and substantial criminal community during the late nineteenth century. Business flourished in the opulent bordellos in the ten-block area west of downtown. As in New Orleans, prostitution interests in San Antonio published a "blue book" of the District's attractions, listing the names, addresses, and fees of the leading women and establishments, though prostitution was never legal in the city. Within the District business owners policed their numbers to discourage competition and to ensure the safety of their customers. As long as prostitution and other forms of vice were restricted to the District, the ladies of the night encountered little interference from police. During the military buildup before the United State's entry into World War I, General John J. Pershing, who commanded the Eighth Army from its headquarters at Fort Sam Houston, launched a drive to clean up the recreations in which his soldiers engaged. Pershing never expected to eradicate prostitution; he directed his efforts toward minimizing the men's risk of venereal infection. Largely in response to the army's concern about the health danger associated with prostitution, the city established a venereal-disease clinic to register and examine prostitutes. The army helped set up the clinic but soon found it more expeditious to open a separate clinic in downtown San Antonio to provide treatment and prophylactics for soldiers. The lack of federal financial support and the attitude of local citizens that venereal disease did not touch their lives doomed the city clinic to failure. In the early 1930s it closed for lack of operating funds. It reopened in 1937, but again it lacked the resources to have any real effect.[7]

[5]*San Antonio Light*, July 10, 1939.
[6]U.S. District Court, San Antonio, case no. 9471, March 9, 1932.
[7]Greg Davenport, "The District: Where Vice Was a Virtue," *SA Magazine*, March, 1978, pp. 50–55; "Dangerous and Wide Open," *Focus*, April, 1938, p. 7.

Although the army periodically expressed concern about venereal disease, it did not interfere with prostitution directly as long as the women stayed off army property. During the Depression, however, competition for customers sharpened, and women frequently tried to solicit on the bases. In 1934, Ruby White, aged thirty-two, who listed her occupation as waitress, was arrested for violating a court order of 1930 banning her from entering Fort Sam Houston. She had very recently completed a thirty-day sentence for an earlier violation of the same court order.[8]

After the ratification of the Eighteenth (Prohibition) Amendment in 1919, the District, in which liquor consumption and gambling had gone hand in hand with prostitution, provided a welcome base for bootlegging. Unlike local officials, however, federal prohibition agents were unwilling to close their eyes to the District. During the 1920s the atmosphere of the District changed not only because of Prohibition but also because of the decline of the large houses of prostitution and the population growth on the West Side. By the end of the decade some of the worst slums in the nation surrounded the District, and a corps of petty criminals who preyed on prostitutes' clients had taken up residence there. Even in vice fashions change, and in the 1920s the garish bordellos no longer attracted customers. Higher-priced prostitutes left the District and operated as call girls catering to patrons in San Antonio's more expensive hotels. Other prostitutes relocated in the "Rattlesnake Hill" neighborhood near Fort Sam Houston.

Throughout its history the District offered the services of prostitutes in various price ranges. Streetwalkers and women who operated out of the less-fashionable establishments depended primarily on patrons from the military bases and from neighborhoods adjoining the District, a clientele that remained through the 1920s and into the Depression. Streetwalkers and prostitutes who solicited from one-room "cribs" remained on the West Side throughout the 1930s. After the large houses of prostitution closed, the District no longer policed itself, and it rapidly deteriorated into reputedly the most violent sector of the city. During this period the San Antonio police regularly patrolled the District (an unpopular assignment known as the "dog watch"), but crime and violence persisted. As one San Antonian described the area at the end of the Depression:

The majority of San Antonio's host of prostitutes live and work in a corner of this slum. Their hovels cover about a square mile of the Mexican quarter.

[8]*San Antonio Light*, July 22, 1934.

Some live in individual coops, but most occupy the jerry-built "apartments." Here they are on permanent display, one every eight or ten feet, awaiting business, their faces grotesque with thick rouge, lipstick and eyebrow pencil, their bodies revealed by sleazy kimonos. They sit on chairs or cots inside their stalls, with the doors wide open; in very warm weather they sit on the steps outside, with their feet cocked up on empty beer cases. Every detail of their squalid little cubicle is visible from the street. When a customer comes, a door is shut, and a blind pulled down, but every sound inside the closed stall must be audible through the paper-thin partitions.[9]

The prostitutes, the author noted, were women of all races and ages ranging from thirteen to forty-five whose prices varied from $0.25 to $1.50. At the lower rates a single customer a day would bring a higher income than steady labor at hand sewing or pecan shelling, but in this occupation as well as others San Antonio apparently suffered from labor abundance. The prostitues frequently had family members who depended on their earnings. Scores of children lived in the District, and very young children could be seen playing around the "cribs" as their mothers solicited clients.

San Antonio prostitutes, frequently but not always through their connection with that vice, committed felonies as well as misdemeanors. During the Depression a few prostitutes came before the courts on murder and assault charges, but sales of liquor and narcotics were the most frequent charges brought against prostitutes. The prosecution of felonies was more consistent than arrests and indictments on misdemeanor charges. Patterns of serious crime can be documented where the less serious but more numerous small crimes cannot. From 1929 through 1939, 1,245 indictments against women were issued in the district and federal courts in Bexar County.[10] The pattern of prosecutions reveals that activity in the

[9]Maitland, "San Antonio," p. 54.

[10]During these years San Antonio was served by three district courts. The 37th Criminal District Court of Bexar County operated throughout the period; the 94th District Court was discontinued in 1935 when it was replaced by the 144th District Court. The U.S. District Court in San Antonio has jurisdiction over Bexar County and thirteen surrounding counties.

Since court records are not indicators of crimes committed, this analysis is a study of a biased sample, a sample composed of accused women. Crimes reported to the police or arrests could not be used because San Antonio has destroyed most of its police records of these years. Because misdemeanors were tried almost entirely in corporation courts, this is primarily a study of serious female crime with impressionistic evidence on lesser crime supplied where possible. Corporation-court records were not used because of their disorganization and because particular applications of the law in Bexar County made misdemeanors difficult to interpret. Specifically, prostitutes were not regularly arrested, and when they were arrested, they were charged with vagrancy rather than soliciting.

The docket books from which data for this analysis were gathered generally indicate

courts closely followed administrative decisions on law enforcement and changes in the criminal code rather than reflecting actual fluctuations in criminal activity or indirect predictors of crime such as unemployment. Indictments in federal and district courts were heaviest from 1929 through 1931, before the brunt of the Depression struck San Antonio and Bexar County. Furthermore, the chronological pattern of indictments in the federal court was distinctly different from the record of prosecutions in the district courts. The serious crimes that women committed in the Depression were motivated primarily by economics, but the Depression did not cause an increase in arrests for these crimes.

The felonies that women committed during the period suggest that the behavior of women as criminals is similar to their behavior as paid workers. Women consider entering the labor market for reasons of economic need, but for some women resistance by husbands, child-care responsibilities, and the lack of appropriate occupational opportunities outweigh economic considerations. Similarly, women may commit or refrain from committing crimes because of family or other social pressures. Regardless of the sources of criminal motivation or deterrents to criminal actions, women in San Antonio selected the crimes that they committed under the same limitations as those of others pursuing legitimate occupations. Prostitution has been the most obviously gender-typed crime in the history of the West, but in other crimes as well female "occupational" concentrations appeared in San Antonio. Women's roles as workers and within the home protected them from some criminal opportunities while exposing them to others. Women lacked the experience, the motivation, or the role image to commit such crimes as auto theft. Crimes such as forgery and shoplifting were more consistent with notions of passive female behavior and with women's roles as homemakers than were the aggressive crimes of robbery and burglary (tables 48–50).[11]

---

neither the gender nor the race of the defendant. In the collection of the data gender was determined on the basis of given names. A case in which a given name was common among both men and women was excluded unless the record indicated sentencing to a women's prison. Ethnicity was determined by nationality of surname. There have been errors in the application of these procedures; the fact of intermarriage among ethnic groups has unquestionably resulted in misclassifications. The major intent of the labeling process, however, has been to separate the Hispanic population from other women. Students of San Antonio's Mexican-American community have determined that intermarriage among Hispanics and Anglos was uncommon until World War II. When intermarriage did occur, wives and children were exposed to the cultural values of the husbands' and fathers' ethnic groups.

[11]Carol Smart, *Women, Crime, and Criminology*, pp. 5–8.

Among the crimes tried in Bexar County's federal and district courts, violations of narcotic and alcohol prohibition statutes were by far the most common offenses. A total of 597 federal cases, or nearly half the total federal and district female felony indictments, were for drug or alocohol violations (table 51). The vast majority of these cases, 517, involved bootleg liquor. Indictments fell off dramatically after Congress repealed Prohibition in February, 1933. In that year the number of women prosecuted in federal court dropped 65 percent from the number prosecuted the previous year. Convictions on failing to pay liquor taxes and maintaining a nuisance were common after 1933, but they did not approach the number of convictions obtained earlier on Prohibition violations. Of all female indictments in federal court during the years studied, 70 percent occurred in the years 1929 through 1932.

While there is no way to estimate income from the liquor traffic, the income possibilities, if not the probabilities, were definitely higher than those of such household industries as hand sewing and pecan shelling. When Emilia Castaneda was arrested for operating a still, she produced the cash to post a $400 bond, more money than the annual income of many San Antonio families. Most women similarly charged were unable to make bond, however. Josephine Parrott and Hortense de la Garza were jailed pending trial on liquor-law violations when they failed to make their $500 bonds (table 52).[12]

While women obviously engaged in bootlegging for the profits, there is no evidence to support the view that they were driven into such work by the Depression. Illegal liquor sales had long been part of the San Antonio vice scene, and it was possible to maintain business almost as usual after the adoption of the Eighteenth Amendment. Occasionally, however, a woman arrested for violating liquor laws could turn the Depression to her advantage before the court. Mrs. Grace Karger, who had sold twelve pints of beer and two pints of whiskey to Prohibition officers, pleaded guilty and received a four-month suspended sentence and one year's probation after she demonstrated that she was "the only support of an aged mother and the victim of a bank failure." Such sentences did not encourage women to pursue the straight-and-narrow path to honesty. Mrs. Brijida Valle was arrested in rural Bexar County on charges of opearting a still soon after completing a suspended sentence on a similar violation.[13]

[12]San Antonio Express, July 30, 1932; May 2, 1932.
[13]San Antonio Express, September 28, 1932.

Officers of the Texas Liquor Control Board posing for a *San Antonio Light* photographer before destroying a San Antonio still, March 6, 1937. Women were active in bootlegging, a "cottage industry," during the Depression.
(*San Antonio Light* Collection, University of Texas Institute of Texan Cultures, San Antonio.)

As the District's reputation in the Depression suggests, prostitution in San Antonio was geographically related to other female crime. Of the 232 women indicted on drug and bootlegging charges in 1929 and 1930, 62 were listed in the city directory of 1930. Of the 62, 8 lived near the intersection of South Concho and Matamoras streets in the heart of the District, and 24 lived on the fringes. City directories for the decade document a high concentration of female householders in the vicinity of the District, and female arrests there might consequently be disproportionate to female arrests elsewhere, but the area did not account for 50 percent of the city's women. Even allowing for the probability that women criminals in the District faced stronger possibilities of detection because police expected to find female crime in the area, the District did represent a concentration of female criminal activities other than prostitution.

Excluding narcotics and Prohibition cases, most female felonies in San Antonio from 1929 through 1939 fell into three broad categories: economic crimes of taking such as burglary and theft, economic crimes of fraud such as forgery and embezzlement, and violent crimes (table 49). After bootlegging, the most common serious offense of women was forgery, for which there were 152 indictments. There were 52 additional crimes of fraud, such as embezzlement, which brought the total in this category to 204, or 17 percent of all indictments of women. Crimes of taking totaled 254, or 21 percent of the prosecutions of women, indicating that women frequently acted aggressively in committing crimes, though clearly they preferred "victimless" crimes. One of every 10 female defendants in federal or district court was tried for a crime of violence. In 1933, when the Federal Bureau of Investigation began gathering statistics, 16 percent of the female crimes in cities reported to the bureau were violent crimes. The proportion was the same at the end of the decade. Only a few cities reported to the FBI in the 1930s, and the crime figures are not considered very reliable by historians or FBI statisticians.[14]

In the pattern of female prosecutions in San Antonio, criminal behavior reflected not only gender concentrations that were consistent with women's roles as family members and workers but also ethnic concentrations that mirrored occupational segregation by ethnicity. Because of the nature of criminal records that have survived from the 1930s, the races of the women who appeared in federal and district courts are not usually known, but Hispanic women can be distinguished from others by name. Overall, the rate of felony indictments among female Mexican Americans was not significantly different from that of other women. Mexican Americans accounted for approximately 30 percent of female residents of Bexar County fifteen years old and older, and Mexican-American women were named in 413, or 33 percent, of the 1,245 indictments issued between 1929 and 1939.[15]

On the one hand, the statistics conflict with common assumptions of a

[14]Federal Bureau of Investigation, *Uniform Crime Reports* 5 (1934); 11 (1940).

[15]If the twenty-five indictments of Hispanics for illegal immigration are deducted from the total number of cases involving Chicanas, the percentage falls to 32 percent. Arrest statistics from the first six months of 1940 are the only information available regarding black female criminals. The arrest rate for black women was somewhat higher than that for Anglo women or Chicanas, and prostitution played a less important role in the criminal activities of black women than in the crimes of other women. When prostitution is removed from consideration, blacks show approximately twice the arrest rates of Anglo women or Chicanas.

negative correlation between income and crime. Although female Mexican Americans were poorer than other women in San Antonio, they were not greatly overrepresented among defendants. The record of court proceedings also suggests that traditional arguments about the influence of familial values on the behavior of Mexican-American women ought to be reexamined. The cloistering of girls and women was recognized by both Anglos and Hispanics in San Antonio as a central and distinguishing characteristic of Mexican-American family life. Rates of juvenile delinquency among Hispanic boys in the 1930s were considerably higher than those among Anglo or black boys, but the rates among Mexican-American girls were markedly lower than those among black or Anglo girls. An Anglo social worker explained the very low juvenile-delinquency rate among Mexican-American females as a consequence of their being confined to the home. Adult indictments reveal, however, that a protective attitude toward girls did not reduce criminal activity in later life. In 1940, after Mayor Maverick's attack on prostitution had begun, 152 Hispanic, 127 Anglo, and 17 black women between the ages of eight and twenty-five were arrested on prostitution charges. Observers of the 1930s, however, estimated that Mexican Americans accounted for about 40 percent, rather than the majority, of prostitutes.[16]

Although the patriarchal structure of the Mexican family apparently did not discourage the commiting of crimes by Hispanic women in San Antonio, it can be seen that familial or cultural values influenced Mexican-American females' choices of criminal occupations. The Mexican-American preference, as reflected in indictments, was for crimes that might be deemed honest crimes in that customers paid for a product or a service, clearly understanding that they were participating in illegal activities. Hispanic women were less likely than others to commit crimes of violence. The criminal occupations of Mexican-American women were particularly those activities that could function as a variation of the tradition of cottage industry that was demonstrated by their extensive participation in home sewing and home shelling. More than half of all Mexican-American female indictments between 1929 and 1939 were for bootlegging, alcohol and narcotics violations together accounting for more than three-fifths of all court appearances by Mexican-American women but only two-fifths of the appearances of other women.

[16]San Antonio Public Welfare Survey, appendix, pt. 5, table 5, p. 1.

Crimes that required going outside the home—such crimes as theft, robbery, forgery, and embezzlement—were much less common offenses of Hispanic than of other women. It was common for groups of black women, armed with small knives, to rob passers-by on streets of the East Side, but such crimes were rarely perpetrated by Mexican-American women. Economic crimes by taking or by fraud constituted 16.5 percent of Hispanic female indictments as opposed to 43 percent of non-Hispanic female indictments. Hispanic as well as black women had limited opportunities to commit the white-collar crimes of forgery and embezzlement. Both crimes depend on access to financial accounts that blacks and Mexican Americans were unlikely to obtain in a racist society. Forgery, fraud, and swindling hinge on creating confidence in the perpetrator's financial abilities or worth, a sitaution of trust that poor black and Hispanic women could not build.

While the attempt to link Hispanic women's participation in particular activities and not in others to their roles as submissive home workers is speculative, another category of court proceedings dominated by Mexican-American plaintiffs and defendants substantiates the view that ethnic values are reflected in court records. In this instance Mexican-American values encouraged Hispanic women to press their cases when other women did not. In 1930 seven convictions on morals charges were reviewed in district courts on appeals from lower courts in Bexar County. All the appeals were instituted by Mexican-American women, revealing a concern for the protection of a woman's moral reputation that other racial groups did not demonstrate. In these cases women had been convicted of improper and illegal behavior after their Hispanic neighbors pressed charges against them. In one such case A. Valdez filed an affidavit with the San Antonio police that "Florence Morales a woman did unlawfully live together and have carnal intercourse with Robert Zepeda, an unmarried man." [17] A Bexar County criminal court convicted Morales of fornication, and the district court reaffirmed the verdict, denying Morales's plea for a reversal.

In the courtroom Mexican-American women were treated no more harshly than other women despite the racism that touched all aspects of life in San Antonio. Substantially more Hispanic women than other female defendants, 56 percent as opposed to 36 percent, were pronounced guilty by the courts, but Mexican-American women were much more likely than

[17]Jacket of case of Florence Morales, October 10, 1930, Bexar County Court at Law, Criminal Court 2, case no. 39239.

others to be tried in federal court, and the federal court had a much higher rate of convictions than that of district courts. When cases are separated into federal and other cases, the rate of convictions is about the same for Hispanic as for other women. The courts did not discriminate against Hispanic women in sentencing or assessing fines. Mexican-American women received twice as many very high fines (over $500) as other women, but they were also more heavily represented among women receiving fines under $100. In view of the fact that Mexican-American defendants were disproportionately represented among women convicted in narcotics and bootlegging cases, in which high fines were the most frequent punishment administered by the courts, the court record suggests a somewhat lenient attitude toward Hispanic women.

The imposition of fines undoubtedly reflected the court's sensitivity to the ability of defendants to pay. A total of 35 female convicts fined by the courts were imprisoned because of failure to pay their fines and were later released on poor-convict discharges; 21 of the 35 were Mexican Americans. Of 230 Hispanic women found guilty, 12 were granted suspensions of their fines, and the sentences of 65 were commuted or suspended. In contrast, 51 of 198 Anglo or black women received suspended or commuted sentences after conviction, and only 6 were granted suspension of fines.

With regard to women generally, students of criminal justice have argued that male judges are less tolerant of deviant behavior among women and therefore punish female convicts more heavily than male offenders. Others have maintained, however, that male judges are inclined to act protectively toward female offenders and not to see women as threatening the social order and consequently impose lighter sentences on women than on men.[18] The latter point of view is consistent with the disposition of the cases of women tried for murder in San Antonio from 1929 through 1939. Gladys Rice, sentenced to two years' imprisonment on a murder conviction, was representative of women sentenced for criminal homicide in Depression San Antonio.

The Rice case also demonstrates that economic grievances may not

[18]Carolyn Engle Temin, "Discriminatory Sentencing of Women Offenders: The Argument for the ERA in a Nutshell," in Laura Crites, ed., *The Female Offender*, pp. 49–66; Rosemary C. Sarri, "Juvenile Law: How It Penalizes Females," in ibid., pp. 67–88; Meda Chesney-Lind, "Young Women in the Arms of the Law," in Lea H. Bawker, ed., *Women, Crime, and the Criminal Justice System*, pp. 171–96; Chesney-Lind, "Chivalry Reexamined: Women and the Criminal Justice System," in ibid., pp. 211–24; Smart, *Women, Crime, and Criminology*, pp. 108–45.

Mrs. Gladys Rice at the police department before her conviction of the murder of Ben H. Kelly, a former judge, 1934.
(*San Antonio Light* Collection, University of Texas Institute of Texan Cultures, San Antonio.)

translate into economic crimes and that economic frustrations may be endured for a considerable length of time before a criminal act follows. On a street in downtown San Antonio one hot summer day in 1934, Gladys Rice walked up to Ben H. Kelly, an elderly attorney and former judge, and shot him three times. Kelly died moments later in a local hospital. Rice, who was about forty years old, was arrested and after a preliminary hearing was held without bond. Her lawyers explained to the press that some years earlier Kelly had acted as Rice's legal counsel in the matter of a modest inheritance. The inheritance had come to nothing in the crash, and Rice had harbored a resentment against Kelly in the belief that he had mismanaged the investment of her estate. During her arraignment and trial Rice elicited sympathy from courthouse employees who had known her previously. As May Eckles noted:

> I finally found out who that Mrs. Gladys Rice is. She is a woman I did some work for several years ago. They had her preliminary hearing in the 37th Court at two thirty and I went up and listened to it. Mrs. Eichelberger was up there and seemed to know her, she kissed her good-bye. Mrs. Eichelberger was the one that sent her to me, she said why don't you go and speak to her but I did not want to do it, it's all too bad.[19]

Rice was subsequently convicted of murder. Although the jury recommended life imprisonment, the presiding judge specified a two-year sentence.

Of 43 women tried on 48 counts of murder in Depression San Antonio, only 5 were convicted. In 1934, Mittie Green was sentenced to five years on a conviction of murder without malice aforethought. Also in 1934, Emma Oliver was found guilty of murder. The jury recommended a five-year sentence, but the presiding judge suspended the sentence. Helen Steiger, who was convicted of premeditated murder in 1938, was denied a suspension of her twenty-year sentence. The bench ordered Steiger to serve her sentence despite the belief of the presiding judge that "it just wasn't right to send a woman to the penitentiary."[20] Perhaps the judge was influenced by knowledge of Steiger's other activities. The docket book carries the notation that Steiger also went under the aliases Honey Meyers, Helen Rogers, and "Chickie." In a separate trial she was later convicted of manslaughter as well. Both Steiger and Oliver were local prostitutes. Oliver was black, and Steiger was white, which again suggests that race alone did not determine a woman's treatment by the courts.

The Clara Uhr case demonstrated the court's determination to guarantee female murder defendants every defense recourse under the law. Mrs. Uhr was charged with hiring her husband's killing. Two soldiers testified that she had offered them $500 to kill her invalid husband, Daniel. The

---

[19]*San Antonio Express*, August 8, 1934; Eckles diary, August 7–8, 1934; 37th District Court Criminal Minutes, case no. 41437.

[20]Interview with Elton R. Cude, May 21, 1979.

jury found the two soldiers guilty of the ax slaying of Daniel Uhr. Their testimony also led to Clara's conviction of first-degree murder, and she was sentenced to death. Shortly after sentencing, however, the court and the district attorney agreed to send her to the San Antonio State Hospital for psychiatric evaluation (apparently doctors had not found her incompetent to stand trial or insane at the time of the crime). Although she had pleaded innocent in the original trial, when granted a new trial, she pleaded not guilty by reason of insanity. After the second trial had begun, the court permitted her to withdraw the insanity plea and enter a guilty plea, after which she was sentenced to life imprisonment. Overall, the five sentences of women convicted of murder suggest both a regional tolerance of violence and a reluctance to punish women harshly. Several men received death sentences on murder convictions in Bexar County during these years, but only one, a black, was executed.[21]

In the variety of crimes that they committed, San Antonio women were not very different from other women in the nation, with the exception of their active role in bootlegging. The vast majority of felonies committed during the Depression years were motivated by economics. While the eleven-year period examined here is too brief to identify long-term trends, it was the period of most radical change in economic conditions in the nation's history, and San Antonio was a city heavily burdened by poverty and lacking in relief services. The county-court system during the Depression had become so overloaded with misdemeanor cases, such as vagrancy, thefts under $50, and thefts of chickens and other livestock, that the courts had practically ceased functioning. In the incomplete records that remain of misdemeanor prosecutions in the county, women were prominent, and the types of cases suggest strong ties to the general state of the economy. With respect to felonies, however, a dependable trial record of which survives, the Depression did not prompt an increase in female offenses. When it was expected that Prohibition would be lifted, the number of female indictments dropped each year, and indictments of women on other charges than bootlegging did not fluctuate widely during the Depression. San Antonio's red-light district accounted for a disproportionate share of all female crimes, not simply prostitution. Although the Mexican-American

[21]94th District Court Criminal Minutes, case no. 40804. June Woolfolk, a black male, received the death sentence for murder on September 23, 1934, and was subsequently executed.

community of San Antonio endured the nation's deepest poverty during the Depression, felony indictments were not significantly higher among Hispanic women than among other women. Mexican-American women did, however, reveal a different profile of criminal occupations from the profiles of Anglo and black females. In their preference for cottage crimes and their disinclination to act aggressively, Mexican-American women played the familial and social roles expected of them despite violations of the law and despite poverty.

[10]

Consequences

Well I guess it's bad now and it's bad primarily, I think, because we have so many.
If one group pulls itself up, there's a great influx coming in.

—Former union organizer, 1979[1]

THE histories of San Antonio women as workers and as family members
reveal the degree to which generalizations about the national Depression
experience camouflage the realities of the 1930s for individual groups. A
privileged few passed through the Depression in ease, but overall San Antonians suffered more than did most other city dwellers. The women perceived and adapted to economic losses differently from men. Anglo, black,
and Hispanic women faced very different circumstances in a city of low
wages, high unemployment, and menacing slums. San Antonio women
adopted many survival strategies: collecting commodities for the needy,
sharing housing, taking in lodgers, seeking employment, applying for relief, striking against wage cuts, and engaging in criminal acts. Women did
not choose freely among these options, however. Family status and caste
heavily determined which of the options a woman might pursue.

Marriage, children, and the absence or death of the spouse were primary personal considerations in meeting the Depression. Black and Hispanic women married earlier than Anglo girls, but only among Mexican
Americans was early marriage accompanied by high fertility. Black women
bore the fewest children and Hispanic women the most, but overall Depression conditions lowered the birthrate. Because they had large families
and because of poor health and nutrition within their families, Mexican-
American mothers were the most likely of San Antonio women to experience the trauma of a child's death. Black women were the most likely to
face the necessity of supporting themselves and their children after widow-
ing, separation, or divorce. Anglo women had the best chances of raising
their children in homes in which fathers were present continuously.

As family status defined women's needs, caste limited women's op-

[1]Anonymous interview, May 30, 1979.

tions. Caste determined occupational opportunities and signified cultural differences. Cultural values prescribed the appropriate roles for Anglo, black, and Hispanic women at particular stages of the life cycle. Economic exigencies occasionally forced compromises of cultural values, but culture proved remarkably strong in the face of the Depression. In San Antonio caste was a strong but not absolute indicator of class. Black and Mexican-American women were predominantly lower class and were narrowly restricted by occupational segregation. Consequently, minority women had broader needs but fewer economic alternatives than their Anglo sisters had.

Some Depression behaviors reached across caste lines and characterized class situations. Middle-class women of all ethnic groups, including the exceptional black and Hispanic women who had achieved that status, "made do." As long as some income flowed into the household, they succeeded in keeping families healthy and intact. In families like Carmen Perry's, coping with the Depression involved the postponement of personal goals for the good of the family. Beatrice Clay and Ruby Cude surrendered the privacy of the nuclear household to relieve the economic hardships of the larger family. Women at the bottom of the economic ladder could not cope so readily with bad times. Many families had survived the 1920s only through the efforts of numerous breadwinners. Wage reductions or unemployment spelled disaster for these families. Working-class women like Veda Butler and her mother found public or private relief agencies their only hope as income dwindled. Middle-class women experienced families drawn together into mutual support groups by the employment decline. Working-class women experienced families separated by unemployment and feared the starvation or institutionalization of their children as family income disappeared.

Women who were in a position to help others during the Depression often gave generously of their time and economic resources. Union auxiliaries held benefit events for the relief of needy union families. Middle- and upper-class women kept the Milk and Ice Fund functioning, fed the hungry and nursed the sick at the Junior League clinic, and promoted the Loyal Legion and the Blue Eagle. Anglo women dominated charitable organizations and public agencies that assisted unemployed during the Roosevelt administration. Although sincere in their efforts, Anglo welfare workers displayed judgmental and frequently condemnatory attitudes toward their clients that mirrored their class and ethnic prejudices. In working with public employment projects, middle-class Anglo women reinforced the occupational segregation by gender and ethnicity that functioned in the private sector.

Female bureaucrats and volunteer relief workers fought to lighten the burden of the Depression for all San Antonians, but most women focused their energies on the needs of their own families. Most San Antonio women saw their roles as nurturers of children, helpmates of careworn husbands, and protectors of the home. Rather than undermining their roles, the Depression challenged housewives to do their very best. While the Depression jeopardized men's positions as primary breadwinners, it reinforced women's importance as home managers even if they were also paid workers.

Whether women were employees or nonpaid workers, their households comprised the primary economic units in which they participated. Although the Depression put pressure on families to cut costs and pool resources by expanding the household beyond the nuclear family, the nuclear household remained the norm in all ethnic groups. Most adult women passed through the Depression as wives and mothers who contributed their homemaking skills rather than wages to the family economy. Other women, seeing their families struggle to make ends meet, had the economic motivation to enter the work force. Most mothers of young children did not consider employment a feasible solution to economic problems, but as the decade progressed, more and more married women entered the labor market.

Anglo women predominated among wives securing employment. Although the economic needs of black and Hispanic women were more intense than those of most Anglos, job opportunities for minority women were narrow and declined as the Depression deepened. Black women did not find marriage a barrier to work-force participation, though black mothers with young children were also likely to remain at home. For black homemakers, unlike Anglo and Mexican-American women, paid work performed in their own homes was a common solution to the dual demands of employment and child care.

During the 1920s, Mexican-American families had depended heavily on the wages of child and young adult workers. The Depression severely reduced the employment opportunities of the young, and child labor had almost completely disappeared by 1940. Young adult workers of all ethnic groups, because their wages were needed by their parents or because they could not support themselves on their own, were discouraged from leaving the parental home by Depression conditions. There were differences in family structure and familial values in Anglo, black, and Mexican-American families, and these factors, as well as family responsibilities and income, affected women's abilities to cope with the Depression and their decision to seek paid labor. Mexican-American girls were more likely to seek work than were black or Anglo girls, but they were the least likely to work as adults. Black women were the most likely of all San Antonio women to work as adults, but black teenaged girls were least likely to work. Anglo women occupied a middle position as both teenagers and adults. The differences in age and marital status among women workers of the three ethnic groups were generally consistent with differing familial expectations among the groups, but they also reflected the impact of occupational segregation on labor-force participation. Additional numbers of Anglo wives entered the labor market during the Depression despite prejudices against their employment because market demand for their skills was increasing.

The woman worker faced the Depression under particular disabilities as compared to the male worker. The realities of occupational segregation dictated that she would be relegated to a lower-paying job. The policies of New Deal agencies and the attitudes of private employers added additional handicaps for the woman worker and reinforced old prejudices. During the Roosevelt administration unemployed women who had able-bodied fathers, husbands, or brothers in their households stood almost no chance of being certified as primary workers under emergency hiring guidelines. As secondary workers, they could not reasonably expect to obtain public emergency jobs. Private employers, viewing the employment of "secondary" workers as unpatriotic during the national economic emergency, also discriminated against women. As the policies in the Bexar County Courthouse offices suggested, it was easiest simply to dismiss married women on the assumption that they were secondary workers. At the federal level the establishment of a separate division of women's work under both the FERA and the WPA reinforced occupational segregation and traditional attitudes that women workers occupied a status or a place in the economy separate from that of men.

In Texas the gender segregation of federal programs translated not only into the sewing-room and home-care projects that were common aspects of all state women's programs but also into an administrative perspective that women should be treated differently. Public agencies regarded women as temporary workers who were propelled into the labor force by the exigencies of the Depression. The largest work projects for women taught no marketable skills despite the fact that the vast majority of women given public work had no other workers in their families. Only black women who entered the controversial servant-training projects were treated as permanent workers. Most women in federal programs were employed at tasks that were thought consistent with the nonpaid work they would do at home after the Depression ended. The contradiction between the real economic situation of these women and the assumptions governing federal programs seems never to have concerned the women who administered New Deal women's work in San Antonio. At the federal, state, and local levels both official policies and unofficial practices denied the facts that some women had always been primary workers and that a substantial number of American families had always depended on the income of more than one family member to survive.

Very few married women in San Antonio questioned the view that their claims to employment were inferior to those of men or of single women. There were no official challenges to the dismissal of married teachers. Of the many letters that San Antonio women wrote to Eleanor Roosevelt and to New Deal administrators in which they voiced pleas for employment assistance, not one came from a woman whom the federal government would have classified as a secondary worker. The refusal of the WPA in San Antonio to certify a woman for sewing-room work because her husband was employed as a WPA laborer more deeply jeopardized that family's well-being than did the wage cuts suffered by many male white-collar workers who were the sole supporters of families.

Despite the tremendous pressures that discouraged the hiring of women and despite a real decline in employment opportunities, women's labor-force participation increased between 1930 and 1940. In the occupations that women pursued, there is a clear pattern of gender and ethnic discrimination, a pattern similar to that of other American cities. Despite the competition for jobs during the Depression, men and women rarely displaced each other in the labor market, and one ethnic group rarely made headway up or down the occupational ladder in displacing members of a different ethnic group. The inflexibility of occupational segregation under the economic pressures of the Depression suggests that caste lines were so strong that individuals, either as employers or as employees, were loath to violate the pattern despite the need to cut costs or to find a job. An alternative explanation to the inviolability of caste, one that cannot be tested from the data available, is that even in the Depression the pay differences by sex and ethnicity were so great that Anglo men and women, at the top of their respective occupational structures, could weather unemployment with or without public assistance, and were not forced to accept the inferior jobs of blacks and Hispanics. Changes that occurred in the occupational structure in San Antonio worked against downward occupational mobility among Anglo women despite the willingness some Anglos may have felt to accept "colored" or "Mexican" jobs. The number of jobs stereotyped as black or Hispanic decreased during the decade, while Anglo "female jobs" increased. Consequently, there was not as much pressure for Anglo women to accept industrial and domestic jobs as there would have been in a static occupational structure. The small changes that occurred in the female occupational structure resulted in declining labor-force participation by black women. The long-term changes in women's jobs in San Antonio and rates of labor-force participation among Anglo, black, and Mexican-American women confirm the persistence of occupational segregation in periods of prosperity as well as depression and confirm that labor-force participation by all women was tied to their specific job opportunities as members of a particular racial or ethnic group.

In broad terms, the women of San Antonio's three major ethnic groupings were segregated into three occupational categories in 1930. Black women were almost exclusively confined to domestic and service jobs, the majority of Mexican-American women were industrial workers, and Anglo women clustered in sales and clerical positions. Consistent with Anglo notions of caste, Anglo women had a significantly broader range of occupations from which to choose than that of black and Hispanic women. Although both black and Mexican-American women had severely restricted occupational options, a comparison of the two groups illustrates the differing notions of caste that Anglos applied to blacks and Hispanics. Black women failed to gain jobs in which their contact with the Anglo public was anything other than a clearly service role. Although Hispanic women collectively had less education than black women had, they did find some jobs as sales clerks, beauticians, and teachers that brought them into contact with Anglo clients or pupils. Because San Antonio's manufacturing sector suffered more severe losses during the Depression than did other economic areas, Hispanic women experienced more severe levels of unemployment than did Anglo women and black women.

Occupational segregation and the suffering that accompanied it in De-

Mrs. Burrell Miles nurses her infant as Cecilia Trevino rolls her hair in a San Antonio beauty shop March 7, 1937. Hair-fashion changes of the 1920s created a demand for beauticians that persisted throughout the Depression. In San Antonio both Anglo and Mexican-American beauticians worked in shops serving Anglo patrons. (*San Antonio Light* Collection, University of Texas Institute of Texan Cultures, San Antonio.)

pression San Antonio were manifestations of gender and ethnic or racial prejudices. The inflexibility of occupational segregation over the Depression decade, in particular the failure of Anglo men to move into women's jobs and the failure of Anglo women to move down the occupational ladder, highlights the weaknesses of economic explanations of discrimination. Despite the intense competition for employment, men seeking work did not accept lower-paying women's jobs, and despite the marginal position of many businesses, employers did not cut costs by replacing men with women or Anglo women with minority women.

Black and Hispanic men faced intense discrimination in the assignment of emergency work, in Depression wage codes, and in the allocation of relief commodities, but the legitimacy of their claims to employment was never questioned on account of gender. Although San Antonio offices, shops, and factories would have been forced to shut down without the labor of women, as was the case in the pecan and garment strikes, women workers overall were viewed as an anomaly by male employers and by female New Deal administrators as well. It was indicative of racist views, however, that black women were understood to be permanent workers. As the household workers' training program demonstrated, Anglos in San Antonio assumed that blacks comprised a permanent underclass in which market labor by women would continue to be necessary and that the labor-force status of black women was consequently different from that of other women. Similar assumptions were not made about Hispanic women, who were less likely to work despite poverty and who were considered employable because of temporal conditions rather than their caste status.

Cultural expectations, economic conditions, and occupational segregation by sex and ethnicity interacted to define women's work. Hispanic women who sought employment generally chose industrial jobs, where they could work with family members, over domestic work, though in some instances manufacturing jobs paid less than service jobs. Hispanic women dominated fine hand sewing not only because they worked cheaply but also because they had learned the skills in Mexican schools or at home. Midwives, who were not reported separately in published census reports, were, however, listed in city directories, and they were all Hispanic. Society had previously defined clerical work as an Anglo female job. Anglo but not Hispanic men accepted the employment of their wives and daughters in offices. Anglo girls prepared for secretarial work in high school. Black girls might obtain similar skills but would find virtually no opportunity to practice them. Similarly, the interaction of culture, economics, and segregation affected women's criminal behavior. Hispanic women dominated the "homework" activities of bootlegging and drug dealing, while Anglo women, who had claim to both middle-class status and clerical positions, committed more crimes of forgery and embezzlement than did other women. Society defined prostitution as an exclusively female crime, the one female occupation in which there were no barriers or protections of race or ethnicity.

Mexican-American women's choices of industrial jobs made them likely targets of union organization. At first, in trying to build a local among Hispanic women, Anglo organizers failed to appreciate the critical importance of ensuring support for unions among the workers' fathers, husbands, and brothers. Anglo organizers for the ILGWU complained of the special difficulty of recruiting leadership from a Mexican-American female rank and file. In reality, Hispanic women developed leadership potential among themselves both before and during the ILGWU push of the 1930s. Mexican-American women, however, remained suspicious of Anglo labor leaders and never fully merged their own leadership with the Anglo union establishment. Emma Tenayuca could mobilize the Mexican-American population, male and female, revealing that rigidly patriarchal community could compromise cultural proscriptions in the face of pressing economic and political issues. The ILGWU, the UGWU, and the CIO could not afford a coalition with the Communist Tenayuca, but her rejection also repudiated the one charismatic voice among Mexican Americans.

The experiences of Mexican Americans and blacks in Depression San Antonio reflect additional caste differences between the two groups. Mexican Americans were feared and unwanted, as deportations, public statements endorsing repatriation, and the elimination of relief for aliens indicated. If they were aliens, they might be denied relief, but they were not segregated by government policy. Individual Mexican Americans were accepted as coworkers and possibly as social companions by Anglos; blacks were not. In laundries and garment factories Anglos occasionally worked alongside Hispanic women, but blacks were always segregated. The WPA trained Hispanic but not black women for clerical jobs. The greater occupational and social diversity of Mexican Americans, despite their overall educational and economic inferiority to blacks, illustrates the primacy of race in caste definitions.

Segregation by sex was much more inflexible for women than it was for men. Men in Depression San Antonio had more success in entering occupations dominated by women than vice versa. In occupational terms the lines of gender segregation were stricter than those of ethnic segregation. Women workers in Depression San Antonio were also more highly segregated by ethnicity than were men. Only in domestic work, where employees most frequently did not have coworkers, were the lines of racial or ethnic segregation blurred. In cities of the Southeast, where there was no Hispanic caste and where there were relatively few European immigrants unaccustomed to American notions of caste, the servant class was not racially mixed. On the one hand, the differences indicated that minority men, black or Hispanic, had broader occupational options than those of

minority women. On the other hand, the one "protection" offered women
by their exploiters was "protection" against working with undesirable
minorities.

For black and Hispanic San Antonians, unsympathetic or unrespon-
sive attitudes among Anglo relief leaders exacerbated the problems of occupational segregation and high unemployment. Late in the Depression the
Social Welfare and Fact-finding Committee, a group of ten local business
leaders, prepared a report summarizing needs and services in Bexar County.
The governments of San Antonio and Bexar County together contributed
only 0.5 percent of the relief resources distributed locally. Nevertheless,
the committee concluded that demands on local funds were far in excess of
what the two governments could support. In attempting to bolster its argument, the committee pointed out that in 1938 the average WPA expenditure for commodities for relief cases in Bexar County was $9.79 while for
Texas as a whole the average expenditure was $14.65. In elaborating on the
locality's inferior relief disbursements, the committee revealed that the
county lacked storage facilities for perishable foods, and such goods allo-
cated for the county by the WPA and other agencies were consequently
redirected to other areas of the state. A modest local appropriation, then,
could have secured substantial improvements in relief. Rather than argue
this case, however, the committee maintained that relief cases in San Antonio were predominantly Mexican Americans who ought not to be considered a local responsibility because they had always been "transient farm
labor" or had been forced off lands in surrounding counties because of
"federal policies." Although the committee did not suggest resettlement of
Anglo or black agricultural workers, it recommended that some Mexican-
American families should move to small towns and farms elsewhere in the
United States and that others should be repatriated. Despite its position,
the committee maintained that it had "no unfriendly or racial feeling whatever toward Latin-Americans." [2]

The antagonism of the Social Welfare and Fact-finding Committee toward Mexican Americans revealed the change in the economic structure of
the city that followed passage of the Fair Labor Standards Act. Although
enforcement of the act did not immediately follow upon its passage, by the
end of 1939 the government had stopped allowing easements to employers
in transition. San Antonio employers who had exploited the local labor sur-

[2]Social Welfare and Fact-Finding Committee, "An Economic and Social Survey of San
Antonio, Texas" (mimeographed report, 1942), appendix A, exhibit 1.

plus at wages of pennies an hour could not operate profitably on hand labor at twenty-five cents an hour. With this change the impoverished population, which had been tolerated because it permitted handwork industries to flourish, became simply a drain on the city and the county. Local officials watched the Mexican-American population grow during the Depression, fearful that it would soon become a majority. Repatriation was recommended because "the schools are already crowded with children of Latin-American extraction" and because "there are many Latin-Americans in San Antonio for whom there is not opportunity for gainful employment in the near future."[3]

The statistics of death and disease in San Antonio clearly reveal the consequences of economic stratification in the city (tables 53 to 56). Average annual death rates from tuberculosis in the mid-1930s were 52.8 for every 10,000 Anglos, 135.7 for blacks, and 302.7 for Mexican Americans. In the densely populated second ward, the heart of the West Side, the approximately 43,000 residents, 87 percent of whom were Mexican Americans, experienced much higher death rates than those of other residents of the city. In that ward the rates were 116.6 for 100,000 Anglos, 207 for blacks, and 390.2 for Mexican Americans. Spokesmen concerned about health conditions among the Hispanic population tried to mobilize public opinion to improve conditions. Anglo reform advocates pointed out that in areas like the second ward, where Hispanic death and disease rates were highest and where the concentration of Mexican-American population was greatest, Anglos and blacks also suffered more disease than did those who lived elsewhere in the city. Unfortunately, well into the World War II years resettlement or deportation was seen as the most logical solution to the problem.

Resettlement and repatriation were responses consistent with Anglo prejudices, but even to many concerned Anglo observers the problems of West Side residents appeared so overwhelming that removal of the population seemed the only reasonable solution. Descriptions of living conditions on the West Side pointed up the futility of treating disease in the absence of basic environmental changes. An investigator for the health department described a dwelling that consisted of "a single room big enough for two beds, the three feet between them occupied by the baby's crib, and a lean-to kitchen almost entirely filled with a small wood stove. This was the

[3]Ibid.

Mexican-American shanties, about 1938. Unsanitary and improperly heated housing contributed to the high rates of death and disease on San Antonio's West Side. (National Archives, Washington, D.C.)

home of an expectant mother with moderately advanced tuberculosis, her nineteen months old child and her husband."[4] In another home the investigator found that the young husband slept on the floor next to his wife's bed because a clinic nurse had told him that to guard against contagion he should not sleep with his tubercular wife.[5]

San Antonio had a higher infant death rate than that of most other American cities, and the unhealthy condition of the Hispanic population was revealed there also. The absence of appropriate statistics prevents the calculation of the infant death rates by ethnicity, but in 1936, 3,219 babies

[4]San Antonio Department of Health, *Annual Report for the Year 1936*, p. 5.
[5]Ibid.

were born to Hispanic mothers, 2,409 to Anglo mothers, and 246 to black mothers. In that year 618 infant deaths were reported in the city, which was calculated to be 104.9 deaths for every 1,000 live births. A total of 464 of the infants were Mexican American, 127 were Anglo, and 27 were black. In 1940 there were 704 infant deaths, 524 of which were Mexican American, 145 were Anglo, and 34 were black. A comparison of birth and death figures suggests the disproportionate ravages of death among both Hispanic and black children.

Infant deaths reflected many of the socioeconomic problems in San Antonio. Owing to dietary deficiencies and the consumption of contaminated food and drink, diarrhea and enteritis were the leading killers of Mexican-American babies, while comparatively few Anglo or black infants died from those diseases. Respiratory infections resulting from overcrowding and poor housing were the second-most-dangerous threat to Mexican-American infants. Mexican-American babies were rarely delivered in hospitals or by doctors, a circumstance that was thought to explain much of their high death rate, but it is clear from the statistics that diseases contracted after birth rather than complications at birth were the primary killers of infants.[6]

The Spanish-speaking residents, who were most in need of medical assistance, food, and clothing, were least equipped to find help. Union organizer Rebecca Taylor estimated that most of the Spanish-speaking population never crossed the San Antonio River into the central city, where Anglo wealth, influence, and private charities were concentrated.[7] Since the most needy residents of the West Side frequently did not speak English (table 16), they were handicapped in finding employment or assistance outside their community. A number of private charities purposely discriminated against blacks, Mexican Americans, or both groups.

In the face of grim statistics and daily fears San Antonio women fought valiantly to keep their families alive and together during the Depression. Women who could share responsibilities and cares with other family members pooled their energies and resources. Women with no families to fall back on for support besought public or private agencies for help, though they frequently did so in vain. Occasionally women abandoned their children after exhausting all other alternatives.

New behaviors that the Depression elicited from women did not nec-

[6]Ibid., pp. 1–6; *American Public Welfare Survey of San Antonio, Texas, 1940*, pp. 1–7.
[7]Interview with Rebecca Taylor, May 30, 1979.

essarily disappear as prosperity returned. Although some women chose courses of action as Depression expedients or postponed undertakings or commitments because of the hard times, the temporary often became permanent. The few lucky wives and daughters who sought and found jobs after their men lost income did not invariably retire when full male employment returned. Some workers, male and female, forced out of jobs during the 1930s chose permanent retirement. In San Antonio especially, poverty continued despite "recovery," and women struggled on with survival skills learned during the Depression. For those women whose lives returned to "normal" after the Depression, the memories remained and produced a determination to protect against a recurrence of similar personal disasters and a grateful appreciation of bounty.

The long-range consequences of occupational segregation in San Antonio were consistent with the statistics of the Depression decade. Just as women workers did not share equally the burdens of unemployment, women did not benefit equally in the recovery. Long-term changes in the occupational structure displaced black and Hispanic women. Hispanic women, for whom segregation barriers were somewhat less strict than were those for black women, did not suffer as heavily from structural changes as did blacks, but both groups lost during the 1940s. In 1950 workforce participation of black and Hispanic women had declined from 1930 levels, while the position of Anglo women in the labor forced had improved. The changes in the composition of the work force reflected the transformation of women's work in the twentieth-century economy. Domestic and industrial occupations had continued to decline in importance as the number of clerical, sales, and professional positions increased. The number of women workers in San Antonio doubled between 1930 and 1950, but the number of black workers increased by less than 30 percent, and the number of Hispanic women workers increased by only 60 percent, despite the rapid growth of the Mexican-American population. Reliance upon black domestic workers and the lack of other employment options for black women were indicated by the fact that black women emerged as a majority of private household workers as the overall place of domestic workers declined.

As San Antonio recovered from the Depression, the garment industry gradually revived, though post-Depression employers relied primarily on machine work. In terms of overall female employment, factory jobs did not occupy as important a position as they had in 1930. The trend toward increased female employment in the clerical sector continued, with clerical workers comprising the largest single female occupational area in 1960. In the redefinition of women's work that occurred between 1930 and 1960, black and Mexican-American women did not compete effectively with Anglo women. Regardless of the level of discrimination directed against Hispanic women in the labor market, the average Mexican American, for whom the median of years of schooling in 1960 was 3.7 years, was ill-equipped to compete for clerical positions. Black San Antonians achieved higher levels of education than those of Hispanics, yet black women were even less successful in entering clerical occupations than were Mexican-American women. Despite their educational disadvantages, Hispanic women moved into clerical work in significant numbers, and this sector of the economy emerging as the second largest employer of Hispanic women in 1960. Black women were also unsuccessful in breaking down the segregation in factory work. In 1960 there were more black female professionals than black female factory operatives. Although proportionally more factory jobs were held by Anglo women in 1930 than in 1960, Mexican Americans continued as the largest group of female factory employees. In contrast, Anglo female craft workers, supervisors, and foreladies outnumbered Mexican-American women in these positions two to one.

Overall the bonds of occupational segregation held black women more strongly than Mexican-American women. Although Anglo and Mexican-American women had moved into household domestic work and non-household service jobs more strongly by 1960, new areas of employment did not develop for black women. Although domestic or service work was not virtually the only occupational option of black women in 1960 as it had been in 1930, black women were still overwhelmingly concentrated (74.0 percent of all workers) in domestic and service jobs. Since the passage of civil-rights legislation of the 1960s, black women have begun to challenge successfully the racial barriers in women's work.

To the present day, however, San Antonio continues as a city of low wages and poor working conditions, especially in industries that employ women. As a local worker observed, the abundance of labor in San Antonio militates against successful unionization in the present much as it did during the Depression. Mexican-American women, who are still the backbone of the garment industry, are seldom more successful in winning satisfactory union contracts than they were in the 1930s. Life has changed for the better for all ethnic groups in San Antonio. The barriers of legalized segregation have fallen; the educational outlook and health conditions of Mexican Americans have improved. Women of all ethnic groups have been accepted as legitimate workers outside the home. In San Antonio as well as in other American cities, however, occupational segregation remains, though it is somewhat more flexible than it was in earlier decades. In San Antonio the discriminations and inequities of race and sex that pervaded the Depression city have left their marks on the customs of the present.

Particular vignettes of life in Depression San Antonio are nearly as descriptive of life today as they are of a former time. The "Battle of the Flowers" is a scene that has changed little from past to present. The annual festivities continue to signify the socioeconomic superiority of Anglos. Although living conditions in San Antonio have improved since the Depression, the poor health conditions on the West Side have by no means been eliminated. By the end of the Depression, Alazan Courts, the city's first public housing project, offered decent housing at two dollars a week to residents of the West Side. Additional public housing followed on the West Side and the East Side, but thousands of San Antonians continued to live in life-threatening surroundings through World War II. Today substandard dwellings remain one of San Antonio's most pressing problems. The bonds of segregation have loosened, but black San Antonians are still concentrated on the city's East Side, and the West Side remains overwhelmingly Mexican-American. Federal money and a promising determination among Anglo, black, and Hispanic leaders to rescue San Antonio from its ignominious Depression reputation have improved living standards. Nevertheless, thousands of present-day San Antonians continue to know firsthand the perils of East Side or West Side life as it was during the 1930s.

In the early twentieth century Anglo San Antonians discriminated against blacks and Mexican Americans on the basis of observable traits that included language, facial characteristics, and skin color. Then and now socioeconomic differences within black and Hispanic communities in San Antonio and elsewhere attest to the pervasiveness, the tenacity, and the consequences of caste in America. Historically, lighter-skinned blacks have fared better economically and occupationally than have their darker brothers and sisters. Similarly, Mexican Americans have experienced differing levels of acceptance or rejection among Anglos based on their skin color and have practiced these discriminations among themselves. "White" or Caucasian-looking Hispanics have fared best in San Antonio, while "brown" or Indian-looking Hispanics have remained the poorest group up to the present. The long, painful lessons of immigration, of slavery and Reconstruction, of populism and the Depression teach that "racial" prejudices precede and outlive whatever economic utility they may at one time serve.

For women the caste structure of the 1930s interacted with local economic conditions to the benefit of Anglo workers. Minority women suffered job losses because of the general business contraction and encountered additional difficulties as a consequence of federal laws and policies. The Fair Labor Standards Act delivered the death blow to handwork industries that had employed Mexican Americans. While decision making remained largely in male hands, Anglo women reinforced caste attitudes both as the employers of domestic workers and as supervisors of relief efforts. As mothers and as teachers women handed down ethnic values and caste prejudices to their children. During the Depression few San Antonio women challenged discrimination by gender or by ethnicity. On the other hand, in many strikes women fought to protect their jobs and their wages in the occupations in which they had been traditionally concentrated. The few women who protested gender and ethnic discrimination rarely attracted sympathizers, but they set the stage for a more open society in the postwar years.

APPENDIXES

Theoretical Perspectives on Caste and Occupational Segregation in a Depressed Economy

In the quality of the family lives of women in Depression San Antonio differences of class and culture were evident. In their work outside the home and in their contacts with relief agencies women experienced discrimination of both class and caste. The inflexibility of occupational segregation and relief administrators' treatment of minority women reveal that individuals observed rules of caste despite the absence of legal disabilities associated with caste. As a group Mexican-American women were the most poorly educated members of the population, and the few who had completed secondary school or college faced intense resistance when seeking white-collar employment.[1] Black women were not legally segregated into domestic occupations or legally barred from working alongside white women in WPA sewing rooms, but the end results were essentially the same. The few professional opportunities open to black women followed from strict attitudes of separation that dictated segregated institutions and services for blacks. European immigrant women felt the stings of national prejudices, but functionally they merged with the majority population. They were not occupationally disadvantaged in San Antonio.

Marriage patterns articulated differences of caste. A European immigrant might marry across national lines, and ethnicity carried no burden of caste in that respect. For blacks, for whom race defined caste, marriage outside the group was virtually impossible. Marriage of Hispanics outside the Mexican-American community was highly unlikely during the 1930s, though law did not forbid exogamous marriages as it did marriages between blacks and whites.

In San Antonio, Mexican-American women held a castelike status between black and white in which the definitions of race and ethnicity overlapped and were confused. In a nation that has steadfastly counted its

---

[1]Madeline Clark, "A Preliminary Survey of Employment Possibilities of the Spanish-American Girls Receiving Commercial Training in the San Antonio Secondary Schools" (Master's thesis, University of Texas, 1938).

inhabitants as black, white, red, or yellow, the Mexican American fits no-where. Various black, white, and red elements of the Mexican population have intermarried through centuries. The simple dichotomies of appear-ance that function in the United States to distinguish whites from minority races do not apply. This nation, however, has had a historical tradition of associating national identity with the idea of race. Mexican nationality has been redefined in the United States to convey a racial identity foreign to this country. The extent of the transvaluation is indicated in the decision of the U.S. Census Bureau to count Mexican Americans as neither black nor white but as persons of "other races" in the enumeration of 1930.

The notion that Mexicans were a race, a concept sometimes clearly articulated and sometimes not, did not relegate them to a status equivalent to that of blacks in San Antonio. Mexican-American children were highly segregated in the public schools, but not by law. De facto segregation and restrictive housing covenants, not to mention poverty, confined most His-panics to separate neighborhoods. Operators of restaurants, hotels, and theaters might and frequently did deny Mexican Americans entrance.

The Mexican American was outwardly an unwanted member of San Antonio's population. With few occupational skills, Mexican-American men and women were considered to contribute little to the city's economy. In reality employers exploited the abundance of low-wage Hispanic labor to develop marginal industries in the 1920s that would not have operated otherwise. In contrast, Anglos viewed blacks as a stable group of workers who performed valued tasks in domestic work and the construction indus-try. Mexican Americans, whose numbers nearly equaled the Anglo popula-tion in 1930, suffered high death and disease rates yet sustained a high birth rate. Consequently, Anglos characterized the Hispanic population as a menace to public health and social order. The black community was small; it did not grow as fast as other population groups, and to Anglo leaders it presented no threat of sexual or social intermingling.

Despite their fears of Mexican-American population growth in San Antonio, Anglos preferred Hispanics over blacks socially. Segregation be-tween Mexican Americans and Anglos was never as solid as the walls be-tween blacks and Anglos. A few Spanish-named families were always on the social register, where the names of blacks would not appear. Hispanics who were accepted into the elite sector of society, however, were not only "old" families of substantial wealth but also Caucasian rather than black or Indian in physical appearance. Both Anglos and Mexican Americans of

Caucasian stock regarded the Indian-looking Hispanic as inferior. Anglos regarded the "Indian" Mexican as an untrustworthy peon, representative of the heavy Mexican immigration to San Antonio after 1920.

The peon appeared to the majority population as backward but basically intelligent. Anglos justified the high level of segregation of Mexican-American children in the public schools on the basis of language difficulties or, more subtly, class differences, while black children were understood to have different mental abilities from those of whites. Although discrimination against both blacks and Mexican Americans marked them as inferior, the legalized segregation of black children in the public schools reflected the qualitative difference between the two strains of prejudice. Segregated schooling of blacks was complete and unquestionable, while Mexican Americans could and frequently did protest separate schooling. Despite their separate status, at the onset of the Depression blacks in San Antonio were better off than Mexican Americans with respect to income, living conditions, and political influence. As the Depression moved into its mature phases, however, liberal Anglos cooperated with other elements in the political structure to bar blacks from primary voting and jury duty, thus silencing the political voice of blacks.

As the contrasts between the segregation of blacks and of Mexican Americans from Anglos illustrate, the prejudices faced by black women differed in kind from the barriers confronted by Hispanic women. All women shared the discrimination of gender. The intensity of occupational segregation by gender and by race or ethnicity in San Antonio, coupled with the severity of the Depression in that city, presented an ideal test case of the assumption that majority groups displace minority groups on the job during periods of economic stagnation. Largely because of articulated hostilities toward women workers and policies banning the employment of women, students of the 1930s have assumed that men and women competed for the same jobs. Ruth Milkman has demonstrated that this was not so nationally, that men and women comprised different labor markets.[2]

With respect to the maintenance of separate labor markets by gender, San Antonio folowed the national pattern despite the staggering unemployment. In addition, the history of Depression San Antonio demonstrates that the economic emergency reinforced rather than eroded the high level of occupational segregation among Anglo, black, and Hispanic women. The

[2]Ruth Milkman, "Women's Work and Economic Crisis: Some Lessons from the Great Depression," *Review of Radical Economics* 6 (Spring, 1976):76.

implications of an inflexible occupational structure were many. Some occupations were more volatile than others, and it was the decline of individual occupations, rather than Anglo women's appropriation of the jobs of blacks or Hispanics, that caused disproportionate unemployment among minority women. The Depression confirmed the claim of minority women to the less desirable domestic and industrial jobs that remained and that they had traditionally dominated in San Antonio. The more privileged Anglo women, suddenly come upon hard times, did not move into the inferior jobs and displace minority workers. Overall, San Antonio shared in a national trend of decline in domestic and industrial opportunities for women, a decline hastened by the Depression, and expansion in clerical opportunities. Changes in female labor-force participation during the 1930s for each racial or ethnic group depended upon changes in that sector of the occupational structure into which they were segregated. Over the decade the number of jobs open to blacks and Hispanics fell, while the number of places for Anglo women increased. Consequently, rates of Anglo female labor-force participation rose while the rates of black and Mexican-American women fell.

My understanding of the nature and the intensity of occupational segregation, upon which my theory of labor-force participation rests, has developed from the work of labor economists. There are two theories of the manner in which discrimination manifests itself in the labor market. Gary Stanley Becker presented a model of discrimination that assumes that individuals or groups must pay for the privilege of segregating themselves from others, either in higher prices for goods such as housing or in lower wages than those that open competition would generate.[3] A worker who places his desire for a segregated workplace above his economic interest accepts a job that pays less than a position in which he would work alongside members of the group he shuns. Becker explained the relatively low wages of white industrial workers in the American South by asserting that they were willing to pay a higher price (that is, to work for a lower wage) for a segregated workplace than the price that northern whites were willing to pay. Although his work was developed with specific reference to racial discrimination and was published in the wake of the ruling in *Brown* v. *Board of Education*, Becker asserted that his theory fit equally the phenomenon of gender segregation.

[3]Gary Stanley Becker, *The Economics of Discrimination.*

A second explanatory model of discrimination was developed by Janice Fanning Madden in the 1970s.[4] Madden's theory grew out of the work of British economist Joan Robinson, who maintained that power rather than preference predicts an individual's place in the occupational structure. In her writings Madden maintained that "male power" prevents women from competing with men in the job market. The monopsony (or power) model, which presumes that the female labor supply is inelastic in comparison to the male supply, posits that occupational segregation does not have to be paid for in lower profits or wages by males and that, unlike the assumption in Becker's discrimination model, there is no built-in mechanism that would encourage a decrease in discrimination over time.

Both of these models are considered here not as they might explain gender or racial differences in the work force but as they might explain both simultaneously. The application of either model is complicated by Depression conditions. The abundant labor market and poor profits of the 1930s appear to have decreased both the worker's and the employer's willingness to pay the costs of discrimination. In terms of a power model, Anglo male power over the job market appears to have increased so that employers could have protected jobs for their own kind.

The rhetoric of the Depression and specific public measures favor an acceptance of the power model over the discrimination model. Federal law dictated one job per family, and married women began to be eliminated from government employment as their higher-paid spouses stayed on. Works Progress Administration programs forbade the employment of aliens, and in increasing numbers San Antonio's Mexican citizens fell back on sparsely funded relief programs. Overall, however, female employment increased during the Depression, and male employment decreased. Mexican-American women, clearly objects of discrimination, lost jobs; black women, who were also disadvantaged, did not lose comparably to Hispanics.

Becker's model cannot be satisfactorily applied to San Antonio workers precisely because is assumes that the members of an in-group and an out-group are competitive with each other and that the measure of discrimination is the differential in the wages that both groups are paid for the same work. The facts of the occupational structure, by gender and ethnicity, reveal that jobs themselves were so highly segregated that men did

[4]Janice Fanning Madden, *The Economics of Sex Discrimination.*

not compete with women, and women of one ethnic group rarely competed with other women. Additional evidence about the work force substantiates that even where members of one group held the same job as members of another group they were frequently segregated into separate firms or workrooms. The fact that one group of workers did not displace another during the Depression, when workers were least inclined to be particular, reflects the tenacity of segregation. The Becker model also assumes that the in-group and the out-group are perfect substitutes in production. Past discrimination, however, had had the effect of making different groups imperfect substitutes. For example, boys had not been encouraged to study typing in school. Ignorance or prejudice compounded real differences in convincing employers and employees that particular groups of people were best suited to particular jobs.

With reference to San Antonio, what both models underestimate is the inflexibility of the segregated job market. Discrimination was observable within this system in that where Anglos held the same jobs as blacks or Mexican Americans they were paid more, but the wage differential paid to Anglos was an inducement to them to accept the same jobs that Mexican American or blacks held, not to work alongside them. With reference to sex segregation, occupational labels were often artificial, and the substitutability condition of Becker's model was more nearly met than job titles alone would indicate. A woman might be the supervisory clerk in an office in which a man with the same responsibilities would have the title office manager. Not surprisingly, the office manager would be salaried at a higher level than the hourly wage rate accorded the chief clerk. In reference to the power model it must be remembered that the group in power was the victim as well as the beneficiary of its prejudices. The crisis of the Depression was not severe enough to induce an Anglo businessman to hire a black high-school graduate to manage the office switchboard, though he clearly could have hired a black female, if not a black male, for less than he paid an Anglo female telephone operator. Anglo male employers, therefore, paid the price either of their own prejudices or of what they understood to be the prejudices of employees and customers. Anglo male power, then, was circumscribed by the thoroughness with which Anglo workers, male and female, shared the values of their employers.

As an explanation of the genesis of occupational segregation, the male power model assumes a situation in which labor demands outstrip the supply resulting in pressure to bring into the labor market a pool of personnel who have not previously been employed or who have been employed elsewhere at wages lower than the pay to be offered. As an employer's business expands in a tight labor market, he redefines tasks with a greater degree of specialization. A woman can be hired for the new job of file clerk for less than the office manager's pay because she has traditionally been out of the work force and is therefore not a competitor for alternative employment. She is induced to enter the work force because for the first time she has been offered employment that will allow her to associate with persons of like educational background and consequently similar socioeconomic standing. The employer will not lose his male employees to other firms despite the competition for male workers because the male worker perceives his superiority over the file clerk and because similar situations are developing simultaneously in other concerns. The employer is, in fact, getting more value from each of his employees because the office manager is now paid his previous salary for completing only the more complicated jobs, such as accounting and payroll preparation, while clerks do much of his former work at a lower wage scale.

The model presented here to explain occupational segregation in Depression San Antonio is one that assumes that Anglo males exercised effective control over the labor market but that this situation did not give employers the freedom to violate certain employee and consumer preferences. In the abundant labor market of the 1930s there were sufficient male workers to fill all jobs. Classical economics holds that wages are a measure of productivity. If, as wage differentials would suggest, the productivity of males exceeded that of females, employers, exercising their power, should have chosen to hire the better but more expensive male workers, and the less productive female workers should have been squeezed out. By 1940, however, women as a percentage of the total work force of San Antonio had improved their position relative to 1930, and men had lost ground. Given the fact that men did not compete effectively with women in the labor market, segregation or another form of discrimination must have operated. The most logical explanation in terms of demand and supply in the labor market is that employers, long associated with differential wage rates depending upon occupational segregation, chose to hire or retain female workers, fully comprehending that wage rates were not an adequate measure of productivity. While this explanation is most appealing, even to a restrained feminist, it cannot be carried to its full limits, for women did not displace men in their traditional occupations even though their overall representation in the work force grew during the Depression. What the occupational structure and its static nature suggest is that employment gains and losses were registered within a strict system of segregation.

As a number of economists have demonstrated, various tasks became defined as female jobs when the tasks involved had grown general and routinized enough that one worker was easily replaced by another so that the expectedly high rate of labor turnover accompanying the female life cycle did not penalize the employer.[5] Madden has suggested that an employer may encourage segregation by sex, a situation desired by his own tastes, through defining jobs into categories on the basis of real or supposed sex differences.[6] Only clerical jobs, for example, might be made available on a part-time basis. Such a view is consistent with Madden's view that male power prohibits competition between males and females by arranging work in a discriminatory fashion. The "more productive" male worker, therefore, does not eliminate the female worker, and overall costs can be kept down because women will work for less than men.

San Antonio entered the Depression with a well-entrenched system of occupational segregation that had been inherited from a pattern of national economic expansion and former local prosperity. Anglo males had defined jobs to ensure the maintenance of their superior economic position. A sudden change in the labor supply not accompanied by Depression, as in the instance of Mexican immigration in the 1920s, encouraged the expansion or reorganization of operations to employ workers at segregated tasks paying lower wages than those either blacks or Anglos would accept.

The definition, over time, of gender or ethnic lables within the occupational structure had built up a set of consumer expectations, reinforced

---

[5] Valerie Kincade Oppenheimer, *The Female Labor Force in the United States*, chap. 3. For a general discussion of dual-labor-market theory, see Francine D. Blau and Carol L. Jusenius, "Economic Definitions of Occupational Segregation," in Martha Blaxall and Barbara Reagan, eds., *Women and the Workplace: The Implications of Occupational Segregation*, pp. 188–89. The place of women in a labor market separate from that of men is seen by some economists as secondary or as a market in which the supply expands or contracts according to general market needs. Other labor theorists maintain that the female labor market is occupationally specific to the point that an abundance of male workers will not drive women from the labor market.

[6] Madden, *The Economics of Sex Discrimination*, pp. 73–77. For discussion of occupational stereotyping by sex, see Harriet Zellner, "The Determinants of Occupational Segregation," in Cynthia B. Lloyd, ed., *Sex, Discrimination, and the Division of Labor*, pp. 125–45; Elizabeth Faulkner Baker, *Technology and Woman's Work*, pts. 1–3.

by the same prejudices that had encouraged the labeling process originally, prejudices that demanded sex-specific of ethnic-specific labor in certain areas. Even in a time of depression it proved difficult to violate such consumer tastes. Until recently receptionists, telephone operators, and womenswear salespersons were expected to be women. It would have been necessary to pay men a premium to persuade them to occupy such "unmanly" jobs and a penalty may have been paid in lost business as well. Because employers could fill such jobs from the cheaper female labor pool, custom and profit maximization were understood to be compatible. The system did not break down in the Depression because employees are reluctant to step down the segregation ladder and, more important, because by then employers had become convinced through prejudice or traditional practice or both that their job definitions fit the skills of their workers by ethnicity and gender. To tamper with the system might encourage unionization or other worker protest despite the Depression.

The point at which custom and profit maximization appear to conflict for the employer of white-collar labor is the point that ethnic or racial discrimination enters. As long as racial discrimination persisted, black women, who for the most part had sufficient educational skills to hold lower-level white-collar jobs, could have been hired for these tasks at lower wages than those demanded by Anglos. Employers reckoned, however, that the costs in lost business and disruption by Anglo employees would have exceeded the savings achieved by employing black clerks or saleswomen. The general decline of wages during the Depression minimized the wage savings that employers might extract by hiring minority over majority workers, but racial and sex wage differentials remained, as the discriminatory codes of the NRA and the WPA demonstrated.[7]

If their occupational distance from Anglos is seen as a measure of their rejection by the dominant population, blacks were distinctly less acceptable to Anglos than were Mexican Americans, and black women were the least desirable coworkers of all. While male workers were much better

[7]Lois Scharf, *To Work and to Wed: Female Employment, Feminism, and the Great Depression*, pp. 46–53, 104, 153. William E. Leuchtenburg, *Franklin Roosevelt and the New Deal, 1932–1940* (New York, 1963), pp. 185–87; Harvard Sitkoff, *A New Deal for Blacks: The Emergence of Civil Rights as a National Issue*, vol. 1, *The Depression Decade* (New York, 1978), pp. 47–57; John E. Kirby, "The Roosevelt Administration and Blacks: An Ambivalent Legacy," in Barton J. Bernstein and Allen J. Matusow, eds., *Twentieth-Century America: Recent Interpretation*, 2d ed. (New York, 1972), pp. 267–89.

dispersed than women workers in all the city's occupations, only black women were overwhelmingly concentrated in a small sector of the occupational structure.

Occupational segregation is not itself an entirely convincing measure of Anglo male power unless the dominant group protected the most desirable occupations for its own members. The aggregate occupational prestige of each group in 1930, whether measured by the occupational scale of the National Opinion Research Center or the Duncan Socioeconomic Index, clearly demosntrates the occupational superiority of Anglos over blacks and Chicanos (table 32).[8] For both men and women the greatest contrasts exist between the status of Anglos and that of the minority groups, differences that correspond with the differences in political and economic power between Anglos and other San Antonians. Small differences in occupational presitge are not, however, a direct measure of socioeconomic status in San Antonio. Women of all ethnic groups consistently scored higher on both scales than did male members of their own ethnic group, and Chicanas scored slightly higher than blacks. In occupational prestige Anglo immigrants of both sexes ranked slightly ahead of native-born Anglos. While no information exists on the economic status of Anglo immigrants, contemporary accounts of Depression San Antonio reveal that blacks fared better economically than Hispanics (table 47).[9] Housing, disease, and death statistics throughout the 1930s indicate that the standard of living of Hispanics was inferior to that of blacks (tables 55–57).[10] Income statistics from the census of 1940 show that women, despite their advantages in occupational status in 1930, ranked far below men in income. Of all experienced workers in the labor force, 59 percent of women as opposed to 43 percent of men earned less than $400 in 1940. At the opposite end of the income scale 0.2 percent of females and 2.8 percent of males earned $3,000 or more.

[8]For table 32, an estimation of the average occupational prestige of each of the eight population groups distinguished in the census of 1930 by sex and race or ethnicity was computed by weighing each individual in the census according to his or her ranking on the Duncan and the NORC scales and dividing the total of the weights on each scale of the eight separate groups by the number of workers in each group. Albert J. Reiss, Jr., et al., discuss both prestige scales in *Occupation and Social Status*.

[9]Audrey Granneberg, "Maury Maverick's San Antonio," *Survey Graphic* 27, no. 7 (July, 1939):423; T. R. Picnot, "The Businessman's Interest in Decent Standards of Living" (mimeographed copy of press release, April 20, 1942).

[10]*Annual Report of the Department of Health, San Antonio, Texas* (1927–40).

For men as well as women the occupational structure revealed the inferior status of blacks and Mexican Americans, though occupational segregation was not as severe among men as it was among women. Mexican-American males accounted for the vast majority of agriculture workers and laborers in San Antonio, these two categories accounting for 35 percent of Hispanic male workers. The other numerically important category of employment for Mexican-American men was domestic and personal service, which occupied 10.8 percent of Hispanic male workers and 35.0 percent of black male workers. Within the skilled crafts both blacks and Mexican Americans had some representation, but Anglos held the clear advantage. Hispanic men held a proportionate share of or dominated positions in baking, blacksmithing, brick and stone masonry, shoemaking, and tailoring. In contrast, blacks held their own in the skilled trades as firemen, boilermakers, and auto mechanics, firemen and boilermakers being the two smallest categories of craftsmen in the census report. Most factory operatives in San Antonio were women, with operatives accounting for only 3.3 percent of the entire male work force. Both blacks and Hispanics were underrepresented as owners or managers of San Antonio's commercial establishments, but Hispanics were represented among retail dealers in a proportion equal to that of Anglos. In the professions blacks and Hispanics of both sexes were clearly disadvantaged, but blacks held proportionately more positions in the professions than did Mexican Americans. The differing definitions of caste applied to blacks and Hispanics demanded a separate black professional sector to serve a segregated population but did not require total segregation of Hispanics from Anglo professional services.

The application of substitution-effect economic models of female labor-force participation to the San Antonio economy demonstrates that Chicana workers were the city's cheapest labor.[11] Since Mexican-American males had earnings inferior to those of Anglo and black men, the value of a daughter's labor in maintaining the home was less and the value of her earning power to the family economy was more than they were in Anglo or black families. The potential wage at which market earnings "substituted" for unpaid homework was therefore lower for Mexican-American than for black or Anglo women. Not until the establishment of WPA sewing rooms

---

[11]Elyce J. Rotella, "Women's Labor Force Participation and the Growth of Clerical Employment in the United States, 1870–1930" (Ph.D. diss., University of Pennsylvania, 1977); Oppenheimer, chap. 5.

and the enforcement of the Fair Labor Standards Act of 1937 were black or Anglo women attracted to San Antonio's garment work and food-processing industries in significant numbers.

The age structure and the marital status of the Mexican-American and black female labor force reveal the relationship between occupational segregation and work-force participation. A number of jobs in pecan shelling and in the needle trades were available for young workers. Much labor in the garment industry functioned through the homework system, and young girls often learned the work by assisting older relatives. Mexican-American women workers consequently entered the job market in their early to middle teens. In contrast, the employer of domestic labor looked for the maturity and responsibility of an adult for home maintenance, child care, and cooking, and young women suffered age discrimination in such employment. In distinction to all other occupations, the woman who kept her home and raised her children was considered best prepared to enter domestic labor. Since most San Antonio domestic workers were black and most black workers were domestics, black girls were less likely to be in the work force than were their youthful Hispanic counterparts. The jobs available for black women encouraged a pattern of labor-force participation in which married black women were in the work force in a much larger proportion than that of married Mexican Americans or Anglos.

Historian Winifred Bolin and others have observed that nationally the Depression was marked by an increase in the work-force participation of married women.[12] San Antonio women participated in this change. Noting that middle-class wives demonstrated an especially sharp increase in the work rates, Bolin argued that middle-class women went to work to satisfy consumer expectations that rose despite the Depression and could not be satisfied in a single-income family. In San Antonio male employment decreased over the decade, which indicates that married women entered the labor market to replace rather than supplement the earnings of family

[12]Winifred D. Wandersee Bolin, "The Economics of Middle-Income Family Life: Working Women During the Great Depression," *Journal of American History* 65 (June, 1978):60–74. The view that wives entered the labor force to replace the lost income of other family members was argued by Alba M. Edwards in *Sixteenth Census of the United States: Population*, vol. 4, *Comparative Occupation Statistics for the United States, 1870 to 1943*. For a detailed discussion of women's labor-force behavior in the Depression see Clarence D. Long, *The Labor Force under Changing Income and Employment*, Publication of the National Bureau of Economic Research (Princeton, N.J., 1958).

members. The vast majority of women workers in San Antonio, married and single, lacked sufficient income to support an improved standard of living. The composition of the local female work force changed during the Depression not because of changing attitudes or desires but because improved employment opportunities for some women coincided with their need to work.

Tables

TABLE 1. San Antonio, Population by Sex and Race, 1920–50

Year	White Female *	White Male *	Black Female	Black Male
1920	73,058	71,741	7,499	6,842
1930	107,920	105,190	9,794	8,184
1940	119,581	114,441	10,555	8,680
1950	197,217	181,680	15,574[†]	13,971[†]

SOURCE: U.S. Bureau of the Census, *Census of Population, 1950: A Report of the Seventeenth Decennial Census of the United States*, vol. 2, pt. 43, *Texas*.

*White category includes Mexican-American population.

[†]Classification used in 1950 is "nonwhite."

TABLE 2. San Antonio, Population by Age, Sex, and Ethnicity or Race, 1930

Age, Years	Native White		Foreign-born White		Black		Other Races (99% Mexican-American)	
	Male	Female	Male	Female	Male	Female	Male	Female
Under 5	4,587	4,428	7	8	536	562	5,401	5,555
5– 9	5,345	5,207	30	32	716	727	5,812	5,875
10–14	4,721	4,687	40	32	649	683	4,260	4,294
15–19	5,244	5,454	107	113	728	982	4,172	4,650
20–24	7,402	6,835	207	204	913	1,216	4,099	4,516
25–29	6,365	6,289	290	291	834	1,203	3,384	3,877
30–34	5,569	5,790	313	285	829	1,060	2,607	2,815
35–44	9,836	9,456	852	707	1,529	1,716	4,559	4,857
45–54	6,453	6,581	862	770	869	969	3,112	3,334
55–64	3,658	3,953	744	673	357	390	1,763	1,780
65–74	1,655	2,165	516	425	131	188	710	734
75 and older	628	774	259	270	66	91	320	301
Unknown	34	32	1	1	7	7	18	22
Totals	61,047	61,651	4,228	3,811	8,184	9,794	40,217	42,610

SOURCE: U.S. Bureau of the Census, *Fifteenth Census of the United States, 1930: Population*, vol. 2, *Texas*, table 12.

TABLE 3. San Antonio, Population by Age, Sex, and Ethnicity and Race, 1940

Age, Years	Native White		Foreign-born White		Black		Other Races	
	Male	Female	Male	Female	Male	Female	Male	Female
Under 5	9,825	9,928	12	11	570	573	34	30
5– 9	9,771	9,646	18	27	613	595	30	37
10–14	10,330	10,273	100	110	631	724	38	30
15–19	11,300	11,435	340	379	750	854	40	29
20–24	11,228	10,486	591	663	767	1,013	29	18
25–29	9,405	9,229	1,020	1,293	809	1,137	29	12
30–34	7,834	8,336	1,396	1,650	801	1,038	26	10
35–39	6,823	7,269	1,663	2,014	780	1,123	31	14
40–44	5,852	6,276	1,438	1,666	787	981	26	11
45–49	5,021	5,449	1,510	1,612	708	766	40	10
50–54	4,132	4,462	1,249	1,356	483	522	27	3
55–59	3,156	3,450	1,206	1,264	331	366	14	2
60–64	2,527	2,926	800	975	215	237	10	2
65–69	1,847	2,358	684	758	204	303	6	1
70–74	1,179	1,502	490	559	125	162	3	0
75 and older	1,127	1,601	567	616	106	161	4	1

SOURCE: U.S. Bureau of the Census, Sixteenth Census of the United States, 1940: Population, vol. 4, pt. 4, Texas, table D-35.

TABLE 4. San Antonio, Marital Status and Sex Ratios of Males and Females Ages Fifteen Years and Older, 1930

Status and Sex	Anglo		Mexican-American		Black	
	Number	Percent	Number	Percent	Number	Percent
Single males	17,908	35.5	9,153	37.3	1,781	28.4
Married males	29,596	58.6	13,681	55.8	3,893	62.0
Widowed and divorced males	3,004	5.9	1,687	6.9	608	9.7
Single females	12,825	25.1	7,509	28.0	1,570	20.1
Married females	29,463	57.5	14,277	53.3	4,095	52.4
Widowed and divorced females	8,762	17.2	5,018	18.7	2,155	27.6
Males per 1,000 females	990		920		803	

SOURCE: U.S. Bureau of the Census, *Fifteenth Census of the United States, 1930: Population*, vol. 3, pt. 2, *Texas*.

TABLE 5. San Antonio, Marital Status and Sex Ratios of Males and Females Ages Fifteen Years and Older, 1940

Status and Sex	Black		White	
	Number	Percent	Number	Percent
Single males	2,021	28.3	30,388	36.0
Married males	4,491	62.8	48,860	57.9
Widowed males	430	6.0	3,472	4.1
Divorced males	209	2.9	1,665	2.0
Single females	1,729	19.7	22,968	25.6
Married females	4,614	52.6	50,021	55.8
Widowed females	1,971	22.5	13,510	15.1
Divorced females	462	5.3	3,087	3.4
Males per 1,000 females	815		942	

SOURCE: U.S. Bureau of the Census, *Sixteenth Census of the United States, 1940: Population*, vol. 2, pt. 6, *Texas*.

TABLE 6. San Antonio, Female Marital Status by Age and Ethnicity or Race, 1930

Ages, Years	Number				
	Single	Married	Widowed	Divorced	Unknown
Native Anglo					
15–19	4,666	735	11	38	4
20–24	3,078	3,438	94	222	3
25–34	2,086	9,000	462	530	1
35–44	1,094	7,049	911	401	1
45–54	598	4,436	1,341	302	4
55–64	330	2,042	1,496	84	1
65 and older	213	756	1,945	24	1
Foreign-born Anglo					
15–19	108	5	0	0	0
20–24	117	84	1	2	0
25–34	145	387	22	22	0
35–44	141	485	66	14	1
45–54	120	502	128	20	0
55–64	70	350	248	5	0
65 and older	50	182	455	8	0
Black					
15–19	767	189	11	15	0
20–24	372	698	62	84	0
25–34	261	1,490	306	206	0
35–44	101	1,059	404	152	0
45–54	44	500	372	53	0
55–64	14	117	242	16	1
65 and older	9	42	220	8	0
Mexican-American (other races)					
15–19	3,818	750	26	55	1
20–24	1,923	2,335	112	145	1
25–34	1,172	4,790	450	278	2
35–44	362	3,519	800	176	0
45–54	147	1,938	1,172	77	0
55–64	57	759	939	21	4
65 and older	42	234	751	8	0

SOURCE: U.S. Bureau of the Census, *Fifteenth Census of the United States, 1930: Population*, vol. 2, *General Report*, pt. 5, table 29.

TABLE 7. San Antonio, Families with Homemakers, 1930

Families	Native-born Anglos		Foreign-born Anglos		Black		Mexican-American	
	Number	Percent	Number	Percent	Number	Percent	Number	Percent
With homemakers	29,574	97.2	3,262	94.4	4,593	94.8	16,240	95.6
With homemakers employed outside home	4,534	15.3	358	11.0	2,493	54.3	2,542	15.7
With homemakers employed in nonagricultural work at home	497	1.7	35	1.1	537	3.4	475	2.9

SOURCE: U.S. Bureau of the Census, *Fifteenth Census of the United States, 1930: Population*, vol. 5, *Texas*.

TABLE 8. San Antonio, Number and Percent of Households Headed by Women, 1930 and 1940*

	1930			
	Native-White	Foreign-born White	Black	Mexican-American and Other Races
Number	5,081	643	1,370	3,199
Percent of families	16.7	18.6	28.3	18.8

	1940	
	White[†]	Nonwhite
Number	12,837	1,933
Percent of families	22.5	32.6

SOURCES: U.S. Bureau of the Census, *Fifteenth Census of the United States, 1930: Population*, vol. 5, *Texas*; *Families in the United States by Type and Size, 1930*; *Sixteenth Census of the United States, 1940: Population*, vol. 2, pt. 6, *Texas*, vol. 4, pt. 4, *Texas*.

*In 1930, 83 percent of native-born Anglo families, 81 percent of Hispanic and foreign-born Anglo families and 72 percent of black families were headed by males. The sex ratios by age reveal that women most heavily outnumbered men in the young-adult years. The imbalance was most pronounced among blacks in the 25-to-29 year age bracket. For Anglos a serious imbalance did not exist until after age 65. Again the absence of young white men who were serving in the military distorted sex ratios in San Antonio. In 1940, after the World War II military buildup had begun, the male-female ratio among native-born whites had increased considerably, though it was unchanged among blacks.

In 1930 the sex ratio among Mexican Americans in the 25-to-29-year age category was considerably lower than that among Anglos but much higher than that among blacks. Although underreporting of both black and Mexican-American males can be suspected, there are reasons to accept the *pattern* of differences by sex and ethnicity if not the actual numbers. The higher reported incidence of female-headed families among blacks is congruent with the absence of males. In rural parts of the state where agricultural work was available in 1930, the sex ratios among blacks and Hispanic young adults were reversed. The literature on Texas migrant workers of the 1920s reveals that male migrant workers frequently traveled without their families but that the practice was most common among black farm workers. The age structure for married men and women shows that husbands overall were older than wives and that until age 50 men were more likely than women to be single. Ruth Alice Allen, *The Labor of Women in the Production of Cotton*, University of Texas Bulletin no. 3134 (Austin, 1931), pp. 27–32; Madeline Jaffee, "Rural Women in Unskilled Urban Labor" (Master's thesis, University of Texas, 1931), pp. 3–5.

†Mexican Americans were counted with whites in 1940.

TABLE 9. San Antonio, Family Size and Composition, 1930

Median family size
  Black: 2.63
  Foreign-born Anglo: 3.19
  Native-born Anglo: 3.06
  Mexican-American: 4.28
Children under 10 years of age per 100 females 15 years of age and older
  Black: 33.6
  Anglo: 38.5
  Mexican-American: 84.2
Families with no children under 10 years of age, number and percent
  Black: 3,499 (72.2%)
  Foreign-Born Anglo: 2,493 (72.2%)
  Native-born Anglo: 19,519 (64.2%)
  Mexican-American: 7,462 (43.9%)
Families with 1 or more children under 21 years of age but no children under 10,
    number and percent
  Black: 953 (19.7%)
  Foreign-born Anglo: 811 (23.5%)
  Native-born Anglo: 6,299 (30.0%)
  Mexican-American: 3,226 (19.0%)

SOURCE: U.S. Bureau of the Census, *Fifteenth Census of the United States, 1930: Population*, vol. 5, *Texas*, tables 5–6.

TABLE 10. San Antonio, Child-Woman Ratios, 1930 and 1940: Number of Children under Ten Years of Age per Female Ages Fifteen through Forty-four Years

1930	1940
Anglo: 0.555	White: 0.646
Mexican-American (other races): 1.093	Black: 0.384
Black: 0.462	

SOURCES: U.S. Bureau of the Census, *Fifteenth Census of the United States, 1930: Population*, vol. 3, pt. 2, *Texas*, table G; *Sixteenth Census of the United States: Population*, vol. 2, pt. 6, *Texas*, table D-35; ibid., vol. 4, pt. 4, *Texas*.

TABLE 11. San Antonio, Relationship of Females in Private Households, All Ages, to Head of Household, 1940

Relationship	Nonwhite		White	
	Number	Percent	Number	Percent
Total	10,719	100.0	117,158	100.0
Head	1,933	18.0	12,837	11.0
Wife	3,385	31.6	42,875	36.6
Child	2,849	26.6	44,222	37.7
Grandchild	308	2.9	2,920	2.5
Parent	287	2.7	3,508	3.0
Other relative	941	8.8	3,245	2.8
Lodger	835	7.8	3,330	2.8
Servant or hired hand	181	1.7	883	0.8

SOURCE: U.S. Bureau of the Census, *Sixteenth Census of the United States, 1940: Population*, vol. 4, pt. 4.

TABLE 12. San Antonio, Number and Percent of Families with Lodgers, 1930

Number of Lodgers per Family	Native Anglo		Foreign-born Anglo		Black		Mexican-American	
	Number	Percent	Number	Percent	Number	Percent	Number	Percent
One or more	2,072	6.8	220	6.4	513	10.6	571	3.4
Two or more	1,438	4.7	144	4.2	358	7.4	332	2.0

SOURCE: U.S. Bureau of the Census, *Fifteenth Census of the United States, 1930: Population*, vol. 3, pt. 6, *Texas*, table 12.

TABLE 13. San Antonio, Number and Percent of Families with Subfamilies and/or Lodgers, 1940

Number of Subfamilies and/or Lodgers*	Number of Families	Percent of All Families
One or more subfamilies	5,060	6.0
One or more lodgers	5,660	6.7
One or more lodgers and one or more subfamilies	1,080	1.3

SOURCE: Based on sample data from U.S. Bureau of the Census, *Sixteenth Census of the United States, 1940: Population: General Characteristics of Families*, table 74.
* A subfamily consists of an adult family member with his or her spouse and/or children.

TABLE 14. San Antonio, Illiteracy in Population, Ages Twenty-one Years and Older, by Race or Ethnicity, 1930

Race or Ethnicity	Number	Percent
Native white of native parentage	262	0.4
Native white of foreign or mixed parentage	139	0.8
Black	788	6.9
Mexican-American	11,369	27.9
Foreign-born white	241	3.2
Chinese	28	16.5

SOURCE: U.S. Bureau of the Census, *Fifteenth Census of the United States, 1930: Population*, vol. 2, *General Report: Statistics by Subjects*.

TABLE 15. San Antonio, School Attendance by Age, Sex, and Race or Ethnicity, 1930

Sex, Ethnicity or Race	Ages									
	5–6	7–13		14–15		16–17		18–20		21 and Older
	Number	Number	Percent	Number	Percent	Number	Percent	Number	Percent	Number
Sex										
Male	582	13,564	90.1	3,065	83.7	2,051	51.5	1,241	18.6	922
Female	596	13,495	89.7	2,965	77.1	1,999	46.7	1,073	14.2	846
Ethnicity or race										
Native-parentage white	617	11,681	95.5	2,899	90.4	2,184	64.1	1,375	21.8	1,010
Foreign or mixed-parentage white	70	1,786	94.2	442	86.3	406	62.8	252	23.6	247
Foreign-born white	4	92	—	39	—	54	—	53	29.6	120
Black	165	1,858	95.2	509	86.1	353	53.6	129	11.2	82
Other*	322	11,642	83.6	2,141	67.8	1,053	30.3	505	9.2	309

SOURCE: U.S. Bureau of the Census, *Fifteenth Census of the United States, 1930: Population*, vol. 2, *General Report: Statistics by Subjects*.
*More than 99 percent Mexican-American.

TABLE 16. San Antonio, Percentage of Foreign-born
Mexican Americans Unable to Speak English, 1930

Sex	Percentage of Mexican-American Population
United States	
Males	46.5
Females	66.0
Males and females	55.0
Texas	
Males and females	64.0

SOURCE: U.S. Bureau of the Census, *Fifteenth Census of the United States, 1930: Population*, vol. 2, *General Report: Statistics by Subjects*.

TABLE 17. San Antonio, Female Work-Force Participation, 1930 and 1940

Race or Ethnicity	Number of Workers	Population	Percent in Work Force
Women Ten Years of Age and Older, 1930			
Black	4,542	8,505	53.4
Native Anglo	13,191	52,015	25.4
Foreign-born Anglo	892	3,771	28.7
Mexican-American	7,316	31,180	23.5
Women Fourteen Years of Age and Older, 1940			
Black	4,862	8,825	55.1
Native white	21,991	76,803	28.6
Foreign-born white	3,641	14,846	24.5

Percentages of Women Fourteen and Older in the Work Force, 1930 and 1940

Race	1930	1940
White (including Mexican-American)	26.8	28.0
Black	57.0	55.1

SOURCES: U.S. Bureau of the Census, *Fifteenth Census of the United States, 1930: Population*, vol. 3, pt. 6, *Texas*; *Sixteenth Census of the United States, 1940: Population*, vol. 3, pt. 5, *Texas*.

TABLE 18. San Antonio, Labor-Force Participation of Mexican-American or
Spanish-surname Women Ages Fourteen Years and Older, 1930−60*

Year	Number of workers	Percent of work force
1930 (Mexican-American women)	7,294	27.1
1950 (Spanish-Surname women)	12,462	23.6
1960 (Spanish-Surname women)[†]	20,226	26.8

SOURCES: U.S. Bureau of the Census, *Fifteenth Census of the United States, 1930: Population*, vol. 3, pt. 6, *Texas*; *Census of the Population, 1950: Special Report on the Spanish-Surname Population*; *Eighteenth Decennial Census of the United States, Census of Population, 1960*: vol. 1, pt. 45, *Texas*.

 *No figures reported for 1940.

 †Figures based on San Antonio Standard Metropolitan Area.

TABLE 19. San Antonio, Marital Status of Women Workers Ages Fifteen Years and Older, 1930 and 1940*

Race or Ethnicity	1930 Single and Unknown Number	Percent of Population	Married Number	Percent of Population	Widowed and Divorced Number	Percent of Population
Black	881	56.2	2,051	50.1	1,604	74.4
Mexican-American	3,784	50.3	1,375	9.6	2,063	41.1
Native Anglo	6,786	56.1	3,457	12.6	2,937	37.7
Foreign-born Anglo	517	68.8	165	8.3	207	20.9

Totals	Single and Unknown	Married	Widowed and Divorced
1930			
Number of female workers	11,968	7,048	6,811
Percent of female workers	46.4	27.3	26.3
Percent of population in labor force	54.6	14.7	42.7
1940			
Number of female workers	12,899	10,364	7,263
Percent of female workers	42.3	34.0	23.8
Percent of population in labor force*	52.2	19.0	38.2

SOURCES: U.S. Bureau of the Census, *Fifteenth Census of the United States, 1930: Population*, vol. 3, pt. 2, *Texas*; *Sixteenth Census of the United States, 1940: Population*, vol. 2, pt. 6, *Texas*.
    *Figures are distorted slightly by the inclusion of 33 female workers ages 14 years.

TABLE 20. San Antonio, Female Labor-Force Participation by Age and Ethnicity or Race, 1930

Age, Years	Native White		Foreign-born White		Black		Other Races	
	Number	Percent	Number	Percent	Number	Percent	Number	Percent
10–14	21	0.4	3	9.4	6	0.9	94	2.2
15–19	1,663	30.5	38	33.6	314	43.1	1,529	32.9
20–24	3,118	45.6	97	47.5	754	82.6	1,550	34.3
25–34	3,696	30.6	188	32.7	1,494	66.0	1,777	26.6
35–44	2,468	26.1	218	30.8	1,117	65.1	1,230	25.3
45–54	1,413	21.5	185	24.0	590	60.9	757	22.8
55–64	598	15.1	116	17.2	199	51.0	292	16.4
65–74	175	8.1	35	8.2	51	27.1	76	10.4
75 and older	23	3.0	11	16.7	12	13.2	9	3.0
Unknown	16		1		5		2	

SOURCE: U.S. Bureau of the Census, *Fifteenth Census of the United States, 1930: Population*, vol. 4, *Texas*, table 9.

TABLE 21. San Antonio, Youthful Workers by Age, Ethnicity or Race, and Sex, 1930

Age, Years	Native White		Foreign-born White		Black		Other Races	
	Female	Male	Female	Male	Female	Male	Female	Male
10–13	6	18	2	1	3	6	22	52
14	15	41	1	0	3	8	72	71
15	70	120	0	3	8	26	158	189
16	177	245	8	2	26	42	259	406
17	322	387	6	4	54	81	314	550
18 and 19	1,094	1,612	24	31	226	221	798	1,449

SOURCE: U.S. Bureau of the Census, *Fifteenth Census of the United States, 1930: Population*, vol. 3, pt. 2, *Texas*.

TABLE 22. San Antonio, Females Ages Fifteen to Forty-four Years: Labor-Force
Participation by Marital Status, 1930

Race or Ethnicity	Single and Unknown		Married	
	Number	Percent	Number	Percent
	Females 15–19			
Totals	3,229	34.5	234	13.9
Native Anglo	1,513	32.3	117	15.9
Foreign-born Anglo	38	35.2	0	0.0
Black	226	29.5	73	38.6
Mexican-American (other races)	1,452	38.0	44	5.9
	Females 20–24			
Totals	3,879	70.7	1,167	17.8
Native Anglo	2,274	73.9	634	18.4
Foreign-born Anglo	87	74.4	9	10.7
Black	292	78.5	334	47.9
Mexican-American (other races)	1,226	63.8	190	8.1
	Females 25–44			
Totals	3,995	74.5	4,467	16.1
Native Anglo	2,460	77.4	2,155	13.4
Foreign-born Anglo	288	79.7	100	11.5
Black	307	84.8	1,338	52.5
Mexican-American (other races)	1,000	65.2	874	10.6

SOURCE: U.S. Bureau of the Census, *Fifteenth Census of the United States, 1930: Population*, vol. 3, pt. 2, *Texas*.

TABLE 23. San Antonio, Female Labor-Force Participation by Color, Age, and Family Status, Sample Statistics, 1940

	Family Status									
	Married, Husband Present				Married, Husband Absent, Widowed, or Divorced				Single	
	Without Children		With Children		Without Children		With Children			
Color and Age	Number	Percent	Number	Percent	Number	Percent	Number	Percent	Number	Percent
Nonwhite women										
18–64	1,800	54.2	180	17.6	1,900	79.8	180	64.3	940	72.3
18–24	320	57.1	40	12.5	280	100.0	60	60.0	480	64.9
25–29	480	72.7	80	25.0	180	81.8	20	100.0	180	75.0
30–34	300	62.5	—	—	220	100.0	60	75.0	100	100.0
35–39	240	50.0	20	16.7	360	78.3	20	50.0	140	77.8
40–44	280	60.9	20	25.0	300	88.2	20	50.0	20	100.0
45–64	180	26.7	20	33.3	560	65.1	—	—	20	100.0
White women										
18–64	5,820	17.7	1,800	7.4	6,960	44.7	1,780	57.1	11,300	64.4
18–24	860	24.3	120	2.6	400	47.6	220	40.7	5,680	60.0
25–29	1,080	33.7	640	9.5	600	73.2	460	74.2	2,060	75.8
30–34	820	25.6	300	5.4	920	76.7	520	68.4	1,240	75.6
35–39	960	22.2	400	10.2	1,300	73.9	260	52.0	680	73.9
40–44	660	13.2	260	11.6	1,200	58.8	240	48.0	580	63.0
45–64	1,460	10.7	80	6.6	2,540	28.5	80	23.5	1,060	53.0

SOURCE: U.S. Bureau of the Census, *Sixteenth Census of the United States, 1943, Population*, vol. 1, *The Labor Force (Sample Statistics), Employment and Family Characteristics of Women*.

TABLE 24. San Antonio, Female Family Heads and Contributory Workers, 1930*

Heads and Workers	Native Anglo	Foreign-born Anglo	Black	Mexican-American (Other Races)
Number female family heads	5,081	643	1,370	3,199
Total women workers	13,191	892	4,542	7,316
First estimation of female contributory workers	8,110 (61.5%)	249 (27.9%)	3,172 (69.8%)	4,177 (57.1%)
Second estimation of female contributory workers	8,099	246	2,932	4,023

*Contributory workers are defined as workers neither living alone nor heading families, who therefore combine their incomes with those of spouses or fathers and possibly other family members. Contributory workers were estimated by subtracting number of female family heads (women living alone or with dependents) from the total number of female workers, on the assumption that all female family heads were in the work force. Consequently, estimates are maximal figures. A second method of estimating the number of female contributory workers produced highly comparable estimates. Under this method the number of divorced and widowed female workers was subtracted from the number of female family heads to produce an estimate of the number of single women workers who maintained independent households. This number was subtracted from the total number of single workers to obtain an estimate of the number of single women workers who boarded in families or remained in the parental home. To these estimates the numbers of married women workers were added. Thus the second estimation of female contributory workers is inflated by two critical assumptions: that all divorced and widowed women workers were family heads and that boarders constitute contributory workers in the families in which they board. Both estimations are distorted by ignoring the unknown number of women workers who lived with their employers and therefore were neither contributory workers nor family heads. The second estimations yielded the following results:

Heads and Workers	Native Anglo Workers	Foreign-born Anglo Workers	Black Workers	Mexican-American Workers
Number of female family heads	5,081	643	1,370	3,199
Number of widowed and divorced women workers	2,937	207	1,604	2,063
Estimated number of single female workers heading households	2,144	436	$-234 = 0$	1,136
Estimated number of single female workers living at home or boarding in families	4,642	81	881	2,648
Number of married women workers	3,457	165	2,051	1,375
Total female contributory workers	8,099	246	2,932	4,023

TABLE 25. San Antonio, Families by Number and Status of Workers, 1930

Families and Workers	Native Anglos		Foreign-born Anglos		Black		Other Races	
	Number of Families	Number of Workers	Number of Families	Number of Workers	Number of Families	Number of Workers	Number of Families	Number of Workers
Total families	30,418		3,454		4,847		16,984	
Families with								
0 workers	2,350		449		161		606	
1 worker	19,290		1,856		2,259		9,637	
2 workers	6,321	12,642	737	1,474	1,684	3,388	3,867	7,734
3 workers	1,799	5,397	283	848	499	1,497	1,654	4,963
4 or more	658	2,632	129	516	234	936	1,221	4,884
Estimated total contributory workers		20,671		2,839		5,821		17,581
Estimated female contributory workers		8,110		249		3,172		4,117
Estimated male contributory workers		12,561		2,590		2,649		13,464
Estimated total noncontributory male workers*		14,209		1,213		889		6,438

SOURCE: U.S. Bureau of the Census, Fifteenth Census of the United States, 1930: Population, vol. 6, Texas.
*Workers who headed one-worker families and thus did not contribute income to a family other than their own.

TABLE 26. San Antonio, Number of Workers in Occupations by Race or Ethnicity, and Sex, 1930

Category	Native White	Foreign-born White	Black	Other Races
		Males		
Professional-service	2,881	337	226	599
Trade	10,346	1,072	578	3,532
Agriculture, forestry, fishing, and extraction of minerals	925	85	129	1,362
Manufacturing and mechanical occupations	10,457	940	1,327	9,880
Transportation and communications	3,996	143	1,232	3,231
Clerical	4,098	179	60	438
Domestic and personal service	1,600	260	2,001	2,396
Public service	6,219	445	164	649
		Females		
Professional-service	2,680	288	174	210
Trade	2,013	139	23	670
Agriculture and extraction of minerals	21	6	2	27
Manufacturing and mechanical occupations	1,013	91	159	3,226
Transportation and communication	883	7	5	13
Clerical	3,754	97	33	239
Domestic and personal service	2,802	264	4,142	2,930
Public service	25	0	4	1

SOURCE: U.S. Bureau of the Census, *Fifteenth Census of the United States, 1930: Population*, vol. 4, *Texas*.

TABLE 27. San Antonio, Women Workers Ages Fifteen Years and Older by Occupational Sector, Age, and Marital Status, 1930

			Single and Unknown			
		Percent	Ages, Years			
Category	Total Number	of Category	15–19	20–24	25–44	45 and Older
All occupations	11,968	100	3,229	3,879	3,995	865
Agriculture and extraction of minerals	27	—	10	6	4	7
Manufacturing and mechanical industries	2,323	19.4	872	720	621	110
Transportation and communication	597	5.0	326	185	83	3
Trade	1,201	10.0	407	364	350	80
Public service	6	—	0	2	4	0
Professional service	2,167	18.1	152	641	1,063	311
Domestic and personal service	2,996	25.0	923	903	905	265
Clerical	2,651	22.2	539	1,058	965	89

SOURCE: U.S. Bureau of the Census, *Fifteenth Census of the United States, 1930: Population*, vol. 4, *Occupations, Texas*, table 18.

Total Number	Percent of Category	Married					Widowed and Divorced	
		Ages, Years					Total Number	Percent
		15–19	20–24	25–34	36–44	45 and Older		
7,048	100	234	1,167	2,633	1,834	1,180	6,801	100
14	—	0	3	2	4	5	12	
935	13.3	28	117	320	265	205	1,171	17.2
219	3.1	27	86	90	15	1	87	1.3
911	12.9	27	136	301	275	172	727	10.7
16	—	0	1	5	5	5	8	
677	9.6	6	86	269	188	128	506	7.4
3,367	47.8	108	518	1,206	917	618	3,731	54.9
909	12.9	38	220	440	165	46	559	8.2

TABLE 28. San Antonio, Employed Persons and Persons Seeking Work, Ages Fourteen Years and Older, by Occupation, Sex, and Race, 1940

	Male			Female		
Category	White	Black	Other Races	White	Black	Other Races
Professional, technical, and kindred						
Employed	3,376	162	2	3,202	137	1
Unemployed	134	17	0	80	14	0
Farmers and farm managers						
Employed	141	3	0	15	0	0
Unemployed	18	1	0	0	0	0
Managers, officials, and proprietors						
Employed	7,991	108	106	1,296	37	7
Unemployed	177	0	0	16	1	0
Clerical sales and kindred						
Employed	11,432	106	45	6,757	56	17
Unemployed	764	5	2	538	7	0
Protective service workers						
Employed	8,285	142	15	12	3	0
Unemployed	94	1	0	0	0	0
Craftsmen, foremen, and kindred						
Employed	9,282	300	2	206	6	0
Unemployed	1,184	45	1	14	0	0
Operatives and kindred						
Employed	8,390	775	12	3,469	149	1
Unemployed	1,140	95	0	699	38	0
Private household workers						
Employed	513	363	13	2,705	3,224	1
Unemployed	130	86	0	415	388	0
Service workers except private household						
Employed	3,150	1,886	32	3,305	535	4
Unemployed	321	184	1	263	30	0
Farm laborers and foremen						
Employed	396	14	0	42	1	0
Unemployed	466	7	0	39	1	0

TABLE 28. (*continued*)

Category	Male			Female		
	White	Black	Other Races	White	Black	Other Races
Laborers except farm and mine						
Employed	3,949	792	6	60	3	0
Unemployed	2,751	262	0	31	6	0
Occupation not reported						
Employed	388	25	0	171	12	0
Unemployed	188	19	1	91	21	0

SOURCE: U.S. Bureau of the Census, *Sixteenth Census of the United States, 1940: Population*, vol. 3, *The Labor Force*, pt. 5, *Texas*, table 13.

TABLE 29. San Antonio Standard Metropolitan Area, Occupational Structure of Employed Persons by Sex and Race, 1950

Category	Male			Female		
	White	Black	Other Races	White	Black	Other Races
Professional, technical, and kindred workers	7,737	271	6	5,556	235	5
Farmers and farm managers	2,126	29	4	81	5	0
Managers, officials, and proprietors	14,295	258	116	2,452	114	3
Clerical workers	8,912	325	14	14,718	153	14
Sales workers	9,864	67	50	4,883	49	23
Craftsmen, foremen, and kindred workers	23,763	816	12	748	29	0
Operations and kindred workers	16,513	1,547	22	6,334	300	5
Private-household workers	126	150	4	2,020	3,183	3
Service workers except private household	6,596	2,747	39	5,448	1,589	6
Laborers except farm and mine	9,861	1,392	5	236	69	0
Occupations not reported	1,115	88	6	491	45	2

SOURCE: U.S. Bureau of the Census, *Seventeenth Census of the United States, 1950: Population*, vol. 2, *Characteristics of the Population*, pt. 43, *Detailed Characteristics*, table 77.

TABLE 30. San Antonio, Numbers of Female Workers by Occupation Group and Ethnic Grouping, 1930

Category	Black	Native white	Foreign-born white	Other Races*
Manufacturing and	159	1,013	91	3,226
Mechanical industries	(3.5%)	(7.7%)	(10.3%)	(44.3%)
Transportation and	5	883	7	13
communication	(0.1%)	(6.7%)	(0.8%)	(0.2%)
Trade	23	2,013	139	670
	(0.5%)	(15.3%)	(15.7%)	(9.2%)
Professions	174	2,680	288	210
	(3.8%)	(20.4%)	(35.5%)	(2.3%)
Domestic and personal	4,142	2,802	264	2,930
service	(91.3%)	(21.3%)	(29.8%)	(40.2%)
Clerical	33	3,754	97	239
	(0.7%)	(28.6%)	(10.9%)	(3.3%)
Total	4,536	13,145	886	7,288

Other occupations, all races: 86

Total workers: 25,941

SOURCE: U.S. Bureau of the Census, *Fifteenth Census of the United States, 1930: Population*, vol. 3, pt. 2, *Texas*, table 12.

*Mexican Americans were classified with "other races" in 1930 and constituted 99 percent of that category in San Antonio.

TABLE 31. San Antonio, Regressions of Occupational Structures by Gender and Race or Ethnicity, 1930*

Category	Anglo Females, Native-born	Anglo Females, Foreign-born	Black Females	Mexican-American Females	Anglo Males, Native-born	Anglo Males, Foreign-born	Black Males	Mexican-American Males
Anglo females, native-born	—	0.84936	0.38842	0.43148	0.50075	0.50536	0.43156	0.28939
Anglo females, foreign-born	—	—	0.52294	0.51029	0.40927	0.50514	0.47177	0.28793
Black females	—	—	—	0.67410	0.04846	0.12762	0.61006	0.17250
Mexican-American females	—	—	—	—	0.48400	0.55016	0.72795	0.69265
Anglo males, native-born	—	—	—	—	—	0.96096	0.50371	0.72539
Anglo males, foreign-born	—	—	—	—	—	—	0.51897	0.72193
Black males	—	—	—	—	—	—	—	0.73331
Mexican-American males	—	—	—	—	—	—	—	—

*The regressions plot the number of persons of each category in a specific occupation against the number of persons in each of the other categories in the same occupation. The entire work force was classified into 156 occupations ($N = 156$).

The series of bivariate regressions used to evaluate occupational segregation in this study were calculated by plotting the number of persons by sex and by race or ethnicity in a specific occupation against the number of persons of another sex-race classification in the same occupation. The total population was classified according to 156 occupational labels. The regression coefficients are presented as a matrix in table 31 above. The square of the coefficient indicates the estimated percentage of similarity between the occupational structures of any two groups. Table 37 presents an assessment of the occupational prestige of each group, which is discussed in appendix A.

A comparison of the occupational structure of single women in all ethnic and racial groups with that of widowed or divorced women suggests that the employment options of these two groups were very different. It was only in the service occupations, where the least skill was required, that widowed and divorced women had a numerical advantage over single workers. The data do not permit a breakdown of the occupational categories by marital status controlling for ethnicity, but even without this information some tentative observations can be drawn. In 1930 single workers were about evenly matched with the widowed and divorced in manufacturing and trade, but single women had a clear advantage in communications, the professions, and clerical work. Some of this imbalance obviously reflects the racial or ethnic differences in labor-force participation by marital status, but it also reflects the skill disadvantage of the returning worker or preference for the younger worker in particular occupations. The majority of black workers were married and the vast majority of blacks were domestic workers, but widowed and divorced service workers outnumbered married service workers, indicating that the concentration of widowed and divorced in this category is not wholly accounted for by the occupational choice of blacks.

TABLE 32. San Antonio, Mean Occupational Prestige of Ethnic Groups, 1930

Source of Ranking	Native-born Anglo		Foreign-born Anglo		Black		Mexican American	
	Females	Males	Females	Males	Females	Males	Females	Males
National Opinion Research Center	43.4	40.3	41.2	39.4	12.8	14.5	18.7	16.9
Duncan Socio-economic Index	66.1	64.3	64.4	64.1	48.6	48.1	52.4	53.4

TABLE 33. San Antonio Standard Metropolitan Area, Female Occupational Structure, 1960

Category	Anglo	Nonwhite	Spanish-surnamed
Total workers	54,559	7,584	19,220
Professional, technical, and kindred	8,554	375	1,079
Farmers and farm managers	136	0	9
Managers, officials	2,918	126	487
Clerical and kindred	19,953	500	4,168
Sales	4,786	115	1,653
Craftsmen, foremen, and kindred	632	67	334
Operatives and kindred	2,653	270	4,982
Private-household workers	5,069	3,616	1,739
Service workers not in private household	6,665	1,993	3,306
Farm laborers and foremen	172	8	94
Laborers except farm and mine	166	49	191
Not reported	2,855	465	1,178

SOURCE: U.S. Bureau of the Census, *Eighteenth Decennial Census of the United States, 1960: Census of Population*, vol. 1, pt. 45, *Texas*.

Note to Tables 34 through 38

Tables 34 through 38 have been compiled from a sample of 1,004 female workers drawn from the John F. Worley Directory Company, *San Antonio, Texas, City Directory, 1934–1935*. Women were classified as Mexican-American on the basis of Spanish surnames; the absence of racial indicators prevented distinguishing blacks from whites. Roughly one-third of the sample, the same proportion as in the female population, were Spanish-surnamed women. There are undoubtedly errors in determining ethnicity from surnames. While there was not a significant number of Hispanic-named persons from national backgrounds other than Mexican, intermarriage between Anglos and Hispanics would cause some errors in the classification. In San Antonio, however, intermarriage was rare during the 1930s, and exogamy involved marriage between Anglo males and Hispanic females rather than between Hispanic males and Anglo females. Benjamin Spencer Bradshaw, "Some Demographic Aspects of Marriage: A Comparative Study of Three Ethnic Groups" (master's thesis, University of Texas, 1960); Leo Grebler, Joan W. Moore, and Ralph C. Guzman, *The Mexican-American People: The Nation's Second Largest Minority*, pp. 300–303, 405–12.

Division of the city-directory sample into Hispanic and non-Hispanic categories highlights the intensity of occupational segregation and its relationship to residential segregation. The directory also provides more specific job labels than does the census report and, therefore, a finer indication of occupational segregation. Of the total names, 310, or 31 percent of the sample, were Hispanic, a slightly higher percentage than the 29 percent of the female workforce who were Hispanic enumerated in the Census of 1930. Only 22 of 127 professional women in the sample and 50 of 310 sales and clerical workers were Mexican American. In contrast, Hispanic women accounted for nearly half of the 571 handworkers, operatives, and service workers in the sample. Table 36, in which Hispanic and non-Hispanic workers are divided into a category of white- and pink-collar positions and a second category of industrial, manufacturing, and service jobs, indicates the occupational disparity between Mexican-American and other women. Hispanic women were much less likely to be white- or pink-collar workers than were other women in the sample. In Depression San Antonio residential segregation by ethnicity and occupation mirrored the pattern of female occupational segregation. Although the census and the Women's Bureau study are not helpful in studying this relationship, city directories yield useful data.

TABLE 34. San Antonio, Female Workers, 1934–35 Directory Sample and 1930 Census Figures*

Female Working Heads of Families

Ethnicity	Number of Women Workers	Women Living Alone or with Children		Number of Families with Males Present	Number of Families with Males Absent	Number of Families with Male Workers	Number of Families with Additional Female Workers
		Number	Percent				
Spanish-surnamed	310	133	73.2	78	149	83	31
Other	694	367	72.2	97	404	195	54

Household Composition of Female Workers, 1930 Census

Race	Number of Working Women	Female Family Heads[+]	
		Number	Percent
Black	4,542	1,370	30.2
Native white	13,191	5,081	38.5
Foreign-born white	892	643	72.1
Other races[‡]	7,316	3,199	43.7

*Of 1,004 observations, 35 are missing. Corrected chi square = 120.21 with 1 degree of freedom. Significance = 0.000. Phi = 0.35445. Contingency coefficient = 0.33409.

[+]Persons living alone were counted as family heads.

[‡]Mexican-American. The categories are those used in the census of 1930.

TABLE 35. San Antonio, Occupational Distribution of 1930 and 1940
Occupational Censuses of Women Workers and 1934–35 City Directory Sample*

Category	Sample	1930 Census	1940 Census
Manufacturing and	208	4,489	4,610
mechanical	(20.8%)	(17.3%)	(16.7%)
Transportation, trade,	365	7,876	8,708
and clerical	(36.4%)	(30.4%)	(31.5%)
Domestic and personal	263	10,138	10,858
service	(26.2%)	(39.0%)	(39.3%)
Professions	127	3,352	3,433
	(12.7%)	(12.9%)	(12.4%)
All other	41	86	-0-
Total	1,004	25,941	27,609

*Of 1,004 observations, 35 are missing. Corrected chi square = 120.21 with 1 degree of freedom. Significance = 0.000. Phi = 0.35445. Contingency coefficient = 0.33409.

TABLE 36. San Antonio, Women's Occupations by Upper- and Lower-Status Categories, 1934*

Occupational Status	Hispanic Women	Other Women
White- or pink-collar		
Number	75	425
Row percent	15.0	85.0
Column percent	25.1	63.4
Total percent	7.7	43.9
Industrial, manufacturing,		
or service occupations		
Number	224	245
Row percent	47.8	52.2
Column percent	74.9	36.3
Total percent	23.1	25.3

*Of 1,004 observations, 35 are missing. Corrected chi square = 120.21 with 1 degree of freedom. Significance = 0.000. Phi = 0.35445. Contingency coefficient = 0.33409.

TABLE 37. San Antonio, Lower-Status Occupations of Hispanic and Other Women, 1934*

Occupational Status	Hispanic Women	Other Women
Domestic and personal service		
Number	69	193
Row percent	26.3	73.7
Column percent	30.9	78.8
Total percent	14.7	41.2
Industrial and manufacturing		
Number	154	52
Row percent	74.8	25.2
Column percent	69.1	21.2
Total percent	32.9	11.1

*N = 468, no missing observations. Corrected chi square = 106.46 with 1 degree of freedom. Significance = 0.000. Phi = 0.48127. Contingency coefficient = 0.43366.

TABLE 38. San Antonio, Geographic Distribution of Women Workers in Directory Sample, 1934

Distribution	Managers and Professionals	Managers and Semi-professionals	Sales and Clerical	Craft and Industrial	Domestic and Service
West Side (75% Hispanic)					
Numbers	12	10	40	124	40
Row percent	5.3	4.4	17.7	54.9	17.7
Column percent	17.4	35.7	15.3	83.2	28.2
East Side (18% Hispanic)					
Numbers	13	6	23	17	32
Row percent	14.3	6.6	25.3	18.7	35.2
Column percent	18.8	21.4	8.8	11.4	22.5
North Side (10% Hispanic)					
Numbers	44	12	107	8	70
Row percent	18.3	5.0	44.4	3.3	0.29
Column percent	63.8	42.9	41.0	5.4	49.3

TABLE 39. San Antonio, Age Distribution of Homeworkers, 1932

Ages	Numbers
16–19	10
20–29	26
30–39	33
40–49	17
50 and older	13
Total	99

SOURCE: Records of the Women's Bureau, Materials Relating to Bulletin no. 126.

TABLE 40. San Antonio, Marital Status of Homeworkers, 1932

Status	Mexican-American	Anglo	Total
Single	27	0	27
Married	35	11	46
Separated	7	1	8
Widowed	14	4	18
Total	83	16	99

SOURCE: Records of the Women's Bureau, Materials Relating to Bulletin no. 126.

Note to Tables 41 through 44

Unemployment, the major economic and social issue of the 1930s, was irregularly documented across the Depression decade, and any attempt to plot levels of unemployment from year to year would be futile. The unemployment counts utilized in these tables have been criticized for their inaccuracy, but taken collectively they are consistent in documenting that officially reported unemployment in San Antonio was higher among men than among women and higher among Mexican Americans and blacks than among Anglos. No comprehensive censuses of unemployment were taken in the early thirties, at the depth of the Depression, and in the 1937 and 1940 counts of unemployed workers a distinction was no longer maintained between Anglos and Mexican-Americans.

The available unemployment counts suggest that unemployment, contrary to local perceptions, continued to worsen through 1937 rather than declining midway through the decade. The relief census of 1935, however, is not comparable to other unemployment counts because only the unemployed who could demonstrate that they had no alternative means of support or that others were dependent on their earnings could be certified for relief. Unlike a census in which a worker simply reported his status, certification for relief involved an application-and-admission process. Families with two or more workers could have only one worker on relief. Relief rolls are thus an incomplete measure of unemployment. A relief census of 1933, counting persons rather than workers on relief, indicated how much more broadly San Antonio was afflicted by want than were other cities. In San Antonio 48,675 persons were on relief rolls as opposed to 36,786 in Atlanta, a larger city, and 81,172 in New Orleans, a city also hard hit but with more than twice the population of San Antonio.

By all the indexes of unemployment men experienced higher levels of unemployment than those experienced by women. There were reasons, however, why women's rates reflected lower levels than those that actually existed. Many homeworkers missed in census counts of workers likewise went unnoticed in unemployment counts. Women who did not head families did not feel the same social expectations of working for wages that men felt and therefore found it easier to leave the work force rather than continue to seek employment in the face of many disappointments. Finally, any woman who had male relatives in her family, even teenage sons, received a secondary rating in applying for emergency work, and secondary workers almost never found relief jobs. Most female workers had nothing to gain financially by listing themselves among the unemployed, while unemployed male workers had to continue their job searches if they hoped to gain public assistance.

Both the unemployment census of 1930 and the relief census of 1935 indicate that unemployment was significantly higher among Mexican Americans than among blacks. Although black women initially displayed higher unemployment rates that those of Hispanic women, by 1935 that was no longer true. In 1933 the percentage of blacks on relief was much higher than the percentage of Mexican Americans. Although the census of 1933 did not restrict itself to workers, the population's need for relief would have reflected the high unemployment among its workers. By 1935 the situation for blacks, male and female, had improved considerably as measured by the percentage of workers on relief. In contrast, the need for relief among Mexican Americans had not lessened. In 1935 approximately one-fourth of all Chicana workers were on relief, and a slightly larger proportion of male Mexican-American workers were also on relief rolls. Social workers, relief workers, and public leaders agreed that unemployment was most intense among Mexican Americans, and the characteristic response to the problem was resentment of their presence in the city rather than sympathy. In terms of emergency jobs, black males proved effective competitors with other men, but a disproportionate share of female jobs went to nonblacks. The statistics also indicate that it was more difficult for women than for men to find relief jobs. By 1940 emergency work for black women had virtually disappeared, though unemployment remained high. Among white women, however, the proportion of workers who secured emergency jobs increased between 1937 and 1940.

TABLE 41. San Antonio, Unemployment, April, 1930*

Category	Native-born White Females	Native-born White Males	Foreign-born White Females	Foreign-born White Males	Black Females	Black Males	Mexican-American Females	Mexican-American Males
Class A [†]	533	1,959	15	144	206	384	209	2,376
Class B [‡]	76	313	2	20	23	45	96	390
Total	609	2,272	17	164	229	429	305	2,766
Percent of gainful workers	4.6	5.6	1.9	4.7	5.0	7.5	4.2	12.5

SOURCE: U.S. Bureau of the Census, *Fifteenth Census of the United States, 1930: Unemployment*, vol. 1
*Six workers of Asian or American Indian extraction were also enumerated among the unemployed.
[†] Class A: Persons out of a job, able to work, and looking for a job.
[‡] Class B: Persons having jobs but on layoff without pay, excluding those sick or voluntarily late.

TABLE 42. San Antonio, Unemployment Relief Census, October, 1933, Number and Percent of 1930 Population

Sex	Anglos		Blacks		Mexican Americans	
	Number	Percent	Number	Percent	Number	Percent
Male	9,149	14.0	2,634	32.2	11,554	28.7
Female	9,224	14.1	3,285	33.5	12,759	29.9

SOURCE: Federal Emergency Relief Administration, *Unemployment Relief Census, October, 1933, Report no. 1*, Washington, D.C., 1934.

TABLE 43. San Antonio, Workers on Relief, March, 1935

Number and Percent	Anglo		Black		Mexican-American	
	Males	Females	Males	Females	Males	Females
Number	2,802	1,002	1,093	751	6,392	1,712
Percent	6.4	7.1	19.1	16.5	28.9	23.4

SOURCE: Philip M. Hauser, *Workers on Relief in the United States in March, 1935*, vol. 1, *A Census of Usual Occupations*, p. 1003.

TABLE 44. San Antonio, Unemployment, 1937 and 1940

Status	White		Black	
	Females	Males	Females	Males
1937				
Totally unemployed (Total: 13,845)	3,865	7,955	975	1,050
Emergency workers	1,295	3,742	199	489
Partly unemployed	1,546	5,125	504	551
1940				
Unemployed (Total: 10,780)	2,185	7,367	506	722
Emergency workers	1,549	—	43	—

SOURCE: U.S. Bureau of the Census, *Census of Partial Employment, Unemployment and Occupations, 1937: Final Report, Texas; Sixteenth Census of the United States, 1940: Population*, vol. 3, pt. 5, *Texas*.

TABLE 45. Bexar County, Amount of Public and Private Assistance and Earnings of Persons Employed On Work Projects Administration Projects, 1933–39

Programs	1933	1934	1935	1936	1937	1938	1939
Public							
Local county relief[a]	(1933–34)	(1934–35)	(1935–36)	(1936–37)	(1937–38)	(1938–39)	(1939–40)
Bexar County School for boys[c]	$ 3,171.30	$ 4,467.59	$ 4,493.32	$ 4,513.65	$ 5,272.95	$ 6,104.06	$ 7,576.77
Bexar County School for girls[c]	4,349.81	6,330.52	5,774.79	5,358.21	5,332.20	6,005.19	5,138.22
Home for the Aged[c]	10,300.00	11,000.00	[b]	11,817.80	12,490.18	11,429.51	13,735.82
Pauper Fund[c]	2,571.83	3,587.06	6,627.17	15,825.79	25,941.22	29,965.49	20,000.95[e]
Total (fiscal)[l]	20,692.94	25,385.17	16,895.23	37,515.45	49,036.55	53,504.25	46,451.76
State and Federal							
Old-age assistance	(1933)	(1934)	(1935)	(1936)	(1937)	(1938)	(1939)
				270,759.00	702,825.25	732,383.00	760,474.00
Federal							
Direct and work relief	822,292.00[g]	1,985,910.00[h]	2,030,412.00[h]	229,596.00[f]			
Work Projects Administration				2,133,000.00[i]	1,307,000.00[i]	2,542,000.00[n]	4,084,000.00[n]
Surplus Commodities (value)	[b]	[b]		426,773.30	610,801.37	728,183.75	763,644.42
Farm Security Administration[j]				4,909.75	463.00	465.00	8,463.50
National Youth Administration[k]				154,374.17	113,169.97	134,770.04	136,777.75

Civilian Conservation Corps							
Total state and federal	[b]	[b]	[b]	[b]	240,000.00	294,096.00	257,730.00
Total	822,292.00	1,985,910.00	2,030,412.00	3,219,412.22	2,974,259.59	4,431,897.79	6,011,089.67
Private							
Total		15,036.00[m]	17,393.00[m]	20,133.00[i]	34,000.50[i]	42,000.00[i]	54,000.00[i]
Grand total federal, state and local private	$822,292.00	$2,000,946.00	$2,047,805.00	$3,239,545.22	$3,008,260.09	$4,473,897.79	$6,065,089.67

SOURCE: American Public Welfare Association, *Public Welfare Survey, San Antonio* (Chicago, 1940).

[a] Data available for fiscal years only.
[b] Data not available.
[c] Includes subsidy to private agencies: 1938–39, $5,100; 1939–40, $7,020.
[d] Operating costs only.
[e] Estimated.
[f] *Federal Emergency Relief Monthly Reports*, 1938 (does not include administration costs).
[g] *Federal Emergency Relief Monthly Reports*, July, 1933–January, 1934 (includes administration costs, January–July, 1933).
[h] *Federal Emergency Relief Monthly Reports*, 1934–35.
[i] "Relief in 116 Urban Areas," *Social Security Bulletin*, April, 1938; September, 1938; March, 1939; April, 1940; excludes Army WPA projects.
[j] Grants only.
[k] Work programs.
[l] Not added in grand total.
[m] "Relief in 120 Urban Areas," *U.S. Children's Bureau Monthly Report*.
[n] Includes Army WPA projects (labor only).

TABLE 46. San Antonio, Estimated Annual Wage Paid per Wage Earner for
Selected Industries, 1929 and 1939*

Industries	1929	1939
All industries	$ 951.60	$ 855.02
Apparel	—	473.94
Clothing, women's	633.70	—
Clothing, men's (except shirts)	509.86	—
Food and kindred products	—	960.49
Beverages (nonalcoholic)	1,291.70	846.30
Bread and bakery products	1,121.83	1,014.84
Confectionary	586.07	611.66
Ice cream	1,443.14	1,431.12
Meat-packing, wholesale	1,040.87	903.15
Nuts, processed or shelled	196.41	—
Food preparation not elsewhere classified	575.02	635.76
Printing and publishing	—	1,546.47
Book and job	1,184.95	—
Newspapers and periodicals	1,944.88	—
Periodicals	—	1,399.06
Ice	1,077.37	943.87
Mattresses and bedsprings	869.44	662.77
Foundry and machine-shop products	1,362.26	

SOURCES: U.S. Bureau of the Census, *U.S. Census of Manufactures, 1930*; *U.S. Census of Manufactures, 1940*.

TABLE 47. San Antonio, Wage or Salary Income Received in 1939 by
Experienced Persons in the Labor Force, by Sex

Income Category	Female		Male	
	Number	Percent of Group	Number	Percent of Group
Total	28,125	100.0	70,246	100.0
$0– $99	7,954	28.3	15,254	21.7
100– 199	2,853	10.1	3,846	5.5
200– 399	5,874	20.9	11,118	15.8
400– 599	3,248	11.5	7,814	11.1
600– 799	2,897	10.3	7,803	11.1
800– 999	1,507	5.4	4,775	6.8
1,000–1,199	873	3.1	3,299	4.7
1,200–1,399	988	3.5	3,554	5.1
1,400–1,599	671	2.4	2,674	3.8
1,600–1,999	784	2.8	3,784	5.4
2,000–2,499	142	0.5	2,716	3.9
2,500–2,999	43	0.2	1,043	1.5
3,000–4,999	46	0.2	1,499	2.1
5,000 and over	11	—	447	0.6
Not reported	234	0.8	620	0.9

SOURCE: U.S. Bureau of the Census, *Sixteenth Census of the United States, 1940: Population*, vol. 3, pt. 5, *Texas*, pp. 540, 544.

TABLE 48. Arrests of Females Ages Eight through Twenty-five by San Antonio Police Department, January 1–June 30, 1940

Charge	Anglo	Mexican-American	Black
Murder	0	1	0
Robbery	1	0	0
Aggravated assault	4	3	4
Burglary	1	0	2
Larceny-theft	11	10	3
Other assaults	1	6	1
Stolen property	0	1	0
Liquor laws	0	1	0
Prostitution	127	152	17
Drunkenness	49	23	10
Sex offenses	5	1	0
Disorderly conduct	14	17	23
Vagrancy	12	7	4
Gambling	1	0	0
Traffic violations	24	3	2
Miscellaneous	3	1	4
Mental cases	2	4	0
Commitments	58	36	7
Delinquent juveniles	15	4	0
Witness	4	1	0
Totals	327	271	77

SOURCE: American Public Welfare Association, *Public Welfare Survey, San Antonio*, (Chicago, 1942), appendix VI, table 1.

TABLE 49. Bexar County, Federal and District Indictments of Women by Charges, 1929–39

Charges	Hispanic-named Women		Other Women		All Women	
	Number	Percent of Charges	Number	Percent of Charges	Number	Percent of Charges
Narcotic and alcoholic beverage violations	263	63.7	334	40.1	597	48.0
Economic crimes by taking	40	9.7	121	14.5	161	12.9
Economic crimes by fraud	16	3.9	189	22.7	205	16.5
Crimes of violence	36	8.7	123	14.8	159	12.8
All other crimes	58	14.0	65	7.8	123	9.9
Totals	413	100.0	832	100.0	1,245	100.0

TABLE 50. Bexar County, Indictments of Women in
District and Federal Courts by Years, 1929–39

Year	District Number	Federal Number	Total Number
1929	43	124	167
1930	48	116	164
1931	45	124	169
1932	61	97	158
1933	67	34	101
1934	63	51	114
1935	75	45	120
1936	56	21	77
1937	33	21	54
1938	36	17	53
1939	56	12	68
Totals	583	662	1,245

TABLE 51. Bexar County, Judgments in Trials of Women in Federal and District Courts, 1929–39

Judgments	Mexican-American Number	Percent	Other Women Number	Percent	All Women Number	Percent
Federal Courts						
Not guilty or case dismissed	73	24.5	82	22.6	155	23.4
Guilty	219	73.5	251	69.0	470	71.0
Case transferred or verdict unknown	6	2.0	31	8.5	37	5.6
Totals	298	100.0	364	100.0	662	100.0
District Courts						
Not guilty or case dismissed	57	49.6	247	52.8	304	52.1
Guilty	12	10.4	50	10.7	62	10.6
Case transferred or verdict unknown	46	40.0	171	36.5	217	37.2
Totals	115	100.0	468	100.0	583	100.0

TABLE 52. Bexar County, Fines Levied and Sentences Pronounced against Women in District and Federal Courts, 1929–39

Fines and Sentences	Hispanic-named Women		Other Women		All Women	
	Number	Percent	Number	Percent	Number	Percent
Fines						
$1– $99	40	31.2	60	37.7	100	34.8
$100–$199	47	36.7	59	37.1	106	36.9
$200–$499	17	13.3	28	17.6	45	15.7
$500 and over	24	18.7	12	7.5	36	12.5
Totals	128	100.0	159	100.0	87	100.0
Cases fined, as percentage of indictments		31.0		19.1		
Sentences in months						
1 – 3	47	32.2	39	23.6	66	27.7
4 – 12	72	49.3	43	26.1	115	37.0
13 –360	27	16.5	31	49.1	108	34.7
361 –life	0	0.0	2	1.2	2	0.6
Cases sentenced, as percentage of indictments		35.4		19.8		

TABLE 53. San Antonio, Number of Live Births and Infant Deaths by Race or Ethnicity, 1930–40

Year	Live Births			Infant Deaths		
	Mexican-American	Anglo	Black	Mexican-American	Anglo	Black
1930	2,486	1,761	209	459	125	27
1936	3,235	2,409	246	464	127	27

Year	Live Births			Infant Deaths	
	White	Black		White	Black
1937	5,686	248		598(105.2)*	25(100.8)
1938	6,175	270		502(81.3)	15(55.6)
1939	6,367	297		624(98.0)	17(57.2)
1940	6,444	341		644(103.0)	32(93.8)

SOURCES: San Antonio Department of Health, *Annual Report*, 1936, 1937, 1940.

*The number in parentheses is the rate per thousand live births.

TABLE 54. San Antonio, Population, Births, Deaths, with Rates, 1930–36 (Birth and death rates per 1,000 population; stillbirth rates per 1,000 births)

Year	Estimated Population	Births (Excluding stillbirths)		Deaths Excluding stillbirths			Stillbirths	
		Number	Rate	Number	Crude Rate	Rate Corrected for Residence	Number	Rate
1930	231,542	5,555	23.99	3,580	15.46	13.28	206	37.08
1931	234,500	5,505	23.47	3,348	14.28	12.58	189	34.36
1932	238,000	5,091	21.39	3,288	13.81	12.27	198	38.86
1933	242,000	5,034	20.80	3,445	14.23	12.88	216	42.91
1934	247,500	5,728	23.14	3,246	13.12	11.79	168	29.33
1935	253,000	5,606	22.16	3,142	12.42	10.79	195	34.78
1936	260,000	5,890	22.65	3,654	14.05	12.11	234	39.73

SOURCE: San Antonio Department of Health, *Annual Report* (San Antonio, 1936).

TABLE 55. San Antonio, Death Rates from Tuberculosis, by Ethnicity or Race and Wards, Annual Average of Three Years, 1936–38

Ward	White			Mexican-American			Black			Mexican-American, per cent of Total Population
		Deaths			Deaths			Deaths		
	Population	Number	Rate per 100,000	Population	Number	Rate per 100,000	Population	Number	Rate per 100,000	
1	13,615	9.0	66.1	10,843	27.1	249.9	113	0.3	265.5	44.1
2	5,144	6.0	116.6	37,159	145.0	390.2	483	1.0	207.0	86.8
3	15,350	8.7	56.7	17,966	45.0	250.0	3,483	3.0	86.1	48.8
4	30,694	15.0	48.9	5,787	6.0	103.7	1,556	1.7	109.5	15.2
5	6,188	1.3	21.0	1,156	3.7	320.1	425	—	—	14.9
6	21,359	9.0	42.1	3,627	8.3	228.8	5,306	10.7	201.7	12.0
7	28,926	16.3	56.4	5,256	12.7	241.6	6,551	7.7	117.5	12.9
8	9,461	3.7	39.1	1,033	2.7	261.4	61	—	—	9.8
Totals	130,737	69.0	52.8	82,827	250.7	302.7	17,978	24.4	135.7	35.8

SOURCES: Population figures from census of 1930; deaths from records of Registrar of Vital Statistics, San Antonio Department of Health, 1936–38.

TABLE 56. San Antonio, Death Rates (including Nonresidents) from Tuberculosis (All Forms) by Ethnicity or Race and Age, Annual Average of Three Years, 1936–38

Age, Years	White			Mexican-American			Black		
		Deaths			Deaths			Deaths	
			Rate per			Rate per			Rate per
	Population	Number	100,000	Population	Number	100,000	Population	Number	100,000
Under 5	9,030	1.7	18.8	10,956	17.0	155.2	1,098	1.3	118.4
Under 1	1,761	1.0	56.8	2,486	8.0	321.8	209	1.0	478.5
5– 9	10,614	—	—	11,687	5.0	42.8	1,443	0.3	20.8
10–19	20,398	2.7	13.2	17,376	43.7	251.5	3,042	3.3	108.5
20–29	27,883	10.7	38.4	15,876	87.3	549.9	4,166	5.7	136.8
30–39	22,358	15.7	70.2	10,338	41.3	399.5	3,654	4.0	109.5
40–49	17,666	20.0	113.2	7,946	29.7	373.8	2,438	5.1	209.2
50 and older	22,788	34.0	149.2	8,648	32.3	373.5	2,137	4.3	201.2

SOURCES: Population figures from census of 1930; deaths from records of Registrar of Vital Statistics, 1936–38.

TABLE 57. San Antonio, Housing Conditions, 1940

Condition	Percent
Dwellings or structures	
In need of major repairs	15.5
With exclusive use of flush toilet	68.5
With shared flush toilet	12.5
With inside nonflush toilet or outside toilet a privy	17.8
With inside running water	79.9
With exclusive use of inside bath or shower	63.5
With shared inside bath or shower	12.6
Without inside bath or shower	23.9
With electricity	85.3
Without refrigeration equipment	23.2
Households cooking with	
Coal or wood	9.9
Gas	68.2
Electricity	0.2
Kerosene, gasoline and other fuels	20.5
No fuel (no cooking)	1.3

Median persons per room:
  White homeowners: 3.32
  White tenants: 3.13
  Nonwhite homeowners: 2.96
  Nonwhite tenants: 2.66

SOURCES: U.S. Bureau of the Census, *Sixteenth Census of the United States, 1940: Housing: General Characteristics, Texas*; tables 1–12.

Sources

Quantitative Sources

The quantitative aspects of this work have rested most heavily on U.S. Census Bureau publications, particularly the reports of the fifteenth and sixteenth censuses. The lack of comparability between the classification systems used for the two censuses presented a number of difficulties. The absence of separate reporting of Hispanics in 1940 made it impossible to document fully the Mexican-American experience through the Depression. Other differences between the two censuses could be minimized by a readjustment of categories, but it should be recognized that no amount of juggling will make the 1930 and 1940 counts entirely comparable.

The differences in the enumeration of workers and of occupations between the two censuses of workers and of occupations between the two censuses are explored fully in the U.S. Bureau of the Census, *Sixteenth Census of the United States, 1943: Population, vol. 2, Comparative Occupation Statistics for the United States.* In this volume, prepared by Alba M. Edwards, changes both in classification and in the instructions to enumerators are discussed.

The most important single difference between the two censuses is the replacement of the "gainful worker" concept that had been used in 1930 with the "labor force," a term that applies beginning in 1940. In 1930 census enumerators were instructed to count as a gainful worker each person ten years old or older who was usually employed in a specific occupation, even if the individual was not employed or seeking work at the time of enumeration. The instructions to enumerators in 1940 singled out the last week of March, 1940, as the period that determined labor-force status. All persons aged fourteen years and older who were either employed or seeking work were counted as labor-force members.

Specific groups included in the 1930 count were deleted from the 1940 count. Inmates in institutions who worked at a specific occupational task were counted as workers in 1930 but not in 1940. Seasonal workers were more likely to be counted in 1930 than in 1940 since they were included in 1940 only if they were at work, were seeking work, or were on temporary layoff during the last week of March. Persons with no previous work experience who were seeking work were enumerated in 1940 but not in 1930. With respect to the effect of the 1940 procedural changes on the enumeration of women, the Census Bureau estimated that some women may have been recorded as paid housekeepers in 1930 who were full-time housewives not earning wages.

In an attempt to minimize the differences between the two censuses, I calculated work rates controlling for age, but calculations controlling simultaneously for age and for occupation could not be made. In 1940 the categories into which specific occupations were grouped were also changed from 1930. In comparing 1930 and 1940, I also rearranged the classifications of specific occupations in larger occupational or industrial categories used in 1940 to conform to the 1930 categories.

Specific occupational labels used in 1940 did not always refer to the same job content that the same labels described in 1930. A few occupations in which women were concentrated were significantly affected by the changes. The occupations dressmaker or seamstress and laundress were not comparably defined in 1930 and in 1940. The differences result from the lack of specificity in 1930 on place of work. Some self-employed or home-employed dressmakers were wrongfully reported as factory seamstresses in 1930, and some shop-employed laundresses were wrongfully reported as private-household employees. These two problems were overcome by collapsing both occupations of dressmaker and of laundress to exclude divisions by place of work. Cautions about other female occupations for which no corrections were made apply to nurses, housekeepers, and lodging or boarding-house keepers. Some hospital maids were wrongfully reported as practical nurses in 1930, though the Census Bureau did not estimate the degree of error. Similarly, at both census dates bureau officials concluded that in some instances servants and housewives had been wrongfully reported as paid housekeepers. The bureau recommended a downward revision of 5 percent of the number of lodging or boarding-house keepers entered in the census of 1930. Significant lack of comparability or error in reporting was not noted for other occupations in which women were heavily represented. One final cautionary note about women's occupations applies, however. In 1930 as in 1920, the Census Bureau checked for error any individual census return that reported a woman in an unusual occupation such as plumber. To cut costs, this procedure was almost never followed in 1940.

With respect to both men and women, in San Antonio especially, the dropping of seasonal workers from consideration in 1940 is a problem. The difference between the two censuses probably results in an exaggeration of the number of workers who appear to have dropped out of the work force during the Depression. Because San Antonio migrant workers also traditionally sought some kind of employment when they were not following the crops, these persons would still have been counted as workers in 1940. Female pecan shellers were most likely to have this seasonal occupation as their only work for wages, but since the census of 1940 was taken during the shelling season, most of these women would also have been counted as members of the labor force in 1940.

Publications of the Bureau of the Census

Fourteenth Census of the United States, 1920
> *Manufactures, 1919: Reports for States, with Statistics for Principal Cities.* 1923.
> *Population, 1920: Composition and Characteristics of the Population by States.* Vol. 3. 1922.
> *Population, 1920: General Report and Analytical Tables.* Vol. 2. 1922.
> *Population, 1920: Occupations.* Vol. 3. 1923.

Fourteenth Census Publications
> Nienburg, Bertha M. *The Woman Home-maker in the City: A Study of Statistics Relating to Married Women in the City of Rochester, N. Y., at the Census of 1920.* 1923.

Census Monographs

Brissenden, Paul F. *Earnings of Factory Workers, 1899 to 1927: An Analysis of Payroll Statistics.* Vol. 10. 1929.

Carpenter, Niles. *Immigrants and Their Children, 1920: A Study Based on Census Statistics Relative to the Foreign Born and the Native White of Foreign or Mixed Parentage.* Vol. 7. 1927.

Hill, Joseph A. *Women in Gainful Occupations, 1870 to 1920: A Study of the Trend of Recent Changes in the Numbers, Occupational Distribution and Family Relationship of Women Reported in the Census as Following a Gainful Occupation.* Vol. 9. 1929.

Ross, Frank Alexander. *School Attendance in 1920: An Analysis of School Attendance in the United States and in the Several States, with a Discussion of the Factors Involved.* Vol. 5. 1924.

Thompson, Warren S. *Ratio of Children to Women, 1920: A Study in the Differential Rate of Natural Increase in the United States.* Vol. 11. 1929.

Fifteenth Census of the United States, 1930

Distribution

Census of Distribution, 1930: Retail Distribution. Special Series.

Employment and Wages in the Retail Industry. 1933.

Special Reports: Population: Age of the Foreign-born White Population by Country of Birth. 1933.

Statistics for Industrial Areas, Counties and Cities. 1933.

Manufactures, 1929

Reports by States. Vol. 3. 1933.

Retail Distribution. 3 parts. Vol. 1. 1933–34.

Wholesale Distribution: State Reports with Statistics for Cities and a Summary for the United States Including County Statistics. Vol. 2. 1933.

Population

Families: Reports by States, Giving Statistics for Families and Dwellings by Counties, for Urban Places of 2,500 or More. Vol. 6. 1933.

General Report: Statistics by Subjects. Vol. 2. 1933.

Occupations, by States: Reports by States, Giving Statistics for Cities of 25,000 or More. Vol. 4. 1933.

Reports by States, Showing the Composition and Characteristics of the Population for Counties, Cities, and Townships or Other Minor Civil Divisions. Vol. 3. 1932.

Supplement: Special Report on Foreign-born Families by Country of Birth of Head with an Appendix Giving Statistics for Mexican, Indian, Chinese, and Japanese Families. Vol. 6. 1933.

Unemployment

General Report: Unemployment by Occupation, April, 1930, with Returns from the Special Census of Unemployment, January, 1931. Vol. 2. 1932.

Unemployment Returns by Classes for States and Counties, for Urban and Rural Areas, and for Cities with a Population of 10,000 or More. Vol. 1. 1931.

Sixteenth Census of the United States, 1940
  Housing
       Characteristics by Monthly Rent or Value. Third Series of Housing Bulletins
           for the States. Vol. 3. 1943.
       Characteristics by Type of Structure: Regions, States, Cities of 100,000 or
           More, and Principal Metropolitan Districts. 1945.
       General Characteristics: Occupancy and Tenure Status, Value of Home or
           Monthly Rental, Size of Household and Race of Head, Type of Structure,
           Exterior Material, Year Built, Conversion, State of Repair, Number of
           Rooms, Housing Facilities, and Equipment, and Mortgage Status. Second
           Series of Housing Bulletins for the States. Vol. 2. 1943.
  Manufactures, 1939
       Reports by Industries. Vol. 2. 1942.
       Reports for States and Outlying Areas. Vol. 3. 1942.
  Population
       Characteristics by Age: Marital Status, Relationship, Education, and Citi-
           zenship. Fourth Series of Population Bulletins for the States. Vol. 4. 1943.
       Characteristics of the Nonwhite Population by Race. 1943.
       Characteristics of Persons Not in the Labor Force, 14 Years Old and Over:
           Age, Sex, Color, Household Relationship, Months Worked in 1939, and
           Usual Major Occupation. 1943.
       Characteristics of the Population: Sex, Age, Race, Nativity, Citizenship,
           Country of Birth of Foreign-born White, School Attendance, Years of
           School Completed, Employment Status, Class of Worker, Major Occupation
           Group, and Industry Group. Second Series of Population Bulletins for the
           States. Vol. 2. 1943.
       Characteristics of Women. Vol. 1. 1943.
       Differential Fertility, 1940 and 1919. 1943–47.
       Edwards, Alba M. *Comparative Occupation Statistics for the United States,*
           1870 to 1940: A Comparison of the 1930 and 1940 Census Occupation and
           Industry Classifications and Statistics: A Comparable Series of Occupation
           Statistics, 1870 to 1930; and a Social-Economic Grouping of the Labor
           Force, 1910 to 1942. 1943.
       Estimates of Labor Force, Employment, and Unemployment in the United
           States, 1940 and 1930. 1944.
       Families, 4 vols. 1943–44.
       Internal Migration, 1935 to 1940. 4 parts. 1943–46.
       The Labor Force: Occupation, Industry, Employment, and Income. Third Se-
           ries of Population Bulletins for the States. Vol. 3. 1943.
       The Labor Force (Sample Statistics): Employment and Family Characteristics
           of Women. Vol. 1. 1943.
       Nativity and Parentage of the White Population. 3 vols. 1943.
Seventeenth Census of the United States, 1950
  Census of Population, 1950
       Number of Inhabitants. Vol. 1. 1952.
       Special Reports. Vol. 2. 1953–57.

1950 Census Monograph Series
>Bancroft, Gertrude. *The American Labor Force: Its Growth and Changing Composition.* July, 1958.

Eighteenth Census of the United States, 1960
>*Population*
>>*Characteristics of the Population.* Vol. 1. 1961.
>>*Subject Reports: IB: Persons of Spanish Surname.* Vol. 2. August, 1963.
>>*IC: Non-white Population by Race.* Vol. 2. August, 1963.

Nineteenth Census of the United States
>*Population*
>>*Characteristics of the Population.* Vol. 1. 1972.

Other Census Bureau Publications
>*Census of Business, 1933*
>>*Retail Distribution: County and City Summaries.* Vol. 3. 1935.
>*Census of Business, 1935*
>>*Retail Distribution: County and City Summaries.* Vol. 2. 1936.
>*Census of Partial Employment, Unemployment, and Occupations, 1937.* 4 vols. 1938.
>*Patients in Hospitals for Mental Disease: 1926–1937 (Statistics of Mental Patients in State Hospitals Together with Brief Statistics of Mental Patients in Other Hospitals for Mental Disease).* 1930–39.
>*Relief Expenditures by Governmental and Private Organizations, 1929 and 1931.* 1932.

Public Documents and Records

Bexar County. Corporation Court no. 1. Docket.
Bexar County Court at Law no. 1. Judge's Criminal Docket.
Bexar County Court at Law no. 2. Judge's Criminal Docket.
Federal Bureau of Investigation. *Uniform Crime Reports.*
Federal Emergency Relief Administration. *Unemployment Relief Census, October, 1933.* Report no. 1. Washington, D.C., 1934.
Hauser, Philip M. *Workers on Relief in the United States in March 1935.* Vol. 1. *A Census of Usual Occupations.* Washington, D.C.: Works Progress Administration, 1938.
Palmer, Gladys L., and Katherine D. Wood. *Urban Workers on Relief.* 2 parts. WPA Research Monograph no. 4. Washington, D.C., 1936.
Records of the Women's Bureau. Correspondence and Survey Materials Relating to Bulletin no. 126. Record Group 86. National Archives.
Records of the Work Projects Administration. Record Group 69. State Series, Texas. National Archives.
State of Texas. 37th District Court. Docket.
———. 94th District Court. Docket.
———. 144th District Court. Docket.
U.S. Bureau of Labor Statistics. *Handbook of Labor Statistics, 1936 Edition.* Washington, D.C., 1937.
U.S. District Court. Western District of Texas. San Antonio Division. Docket.

Sources on San Antonio

American Public Welfare Association. *Public Welfare Survey of San Antonio, Texas*. Chicago, 1940.

Archdiocese of San Antonio, 1874–1949. San Antonio, 1949.

Archdiocese of San Antonio, 1874–1974. San Antonio, 1974.

Arnold, Charles August. "The Folk-lore, Manners and Customs of the Mexicans in San Antonio, Texas." Master's thesis, University of Texas, 1928.

Aschbacher, Frances M. *San Antonio Guide*. San Antonio: Aschbacher Publishers, 1954.

Blackwelder, Julia Kirk. "Women in the Work Force: Atlanta, New Orleans, and San Antonio, 1930 to 1940." *Journal of Urban History* 4 (May, 1978):331–58.

Bradshaw, Benjamin Spencer. "Some Demographic Aspects of Marriage: A Comparative Study of Three Ethnic Groups." Master's thesis, University of Texas, 1960.

Callahan, Sister Mary Generosa. *A History of the Sisters of Divine Providence, San Antonio, Texas*. Milwaukee: Bruce Press, 1955.

Chappelle, Angela Marie. "Local Welfare Work of Religious Organizations in San Antonio, Texas." Master's thesis, University of Texas, 1939.

City Federation of Women's Clubs. Minutes. 1933–39.

———. Miscellaneous correspondence and reports. Daughters of the Republic of Texas Library, San Antonio.

Cotner, Robert C., ed. *Texas Cities and the Great Depression*. Austin, 1973.

Croxdale, Richard, and Melissa Hield, eds. *Women in the Texas Workforce: Yesterday and Today*. Austin: People's History in Texas, Inc., 1979.

Davenport, Greg. "The District Where Vice Was a Virtue." *SA Magazine*, March, 1978, pp. 50–55.

De Zavala, Adina. *The History and Legends of the Alamo and Other Missions in and Around San Antonio*. San Antonio, 1917.

Dickens, Edwin Larry. "The Political Role of Mexican-Americans in San Antonio." Ph.D. diss., Texas Tech University, 1969.

Directory of San Antonio Social Agencies. N.p., n.d.

"Disease and Politics in Your Food: The Case of San Antonio." *Focus*, April, 1938, pp. 3–5.

Dudds, C. H. *Charity Begins: A Brief Record of Welfare in Bexar County*. San Antonio, ca. 1974.

Eckles, May. "A Diary Setting Out the Life of May Eckles." Typed copy. Daughters of the Republic of Texas Library, San Antonio.

Farris, Buford Elijah. "A Comparison of Anglo and Mexican-American Stratification Systems in San Antonio and Their Effects on Mobility and Intergroup Relations." Master's thesis, University of Texas, 1972.

Fehrenbach, T. R. *The San Antonio Story*. Tulsa: Continental Heritage Press, 1978.

Finney, Floy Claiborne, "Juvenile Delinquency in San Antonio, Texas." Master's thesis, University of Texas, 1932.

Garcia, Richard A. "Class, Consciousness and Ideology: The Mexican Community of San Antonio, Texas, 1930–1940." *Aztlan* 9 (1979):23–69.

Gonzales, Kathleen M. "The Mexican Family in San Antonio, Texas." Master's thesis, University of Texas, 1928.

Granneberg, Audrey. "Maury Maverick's San Antonio." *Survey Graphic* 28 (July, 1939):423.

Hagner, Lillie May. *Alluring San Antonio through the Eyes of an Artist*. San Antonio: Naylor, 1940.

Handman, Max Sylvius. "Economic Reasons for the Coming of the Mexican Immigrant." *American Journal of Sociology* 35 (January, 1930):605ff.

———. "San Antonio: The Old Capital of Mexican Life and Influence." *Survey* 6 (May 1, 1931):163–66.

Handy, Mary Olivia. *The History of Fort Sam Houston*. San Antonio: Naylor, 1951.

Hernandez, Mary Esther. "Some Connections between San Antonio and the Mexican Revolution." Master's thesis, University of Texas, 1973.

Interview of Charlotte Graham with Glenn Scott, August, 1978. People's History in Texas, Inc. Copy

John F. Worley Directory Co. *San Antonio, Texas, City Directory*. San Antonio, 1931–40.

Johnston, Leah Carter. *San Antonio*. N.p., n.d.

Jones, Lamar Babington. "Mexican-American Labor Problems in Texas." Ph.D. diss., University of Texas, 1965.

King, Genevieve. "The Psychology of Mexican Community." Master's thesis, University of Texas, 1936.

Knippa, Lyndon Gayle. "San Antonio, Texas, during the Depression, 1933–1946." Master's thesis, University of Texas, 1971.

Knox, William J. "The Economic Status of the Mexican Immigrant in San Antonio, Texas." Master's thesis, University of Texas, 1927.

Landes, Ruth. *Latin Americans of the Southwest*. St. Louis: Webster, 1965.

Landolt, Robert Garland. "The Mexican-American Workers of San Antonio, Texas." Ph.D. diss., University of Texas, 1965. Published as *The Mexican-American Workers of San Antonio: The Chicano Heritage*. New York: Arno, 1976.

Lane, John Hart, Jr. "Voluntary Associations among Mexican Americans in San Antonio, Texas: Organizational and Leadership Characteristics." Ph.D. diss., University of Texas, 1968.

Loeffler, H. W. "San Antonio's Mexican Child." *Texas Outlook* 29 (March, 1945):28.

McCallum, Nancy Lou. "History of the Methodist Episcopal Church South in San Antonio." Master's thesis, University of Texas, 1936.

McMillan, Mary Maverick. "San Antonio during the Depression, 1929–1933." Master's thesis, University of Texas, 1971.

Maitland, Ralph. "San Antonio: The Shame of Texas." *Forum* 102 (August, 1939):51–55.

Menefee, Sedden C., and Orin C. Cassmore. *The Pecan Shellers of San Antonio: The Problem of Underpaid and Unemployed Mexican Labor*. Washington, D.C.: Works Progress Administration, 1940.

Morrison, Andrew. *The City of San Antonio*. N.p., n.d.

Mullenix, Grady Lee. "A History of the Texas State Federation of Labor." Ph.D. diss., University of Texas, 1955.

Murray, Winifred M. *A Sociocultural Study of 118 Mexican-American Families Living in a Low-Rent Public Housing Project in San Antonio, Texas*. 1954. Reprint ed., New York: Arno, 1976.

Myers, Carol Dee. "History of the Anglo-Baptist Churches in San Antonio, Texas." Master's thesis, University of Texas, 1956.

"Organizing for Strength." *Focus*, April, 1938, pp. 6–8.

Perales, Alonso S. *Are We Good Neighbors?* San Antonio, 1948.

Picnot, T. R. "The Businessmen's Interest in Decent Standards of Living." Mimeographed press release. April 20, 1942. San Antonio Public Library.

————. "An Economic and Industrial Survey of San Antonio, Texas." Mimeographed report. N.d. San Antonio Public Library.

————. "The Socio-Economic Status of Low Income Groups of San Antonio." Mimeographed address. N.d. San Antonio Public Library.

La Prensa, 1934–38.

Ramsdell, Charles. *San Antonio: A Historical and Pictorial Guide*. Austin, 1959.

San Antonio Chamber of Commerce. *The San Antonian*.

San Antonio Department of Health. *Abstract of U.S. Public Health Service Survey, City of San Antonio*. San Antonio, 1935.

————. *Annual Report*. San Antonio, 1936, 1937, 1940.

San Antonio Evening News. Historical edition, 1936.

San Antonio Express. 1929–40.

San Antonio Home and Club. 1930–40.

San Antonio Housing Authority. *Annual Report*. 1940.

————. *Housing Survey*. 1939.

San Antonio Light. 1929–40.

San Antonio Open Forum. Minutes, February 7–May 7, 1947.

San Antonio's 1937 Social Directory. N.p., n.d.

San Antonio Social Workers Association. *Directory of San Antonio Social Agencies, 1929–1930*.

San Antonio Weekly Dispatch.

Sanchez, George I. *Concerning Segregation of Spanish-speaking Children in the Public Schools*. Inter-American Education Occasional Papers, no. 9. Austin, December, 1951.

Shapiro, Harold Arthur. "The Workers of San Antonio, Texas, 1900–1940." Ph.D. diss., University of Texas, 1952. Published ed., New York: Arno, 1976.

Smith, Jamie Russell. "The Role of Women's Clubs in the Community Life of San Antonio." Master's thesis, University of Texas, 1939.

Sowell, Emmie Irene. "A Study of Boys' Clubs in Special Reference to San Antonio." Master's thesis, University of Texas, 1940.

Watterson, Wayt T., and Roberta S. Watterson. *The Politics of New Communities: A Case Study of San Antonio Ranch*. Praeger Special Studies in U.S. Economic, Social, and Political Issues. New York, 1975.

Waugh, Julia Nott. *The Silver Cradle*. Austin: University of Texas Press, 1955.

Wertenbaker, Greer Peyton. *San Antonio: City in the Sun*. New York: McGraw-Hill, 1946.

White, Owen P. "Machine Made." *Colliers*, September 18, 1937, pp. 32–33.

Williamson, Sarah Bailey. "Children's Free Clinic of the San Antonio Junior League." Master's thesis, University of Texas, 1934.

Wilson, Orlando Winfield. *Distribution of Police-Patrol Force*. Chicago: Public Administration Service, 1941.

Woman's Club of San Antonio. *Year Book*. 1930–36.

Woods, Sister Frances Jerome. *Mexican Ethnic Leadership in San Antonio, Texas*. Washington, D.C.: Catholic University Press, 1949.

Wozniak, Sister Jan Maria. "St. Michael's Church: The Polish National Catholic Church in San Antonio, Texas, 1855–1950." Master's thesis, Unviersity of Texas, 1964.

General Works

Abbott, Grace. *Public Assistance*. Chicago: Public Welfare Association, 1940.

Allen, Ruth Alice. *Chapters in the History of Organized Labor in Texas*. Austin, 1941.

———. *The Labor of Women in the Production of Cotton*. University of Texas Bulletin no. 3134. Austin, 1931.

———, and Sam B. Barton. *Wage Earners Meet the Depression*. Bureau of Research in the Social Sciences Study. Austin: University of Texas Press, 1935.

Almquist, Elizabeth McTaggart. *Minorities, Gender, and Work*. Lexington, Mass.: Lexington Books, 1979.

Baker, Elizabeth Faulkner. *Technology and Woman's Work*. New York: Columbia University Press, 1964.

Banks, Ann, ed. *First-Person America*. New York: Knopf, 1980.

Banner, Lois W. *Women in Modern America: A Brief History*. New York: Harcourt Brace, 1974.

Barrera, Mario. *Race and Class in the Southwest: A Theory of Racial Inequality*. Notre Dame: University of Notre Dame Press, 1979.

Bawker, Lea, ed. *Women, Crime, and the Criminal Justice System*. Lexington, Mass.: Lexington Books, 1978.

Bayor, Ronald H. *Neighbors in Conflict: The Irish, Germans, Jews and Italians of New York City, 1929–1941*. Baltimore, Md.: Johns Hopkins University Press, 1978.

Becker, Gary Stanley. *The Economics of Discrimination*. 2d ed. Chicago: University of Chicago Press, 1971.

———, and William M. Landes, eds. *Essays in the Economics of Crime and Punishment*. New York: National Bureau of Economic Research, 1974.

Bergman, Andrew. *We're in the Money: Depression America and Its Films*. New York: New York University Press, 1971.

Bernstein, Barton J., and Allen J. Matusow, eds. *Twentieth-Century America: Recent Interpretation*. 2d ed. New York: Harcourt, Brace & World, 1972.

Bernstein, Irving. *The Lean Years: A History of the American Worker, 1920–1933*. Boston: Houghton Mifflin, 1960.

———. *Turbulent Years: A History of the American Worker, 1933–1941*. Boston: Houghton Mifflin, 1970.

Billingsley, Andrew. *Black Families in White America*. Englewood Cliffs, N.J.: Prentice-Hall, 1968.

Bird, Caroline. *The Invisible Scar*. New York: Longman, 1966.

Blackwelder, Julia Kirk. "Letters from the Great Depression." *Southern Exposure* 6 (Fall, 1978):73–77.

———. "Quiet Suffering: Atlanta Women in the 1930s." *Georgia Historical Quarterly* 61 (Summer, 1977):112–24.

Blau, Peter Michael, and Otis Dudley Duncan. *The American Occupational Structure*. New York: Free Press, 1967.

Blaxall, Martha, and Barbara Reagan, eds. *Women and the Workplace: The Implications of Occupational Segregation*. Chicago: University of Chicago Press, 1976.

Boserup, Ester. *Woman's Role in Economic Development*. London, 1970.

Bowen, William G., and T. Aldrich Finegan. *The Economics of Labor Force Participation*. Princeton, N.J., 1969.

Branca, Patricia. "A New Perspective on Women's Work: A Comparative Typology." *Journal of Social History* 9 (Winter, 1975):129–53.

Branch, Mary Sydney. *Women and Wealth: A Study of the Economic Status of the American Woman*. Chicago: University of Chicago Press, 1934.

Briggs, Vernon M. *The Chicano Worker*. Austin: University of Texas Press, 1977.

Burma, John H. *Spanish-speaking Groups in the United States*. Durham, N.C.: Duke University Press, 1954.

Cantor, Milton, and Bruce Laurie, eds. *Class, Sex, and the Woman Worker*. Westport, Conn.: Greenwood, 1977.

Carillo-Beron, Carmen. *Changing Adolescent Sex-role Ideology through Short Term Bicultural Group Process*. San Francisco: R & E Research Associates, 1977.

———. *Traditional Family Ideology in Relation to Locus of Control: A Comparison of Chicano and Anglo Women*. San Francisco: R & E Research Associates, 1974.

Carroll, Bernice A. *Liberating Women's History: Theoretical and Critical Essays*. Urbana, Ill.: University of Illinois Press, 1974.

Chafe, William H. *The American Woman: Her Changing Social, Economic, and Political Roles, 1920–1970*. New York: Oxford, 1972.

———. "Flint and the Great Depression." *Michigan History* 53 (Fall, 1969):225–39.

———. *Women and Equality: Changing Patterns in American Culture*. New York: Oxford, 1977.

Chandras, Kananur V., ed. *Racial Discrimination against Neither White-Nor-Black American Minorities*. San Francisco: R & E Research Associates, 1978.

Clinchy, Everett Ross, Jr. "Equality of Opportunity for Latin-Americans in Texas." Ph.D. diss., Columbia University, 1954.

Conk, Margo Anderson. *The United States Census and Labor Force: A History of Occupation Statistics, 1870–1940*. Studies in American History and Culture, no. 11. Ann Arbor, Mich.: UMI Research Press, 1980.

Conklin, Paul. *Tomorrow a New World*. Ithaca, N.Y.: Cornell University Press, 1959.

Cott, Nancy F., and Elizabeth H. Pleck, eds. *A Heritage of Her Own*. New York: Simon and Schuster, 1979.

Crites, Laura, ed. *The Female Offender*. Lexington, Mass.: Lexington Books, 1976.

De Jong, Peter Y., Milton J. Brawer, and Stanley S. Robin. "Patterns of Female Intergenerational Occupational Mobility: A Comparison with Male Patterns of Intergenerational Occupational Mobility." *American Sociological Review* 36 (December, 1971):1033–42.

Derber, Milton, and Edwin Young, eds. *Labor and the New Deal*. Madison: University of Wisconsin Press, 1957.

Dublin, Thomas. *Women at Work: The Transformation of Work and Community in Lowell, Massachusetts, 1826–69*. New York: Columbia University Press, 1979.

Elder, Glen H., Jr. *Children of the Great Depression: Social Change in Life Experience*. Chicago: University of Chicago Press, 1974.

Epstein, Cynthia Fuchs. *Woman's Place*. Berkeley: University of California Press, 1971.

Federal Writers' Project. *These Are Our Lives*. 2d ed. Chapel Hill: University of North Carolina Press, 1967.

Fogel, Walter. *Mexican Americans in Southwest Labor Markets*. Advance Report no. 10, UCLA Mexican-American Study Project. Los Angeles, 1967.

Fredrickson, George M. *The Black Image in the White Mind: The Debate on Afro-American Character and Destiny*. New York: Harper Row, 1971.

Freundorf, Martha Norby. "Married Women in the Labor Force." *Journal of Economic History* 39 (July, 1979):401–17.

Fuller, Elizabeth. *The Mexican Housing Problem*. 1920; reprint, New York: Arno, 1974.

Galbraith, John Kenneth. *The Great Crash, 1929*. Boston: Houghton Mifflin, 1955.

Gans, Herbert. *The Urban Villagers: Groups and Class in the Life of Italian-Americans*. New York: Free Press, 1962.

Garcia, Richard A. *The Chicanos in America, 1540–1974: A Chronology and Fact Book*. Dobbs Ferry, N.Y.: Oceana, 1976.

Gilfend, Mark I. *A Nation of Cities: The Federal Government and Urban America, 1933–1965*. New York: Oxford, 1975.

Gitelman, Harvard M. "No Irish Need Apply: Patterns and Responses to Ethnic Discrimination in the Labor Market." *Labor History* 14 (1973):56–68.

Goldin, Claudia. "Female Labor Force Participation: The Origin of Black and

White Differences, 1870 and 1880." *Journal of Economic History* 37 (March, 1977):87–100.

————. "Household and Market Production of Families in a Late 19th-Century American City." *Explorations in Economic History* 16 (1979):111–31.

Glasco, Lawrence. "The Life Cycles and Household Structure of American Ethnic Groups: Irish, Germans, and Native-born Whites in Buffalo, New York, 1855." *Journal of Urban History* 1 (1975):339–64.

Gordon, David M. *Theories of Poverty and Underemployment: Orthodox, Radical and Dual Labor Market Perspectives*. Lexington, Mass.: Lexington Books, 1972.

Gordon, Michael, ed. *The American Family in Social-Historical Perspectives*. New York: St. Martin's, 1973; 2d ed., 1978.

Grebler, Leo, Joan W. Moore, and Ralph C. Guzman. *The Mexican-American People: The Nation's Second Largest Minority*. New York: Free Press, 1970.

Green, George N. "ILGWU in Texas, 1930–1970." *Journal of Mexican-American History* 1 (Spring, 1971):144–69.

Griffen, Clyde, and Sally Griffen. *Natives and Newcomers: The Ordering of Opportunity in Mid-19th-Century Poughkeepsie*. Cambridge, Mass.: Harvard University Press, 1977.

Gutman, Herbert G. *The Black Family in Slavery and Freedom, 1750–1925*. New York: Pantheon, 1976.

Hall, Richard H. *Occupations and Social Structure*. 2d ed. Englewood Cliffs, N.J.: Prentice-Hall, 1969.

Handlin, Oscar, and John Burchard, eds. *The Historian and the City*. Cambridge, Mass.: MIT Press, 1963.

————, and Mary Handlin. *Facing Life: Youth and the Family in American History*. Boston: Little, Brown, 1971.

Hareven, Tamara K. *Family and Kin in Urban Communities, 1700–1930*. New York: New Viewpoints, 1977.

————. *Transitions: The Family and the Life Course in Historical Perspective*. New York: Academic Press, 1978.

Harley, Sharon, and Rosalyn Terborg-Penn, eds. *The Afro-American Woman: Struggles and Images*. Port Washington, N.Y.: National University Publications, 1978.

Heleniak, Roman. "Local Reaction to the Great Depression: New Orleans, 1929–1933." *Louisiana History* 10 (Fall, 1969):307–37.

Heller Committee for Research in Social Economics of the University of California and Constantine Panunzio. *How Mexicans Earn and Live: A Study of the Incomes and Expenditures of One Hundred Mexican Families in San Diego, California*. Cost of Living Studies, no. 5. University of California Publications in Economics, vol. 13, no. 1, pp. 1–114. Berkeley, Calif., 1933.

Hoffman, Abraham. *Unwanted Mexican Americans in the Great Depression: Repatriation Pressures, 1929–1939*. Tucson: University of Arizona Press, 1974.

Hoover, Herbert Clark. *The Memoirs of Herbert Hoover: The Cabinet and the Presidency, 1920–1933*. New York: Macmillan, 1952.

Humphries, Jane. "Women: Scapegoats and Safety Valves in the Great Depression." *Review of Radical Economics* 8 (Spring, 1976):98–121.

Hutchinson, Edward Prince. *Immigrants and their Children, 1850–1950*. Census Monograph Series. New York: Wiley, 1956.

Hyman, Herbert H., and John Shelton Reed. " 'Black Matriarchy' Reconsidered: Evidence from Secondary Analysis of Sample Surveys." *Public Opinion Quarterly* 33 (Fall, 1969):346–54.

Jaffe, Madeline. "Rural Women in Unskilled Urban Labor." Master's thesis, University of Texas, 1931.

John, Angela V. *By the Sweat of Their Brow: Women Workers at Victorian Coal Mines*. London: Croom Helm, Ltd., 1980.

Katz, Michael B. "Occupational Classification in History." *Journal of Interdisciplinary History* 3 (Summer, 1972):63–88.

Katzman, David M. *Seven Days a Week: Women and Domestic Service in Industrializing America*. New York: Oxford, 1978.

Kibbe, Pauline Rochester. *Latin Americans in Texas*. Albuquerque: University of New Mexico Press, 1946.

Kirby, John B. *Black Americans in the Roosevelt Era: Liberalism and Race*. Knoxville: University of Tennessee Press, 1980.

Klaczynska, Barbara. "Why Women Work: A comparison of Various Groups— Philadelphia, 1910–1930." *Labor History* 17 (Winter, 1976):73–87.

Klatzmann, Joseph. *Le Travail à Domicile dans L'Industrie Parisienne du Vêtement*. Paris: Center for Studies in Economics, 1957.

Kleinberg, Susan J. "The Systematic Study of Urban Women." *Historical Methods Newsletter* 9 (December, 1975):14–25.

Kolachek, Edward D. *Labor Markets and Unemployment*. Belmont, Calif.: Sage, 1973.

Komarovsky, Mirra. *Blue Collar Marriage*. New York: Random House, 1964.

Kupinsky, Stanley, ed. *The Fertility of Working Women: A Synthesis of International Research*. New York: Praeger, 1977.

Lacasse, Francois D. *Women at Home: The Cost to the Canadian Economy*. Ottawa, 1970.

Lemons, Stanley J. *The Woman Citizen: Social Feminism in the 1920s*. Urbana: University of Illinois Press, 1973.

Lerner, Gerda, ed. *Black Women in White America: A Documentary History*. New York: Pantheon, 1972.

Leuchtenburg, William E. *Franklin D. Roosevelt and the New Deal, 1932–1940*. New York: Harper and Row, 1963.

Levine, Elaine Sue. *Ethnic Esteem among Anglo, Black, and Chicano Children*. San Francisco: R & E Research Associates, 1976.

Lewis, H. Gregg, ed. *Aspects of Labor Economics*. Princeton: Princeton University Press, 1962.

Lindborg, Kristina, and Carlos J. Ovando. *Five Mexican-American Women in Transition: A Case Study of Migrants in the Midwest*. San Francisco: R & E Research Associates, 1977.

Lloyd, Cynthia B., ed. *Sex, Discrimination, and the Division of Labor*. New York: Columbia University Press, 1979.

————, and Beth T. Niemi. *The Economics of Sex Differentials*. New York: Columbia University Press, 1979.

————, et al., eds. *Women in the Labor Market*. New York: Columbia University Press, 1979.

Lyle, Jerolyn R., and Jane L. Ross. *Women in Industry: Employment Patterns of Women in Corporate America*. Lexington, Mass.: Lexington Books, 1973.

Lynd, Robert S., and Helen Merrell. *Middletown in Transition: A Study of Cultural Conflicts*. New York: Harcourt Brace, 1937.

McAdams, Ina May. *Texas Women of Distinction: A Biographical History*. Austin: McAdams Publishers, 1962.

Madden, Joyce Fanning. *The Economics of Sex Discrimination*. Lexington, Mass.: Lexington Books, 1973.

Madsen, William. *The Mexican Americans of South Texas*. New York: Holt, Rhinehart, and Winston, 1964.

Martin, Elmer P., and Joanne Mitchell. *The Black Extended Family*. Chicago: University of Chicago Press, 1978.

Martinez, Rosa, ed. *Essays on la Mujer*. Los Angeles: Chicano Studies Center, UCLA, 1977.

Menefee, Selden C. *Mexican Migratory Workers of South Texas*. Washington, D.C.: Work Projects Administration, 1941.

Mincer, Jacob. "Labor Force Participation of Married Women: A Study of the Labor Supply." In H. Gregg Lewis, ed. *Aspects of Labor Economics*, pp. 63–106. Princeton: Princeton University Press, 1962.

Mirandel, Alfredo, and Evangelina Enriquez. *La Chicana: The Mexican-American Woman*. Chicago: University of Chicago Press, 1979.

Moore, Joan W. "Colonialism: The Case of the Mexican Americans." *Social Problems* 17 (Spring, 1970):463–72.

Mott, Frank L. *Women, Work, and Family: Dimensions of Change in American Society*. Lexington, Mass.: Lexington Books, 1978.

Myrdal, Gunnar. *An American Dilemma: The Negro Problem and Modern Democracy*. New York: Harper and Bros., 1944.

Oakley, Ann. *Woman's Work: The Housewife, Past and Present*. New York: Pantheon, 1974.

Oaxaca, Ronald L. "Male-Female Wage Differentials in Urban Labor Markets." Ph.D. diss., Princeton University, 1971.

Oppenheimer, Valerie Kincade. *The Female Labor Force in the United States: Demographic and Economic Factors Governing Its Growth and Composition*. 1970; reprint ed., Westport, Conn.: Greenwood Press, 1976.

Parigi, Sam Frank. *A Case Study of Latin American Unionization in Austin, Texas*. 1964; reprint, New York: Arno, 1976.

Patterson, James T. *The New Deal and the States: Federalism in Transition*. Princeton: Princeton University Press, 1969.

Pells, Richard H. *Radical Visions and American Dreams: Culture and Social Thought in the Depression Years.* New York: Harper and Row, 1974.

Piotrkowski, Chaya S. *Work and the Family System: A Naturalistic Study of Working-Class and Lower-Middle-Class Families.* New York: Free Press, 1979.

Pollak, Otto. *The Criminality of Women.* 2d ed. New York: Barnes, 1961.

Poster, Mark. *A Critical Theory of the Family.* New York: Seabury Press, 1978.

Pruette, Lorine, ed. *Women Workers through the Depression: A Study of White Collar Employment Made by the American Women's Association.* New York: Macmillan, 1934.

Rainwater, Lee, and Yance, William L., eds. *The Moynihan Report and the Politics of Controversy.* Cambridge, Mass.: M.I.T. Press, 1967.

Ransford, Edward H. *Race and Class in American Society.* Cambridge, Mass.: Shenkman, 1977.

Reisler, Mark. *By the Sweat of Their Brow: Mexican Immigrant Labor in the United States, 1900–1940.* Westport, Conn.: Greenwood Press, 1976.

Reiss, Albert J., Jr., et al. *Occupations and Social Status.* New York: Free Press, 1961.

Rodriguez, Roy C. *Mexican-American Civic Organizations: Political Participation and Political Attitudes.* San Francisco: R & E Research Associates, 1978.

Romasco, Alfred. *The Poverty of Abundance: Hoover, the Nation, the Depression.* New York: Oxford, 1965.

Ross, Arthur M., and Herbert Hill, eds. *Employment, Race, and Poverty.* New York: Harcourt, Brace and World, 1967.

Rotella, Elyce J. "Women's Labor Force Participation and the Growth of Clerical Employment in the United States, 1870–1930." Ph.D. diss., University of Pennsylvania, 1977.

Rubel, Arthur J. *Across the Tracks: Mexican-Americans in a Texas City.* Austin: University of Texas Press, 1966.

Ryan, Mary P. *Womanhood in America: From Colonial Times to the Present.* New York: New Viewpoints, 1975.

Scharf, Lois. *To Work and to Wed: Female Employment, Feminism, and the Great Depression.* Westport, Conn.: Greenwood, 1980.

Schlesinger, Arthur M., Jr. *The Age of Roosevelt.* 3 vols. Boston: Houghton-Mifflin, 1957–60.

Schnore, Leo F. *The Study of Urbanization.* New York: Wiley, 1965.

Scoville, James G. *The Job Content of the U.S. Economy, 1940–1970.* New York: McGraw-Hill, 1969.

Seifer, Nancy. *Nobody Speaks for Me! Self-Portraits of American Working Class Women.* New York: Simon and Schuster, 1976.

Seldes, Gilbert. *The Years of the Locust: America, 1929–1932.* Boston: Little, Brown, 1933.

Sellin, Thorsten. *Research Memorandum on Crime in the Depression.* New York: Social Science Research Council, 1937.

Seward, Rudy Ray. *The American Family: A Demographic History*. Beverly Hills, Calif.: Sage Publications, 1978.

Simmons, Ozzie G. "Anglo-Americans and Mexican-Americans in South Texas." Ph.D. diss., Harvard University, 1952.

Simon, Rita. *Women in Crime*. Lexington, Mass.: Lexington Books, 1975.

Sitkoff, Harvard. *A New Deal for Blacks: The Emergence of Civil Rights as a National Issue*, vol. 1, *The Depression Decade*. New York: Oxford, 1978.

Smart, Carol. *Women, Crime, and Criminology: A Feminist Critique*. London: Routledge and K. Paul, 1976.

Smuts, Robert W. *Women and Work in America*. New York: Columbia University Press, 1959.

Sobel, Charles F. "Marginal Workers in Industrial Society," *Challenge* 22 (March–April, 1979):23–32

Spicer, Edward H., and Raymond H. Thompson, eds. *Plural Society in the Southwest*. New York: Interbook, 1972.

Stack, Carol B. *All Our Kin: Strategies for Survival in a Black Community*. New York: Harper and Row, 1974.

Sternsher, Bernard. *Hitting Home: The Great Depression in Town and Country*. Chicago: Quadrangle Books, 1970.

Stouffer, Samuel A., and Paul F. Lazarsfeld. *Research Memorandum on the Family in the Depression*. New York: Social Science Research Council, 1937.

Sullivan, Mary Loretta, and Bertha Blair. *Women in Texas Industries*. Women's Bureau, Bulletin no. 126. Washington, D.C., 1936.

Sweet, James A. *Women in the Labor Force*. New York: Seminar Press, 1973.

Tentler, Leslie Woodcock. *Wage-Earning Women: Industrial Work and Family Life in the United States, 1900–1930*. New York: Oxford, 1979.

Terkel, Studs. *Hard Times: An Oral History of the Great Depression*. New York: Pantheon, 1970.

Terrill, Tom E., and Jerrold Hirsch. *Such as Us: Southern Voices of the Thirties*. Chapel Hill: University of North Carolina Press, 1978.

Thompson, Warren S. *Research Memorandum on Internal Migration in the Depression*. New York: Social Science Research Council, 1937.

Tilly, Louise A., and Joan W. Scott. *Women, Work, and Family*. New York: Holt, Rhinehart, and Winston, 1978.

Tobin, Sidney. "The Early New Deal in Baton Rouge as Viewed by the Party Press." *Louisiana History* 10 (Fall, 1969): 307–37.

Trout, Charles H. *Boston: The Great Depression and the New Deal*. New York: Oxford, 1977.

Walkowitz, Daniel J. *Worker City, Company Town: Iron and Cotton Worker Protest in Troy and Cohoes*. New York, 1855–84; Urbana: University of Illinois Press, 1978.

Warren, Harris Gaylord. *Herbert Hoover and the Great Depression*. New York, 1959.

Webb, John N., and Malcolm Brown: *Migrant Families*. Washington, D.C.: Works Progress Administration, 1938.

Wertheimer, Barbara. *We Were There: The Story of Working Women in America*. New York: Pantheon, 1975.

Westin, Jeane. *Making Do: How Women Survived the '30s*. Chicago: Follet, 1976.

White, Clyde R., and Mary K. White. *Research Memorandum on Social Aspects of Relief Policies in the Depression*. New York: Social Science Research Council, 1937.

Wolters, Raymond. *Negroes and the Great Depression*. Westport, Conn.: Greenwood, 1970.

Yans-McLaughlin, Virginia. *Family and Community: Italian Immigrants in Buffalo, 1880–1930*. Ithaca: Cornell University Press, 1977.

Index